The inner world outside

Paul Holmes is a psychiatrist and psychotherapist trained in both psycho-analytic and psychodramatic methods of treatment. In *The Inner World Outside* he draws on his experiences to give a clear introduction to object relations theory and to demonstrate its relevance to the practice of psychodrama.

Object relations theory, with its emphasis on the influences of external reality and early relationships on psychological development, provides a model of the individual's inner world. This world can be safely externalized on the psychodrama stage allowing for the exploration of early relationships which may still be causing problems in adult life.

The Inner World Outside presents the first unified account of the clinical methods (or techniques) of psychodrama with the psychological under-standing produced by modern psychoanalysis. The book includes a description of a single psychodrama session, an account which is linked, chapter by chapter, to the presentation of the relevant psychoanalytic theories. The problems 'George' has with his boss and his wife, as well as scenes from his childhood, are enacted on the psychodrama stage, providing material which, together with the reactions of other group members and the psychodrama director, is used to illustrate basic psychoanalytic concepts in action.

The book highlights the links between the theories of J.L. Moreno, the founder of psychodrama, and those of psychoanalysis, presenting a stimulating new synthesis which will be of interest to many schools of psychotherapists. It will also be useful to other mental health professionals, including those working in social work, nursing, psychiatry and education.

Paul Holmes is a Consultant Child and Adolescent Psychiatrist working in the National Health Service and a psychotherapist in private practice.

The inner world outside

Object relations theory and psychodrama

Paul Holmes

Tavistock/Routledge
London and New York

First published in 1992
by Routledge
11 New Fetter Lane, London EC4P 4EE

Simultaneously published in the USA and Canada
by Routledge
a division of Routledge, Chapman and Hall Inc.
29 West 35th Street, New York, NY 10001

© 1992 Paul Holmes

Typeset in Times by
NWL Editorial Services, Langport, Somerset

Printed and bound in Great Britain by
Biddles Ltd, Guildford and King's Lynn

British Library Cataloguing in Publication Data
A catalogue record for this book is available from the British Library

Library of Congress Cataloging in Publication Data
Holmes, Paul, 1947–
  The inner world outside: object relations theory and psychodrama
  /Paul Holmes
  p. cm.
  Includes bibliographical references and index.
  1. Psychodrama. 2. Object relations (Psychoanalysis)
  3. Psychodrama – Case studies. 4. Object relations (Psychoanalysis) –
  Case studies. I. Title
  [DNLM 1. Object attachment. 2. Psychoanalytic Therapy.
  3. Psychodrama. WM 460.5.02 H752i]
  RC489.P7H65 1992
  616.89'1523–dc20
  DNLM/DLC   91–5232
                                                        CIP

ISBN 0–415–05550–4 (hbk)
ISBN 0–415–05551–2 (pbk)

This book is dedicated to Dr Ezequiel Murillo Garcia who gave me the space and encouragement to write it in Mexico City in 1990.

And to Marcia Karp and Ken Sprague, who introduced me to the power and magic of psychodrama at the Holwell Centre, Devon.

Contents

Acknowledgements

I have been lucky enough, over my twenty years' involvement with psychotherapy, to have worked with many creative, well-informed, and encouraging teachers, supervisors, colleagues, personal therapists, patients, and friends. I know that I have gained much from these people, although I feel that it would be invidious or unprofessional to list their names. I have also had less satisfactory experiences with teachers, supervisors, and therapists. I am sure too that I have failed some of my own patients and students. I know that I have learnt much and matured a little as a result of all these experiences.

I would, however, like publicly to acknowledge the help I received from many friends during my stay in Mexico City. I would like to thank David and Rowena Resnikoff, Gustavo Fuentes and Herminia Loza, Manuel Acuña, Gregorio Fritz, Manlio Guerrero, Margarita Guitart Padilla, Moises Riuera Ortiz, Ken Davy, Jorge Bravo Soto, and Laura Cortes. I am also grateful for the friendship of my psychodramatic 'cousins' Yuyo Bello and Jaime Winkler and their students at the Escuela Mexicana de Psicodrama y Sociodrama.

I would like especially to thank my parents who, in their different practical ways, helped with the arrangements necessary for the visit to Mexico, my editor at Tavistock/Routledge, Edwina Welham, for her unfailing support and encouragement from the start of this project, and the Universidad de las Americas A.C. in Mexico City who provided me with computing facilities at a moment of crisis.

NOTE

I am a male psychodramatist and in this book I describe a psychodrama session with a male protagonist. I therefore decided to use the male gender throughout this book unless the context clearly refers to a woman. It is, however, worth noting that in this country the majority of psychotherapists are women.

I would like to thank the following for permission to reproduce material: Beacon House, Inc. for the writings of J.L. Moreno and Figure 11.4, E. Goldman and D. Morrison for Figure 3.1, D.H. Malan for Figure 3.2, Yaffa Character Licensing for Figure 3.3, the poet ME for her poem 'Roles?'.

1 Introduction
Psychodrama and psychoanalytic theory

The group

George arrived late, out of breath and rather red in the face. The group was due to start in a couple of minutes. Thelma gave him a cup of coffee which he accepted gratefully.

'You'll be late for your own funeral one day,' said Joyce, adding, 'but at least this week you're on time for the start of the group.'

Maggie interrupted, 'Oh leave him alone, he tries to get here on time.'

'Well he might try harder. I don't like it when people come after we've started.'

The rest of the group looked on. Tussles such as this were becoming an all too regular start to the group sessions.

Paul, the group leader, came into the coffee room from his office where he'd been having an animated, and rather tense, argument, unconnected with the psychodrama group, with Tom, a social work colleague.

Paul suggested that they move up to the 'theatre', the largest room in the Victorian house in which his clinic was based. Coffee cups were quickly drained and the group trailed up the stairs. Debby rushed to the lavatory. She knew that it was going to be a long evening.

The group had been meeting every week for eight months. People had joined for various reasons. Joyce, an attractive middle-aged woman, had become depressed after the collapse of yet another relationship. As she got older she was having to come to terms with the reality of never becoming a mother. Her family doctor had suggested therapy. Joan had heard about psychodrama through a friend. David, a successful lawyer, had joined the group to work on problems related to difficulties in close personal relationships. Debby on the other hand joined to learn more about psychodrama. Her children were growing up and leaving home and she wondered about becoming a psychodramatist. All the members of the group hoped that their lives could be improved by joining the group, but not all were clear in what way.

The group was 'semi-closed', members agreeing to join for a contractual period of a term of twelve sessions. New members joined at the start of the term. Initially there were ten in the group, but Roy, an anxious unemployed young man, had left after three sessions saying: 'Psychodrama is not for me. It scares me.'

Jane, a single parent, left after the first term because of difficulties in finding baby sitters for her young children. For a term the group had eight members, and at the start of the third term George had joined. He wanted to work on his difficulties both at work and in his marriage. He made others in the group angry at times and his arrival had a marked effect on the group dynamics.

The group sat around in the 'theatre', a comfortable room with many cushions. The chairs had been removed before the session, but some of the toys that related to Paul's work as a child psychiatrist remained. While they waited for Debby to finish in the lavatory there was a rather subdued discussion during which Thelma was asked how her week had been after her psychodrama in the last session. Debby arrived and Paul looked around the group.

He was aware of the rather quiet and reserved mood pervading the room. This fitted with his mood after the row with Tom. People were tired, the evenings were drawing in, and the weather outside was awful. The group lacked energy, no one was making it obvious that they needed to 'work'. Paul himself felt tired and lacking in creativity (it had been a long week so far). He checked his impression that no one felt ready to become the evening's protagonist.

More energy was needed so Paul decided on a playful warm-up. He asked the group to think of a toy from their childhood and to start moving around the room being that toy. Thelma at once began to suck her thumb and look floppy, while Peter walked around moving his arms like the pistons of a toy train, hooting his horn every now and then, 'Toot!'.

Debby was jumping around the room saying, 'I'm Tigger! I'm Tigger!'

For a time neither David nor George would join in, standing together in a corner. Paul then asked the 'toys' to interact at which point Tigger went over to the two men and began to push them gently. David then became a toy car, rushing round the room hooting, braking suddenly, and having near 'accidents' with the other toys. George remained still and tense, but began slowly to rock on his heels. It became apparent to Paul that he was now in the role of a toy. After a few minutes the whole group seemed more alive; there was laughter in the room as the toys interacted and people's impersonations became more relaxed and extravagant.

Paul said, 'Let's stop now.'

The group sat around in a circle.

'Anyone like to tell us about their toy?'

Debby started: 'Yes, I was Tigger from the Winnie the Pooh books. I was given him by my parents when I was about four. I've still got him, but he's very tatty now.'

Thelma added: 'I was a rag doll that I used to sleep with, I've no idea what happened to her. I think my mother threw her out when she became too dirty.'

One by one people said a little about their toys. Questions were asked:

'Did you miss the doll?'

and answered:

'Yes. I was much more careful of my children's toys.'

Even George, who was still tense and quiet, talked a little about his wooden toy soldier: 'With his smart red tunic, he looked so proud and strong.'

'Well, does anyone wish to explore their toy and the memories it stirred up in you?'
No response. A psychodrama director's nightmare. A session and no one ready
or willing to become a protagonist.

Continued on page 14

(Note: To make it easier to read this account of a psychodrama session at one sitting, the number of the first page of the next chapter is given at the end of each section.)

The OUTER WORLD INSIDE and the INNER WORLD OUTSIDE

These words, the original but over-long title of this book, sum up the ideas I present in the following chapters. The psychoanalytic model of object relations theory is used to explain how the inner world of the individual derives from experience of the outer world, while an account of a single psychodrama session is used to demonstrate how this inner world may be externalised both in life and in psychotherapy.

A PERSONAL INTRODUCTION

This book is the result of my attempt to understand and to integrate my experience (as both patient and therapist) of two apparently very different forms of psychotherapy: psychodrama and psychoanalytic psychotherapy.

My first encounter with psychoanalytic therapy occurred long before I trained as a psychiatrist or psychotherapist. While an undergraduate, I went to see the doctor in the student health service. He referred me to a psychoanalytic group in an attempt to help me resolve certain personality conflicts and the resulting depression. My experience of analytic groups and individual psychoanalysis continued (on and off) for the next fifteen years. And some things never changed!

I later trained as an analytic psychotherapist, in part as a result of my own positive experiences of the therapeutic process. This is not an uncommon route into the profession of psychotherapy.

On the other hand, my first direct contact with psychodrama was almost accidental, as is perhaps appropriate for a therapy which so values spontaneity. I was looking for somewhere to go for a week's holiday when I saw a poster for a psychodrama course at the Holwell Centre in Devon, run by Marcia Karp (who subsequently became my trainer).

I remembered that some years previously I'd bought (by post) a copy of an early version of Adam Blatner's first book *Acting-In*. (At that time it was a duplicated document published privately and entitled 'Psychodrama, role playing and action methods' [Blatner 1970].) I had found its contents interesting but I had done nothing more about psychodrama.

So it was with a degree of trepidation and excitement that I went down to Holwell Centre, which is based in a farmhouse high on the moors of north Devon. It was there that I had my first taste of real psychodrama.

The week was a revelation. I enjoyed the atmosphere of the Centre, humour and warmth of the sessions. I liked psychodrama's lack of intere diagnosis and labelling, and its theatricality reminded me of the years I had spent directing drama in the students' union when I should have been doing research in my laboratory on the functions of the cerebral cortex of rabbits. In fact, it was my enjoyment of my theatrical activities, with all the associated complexities of human relationships, that had encouraged me, a few years previously, to leave the neurophysiology laboratory and continue my medical studies.

I was trained first as an individual psychoanalytic psychotherapist while I was also working as a psychiatrist at the Maudsley Hospital in London. I subsequently trained as a psychodramatist. These two forms of psychotherapy appeared to me to exist in very different philosophical, theoretical, and practical camps and for several years I practised these methods of treatment in isolation from each other. I think that I found it easier and more appropriate to follow the advice and instructions of my different supervisors and mentors.

Analytic psychotherapy abhors certain actions, such as touching each other during a session or friendships developing between a patient and his therapist. Such behaviour is called 'acting out' and is considered to be counter-productive to the therapeutic process (see Sandler *et al.* 1973).

As a young professional I valued the safety provided by the rules about the patient–therapist relationship: rules and expectations which also fitted with my training as a doctor and psychiatrist. Psychoanalysis also offered me a well-developed psychology of the mind and of emotional disturbance whose clarity and logic appealed to my background in neurophysiology.

Psychodrama on the other hand is, by its very nature, dramatic. Action and movement are encouraged. Indeed, a static psychodrama session, dominated by talking, might be considered to be a failure. I enjoyed the excitement of the drama. Relationships are allowed to grow between group members. I found this openness very rewarding and supportive.

Perhaps it is no wonder that I tried to keep these two powerful therapies separate in my clinical practice.

I continued to see myself mainly as a psychiatrist and as an analytic psychotherapist. Psychodrama provided me with a forum for my personal development and therapy, although I also ran groups for adolescents in a hospital (Holmes 1984, 1987). In time, however, I decided to train as a psychodramatist with Marcia Karp and her husband Ken Sprague. Marcia followed the theories and practice of her trainers, J.L. Moreno and Zerka Moreno (with perhaps some additional influences from Carl Rogers).

At the Holwell Centre there was little talk of the theories of the psychoanalysts. Indeed, J.L. Moreno had a deep-seated antagonism to Sigmund Freud, his followers, and most of his theories, an attitude that I initially felt was shared by many of Moreno's students and trainees.

While I was a psychodramatist in training I developed an increasing conviction about the techniques and methods of psychodrama. However, I continued to have little real understanding or appreciation of the meta-psychological theories of Moreno. I was a psychoanalytic therapist who happened to run psychodrama groups.

In time I discovered how much of my psychoanalytic training and knowledge I was using in my clinical practice as a psychodrama director. I also found that I had made significant philosophical shifts towards a more humanistic (and less medical) approach to my clinical work. It was increasingly necessary therefore to develop my own integration of psychodrama and psychoanalysis.

To my delight, and perhaps surprise, I found my trainers, colleagues, and friends in the psychodrama movement most supportive. I now see myself as committed to the theories and clinical practice of both therapeutic camps, and I still work, when opportunities present themselves, both as an individual psychoanalytic therapist and as a psychodramatist.

This book is one consequence of my personal journey.

PS

The reader may be surprised to find a postscript so near the start of a book. However, the very nature of psychodrama allows for the unexpected.

This book was written in Mexico during a period of my life when I was cut off from regular contact with British psychodrama. On my return to Britain, and after reading the final draft, I became aware once more that the theories I present explain only part of the richness of the psychodramatic process.

The book reflects my rather concrete, and perhaps at times over-rational, approach to an understanding of the psyche. For example, the text only hints at the uses of symbolism and myths in psychodrama and at the powerful aspects of the interpersonal relationships that are an undercurrent in any group. For me these are important aspects of the magic of psychodrama, which must not be ignored when the totality of the process is considered.

FREUD AND MORENO: TWO VIENNESE PHYSICIANS

Both Freud and Moreno trained as doctors in Vienna. Freud became a neurologist and initially published research in neuropathology. His creation, psychoanalysis, has its roots in a biological and organic view of human nature. There are those, however, who would claim that his apparent scientific stance is the creation of his British translators.

Moreno's creations, psychodrama and sociodrama, belong to a very different philosophical arena, that of the existential schools of psychotherapy and human relations (Moreno 1959:207–17).

He was influenced by the philosopher and theologian Martin Buber's view that, to avoid a sense of alienation, emphasis must be placed on the 'I–Thou' relationship rather than the 'I–It' relationship.

Anything – a tree, for example, or the eyes of a cat – can belong in the 'Thou', just as *anyone* can be an 'It' for us. Something figures as 'It' when, for example, it is considered solely as an object of perception, possessed of properties deemed to exist independently of ourselves. It is 'Thou' when it 'has to do with me', in a dual sense that I am essential to its being and it is to mine. A subject deprived of its object is deprived of its reality.

Existentialism (Cooper 1990:34)

The schools of psychotherapy, each with an associated meta-psychology, created by Freud and Moreno, have very different styles. Malcolm Pines, following the ideas of Nietzsche, described how Freud can be seen as Apollonian and Moreno as Dionysian:

In Greek mythology Apollo is the God of distance, of space, of objectivity, of irony. Apollo shoots his arrow from afar. He symbolises knowledge freed from bondage to the Will. Dionysias, Pan ... brings from his Asiatic sources a super-abundance of creative energy with which to celebrate life that leads to a desire for destruction in order to bring about change.... Thus the Apollonian seeks unity within a classical framework.... At the other pole Dionysias is always surrounded by a Bacchantic crowd, bringing cathartic release from the oppression of individuality.

'Psychoanalysis, psychodrama and group psychotherapy: step-children of Vienna' (Pines 1987:16–17)

The integration of the Apollonian and Dionysian approaches to psychotherapy described in this book does not take equally from both psychotherapeutic schools. The therapeutic techniques used in the session were those of psychodrama, while the theoretical understanding of the process was derived, on the whole, from object relations theory, a development of classical Freudian psychoanalytic theory.

Let us for a moment consider psychodrama and object relations theory separately.

SO WHAT IS PSYCHODRAMA?

J.L. Moreno defined psychodrama as:

The science which explores the 'truth' by dramatic methods. It deals with interpersonal relations and private worlds.

Who Shall Survive? (Moreno 1953:81)

Zerka Moreno (Moreno's widow and the co-creator of modern psycho-drama) describes psychodrama as the process in which you can explore life, taking risks without the fear of punishment (personal communication).

It is a form of group psychotherapy in which action techniques are used. Group members do not sit in a circle on chairs discussing life and its problems. Life is brought into the room and enacted using group members as the cast of the drama. The process is rich, enlivening, and fun. Solutions are found to problems using the creativity and spontaneity of the group.

The group leader (or therapist) is called the 'director' because psychodrama is a dramatic form of therapy. It uses some of the conventions and language of the theatre; the group is held in a 'psychodrama theatre'. Within this theatre there is a stage, ideally with coloured lights that can be changed, dimmed, or turned off. The group becomes, at times, an audience, at other times members of the cast. Seating, which may often be just cushions, is arranged in a relaxed and flexible way. There are no formal props, just a selection of hard chairs, boxes, blankets, and anything else that comes to hand.

In the early 1920s, in Vienna, J.L. Moreno created his 'Theatre of Spontaneity' (*Das Stegreiftheater*). This was the forerunner of psychodrama. His account of this project was published anonymously in 1923 and later (under his name) in English (Moreno 1947). He designed a stage to meet the needs of this theatre. This stage was never built, and indeed legal battles over the authorship of the design resulted in one of Moreno's more flamboyant public rows. Interesting accounts of this conflict can be found in René Marineau's biography and Moreno's own autobiography (Marineau 1989:82; Moreno 1989:77).

Moreno left Europe in 1925 to seek a new life in the United States. It was there in 1936 that he finally built a psychodrama stage in the theatre of his private hospital, the Beacon Hill Sanatorium, in New York State. This stage was less grand and more practical than that in the Viennese plans. However, some of the original features survived. The theatre was designed so that everyone could be an equal participant (a fundamental aspect of Moreno's views of theatre and therapy) and the stage had different levels which could be used to represent, among other things, different stages of a protagonist's life, the judge on high in a court room, or heaven and hell.

My own psychodrama 'theatres' (or spaces) have always been more mundane, without the luxury of fixed, raised levels; indeed, sometimes I've worked in rooms full of the day-to-day furniture of an educational establishment or the discarded food from a medical lunch. The group which is described in this book was held in my office in a child guidance clinic in London. This room had its own character, which, while solid and Victorian, was almost never theatrical, except, that is, when used for psychodrama. Then its safe clinical aspects would be transformed by the magical process enacted within its four walls. It is wonderful what can be created with chairs, wooden stools, and a desk. Heaven can be made and entered by standing on a filing cabinet. The magic of the creative process within the group can make the 'theatre' in which the drama occurs.

Psychodrama usually has no formal audience; any member of the group might become an active participant in the drama, moving from being an observer to playing a crucial role for the protagonist, or 'chief person in a drama ... principal performer' (*Concise Oxford Dictionary* 1990). Psychodrama is after all a form of group psychotherapy, and does not allow for passive observers. The emotional energy, the creativity, and the honesty of the drama should involve all who watch it.

This book does not aim to offer you much more by way of a description of classical psychodrama than the account that starts each chapter. This psychodrama session is fictitious, a compilation of many experiences, and many groups. I did indeed run a psychodrama group in my office in London, but not with these people. All the events described have occurred in groups but the details have been shuffled. I hope that I alone remain recognisable and that the resulting account rings true to the experienced psychodramatist.

I am aware that many, perhaps especially those with a training in analytic psychotherapy, will raise questions about my understanding and inter-pretation of events described in this book and their psychological significance. Such questions could be the start of a productive dialogue between the schools of Freud and Moreno.

Excellent accounts of psychodrama have been provided by others (see 'Psychodrama bibliography' at the end of this book). Reading is, however, one thing, experience another. Written descriptions of psychodrama can never provide the full flavour of this powerful therapeutic technique. If, as someone new to psychodrama, you really wish to know more you will have to join a group and experience the process.

AND WHAT IS OBJECT RELATIONS THEORY?

Object relations theory is a psychology of the mind developed by certain of Freud's successors: in Britain by Melanie Klein, W.R.D. Fairbairn, D.W. Winnicott, Harry Guntrip, and John Bowlby (among others), and in the United States by psychoanalysts such as Otto Kernberg.

Their theories are concerned with the consequences of an individual's relationships with the external world on their internal psychic world. The psyche and the personality are seen as being, in part, a result of the relationships made with people in the external world, which are remembered, or internalised, as 'object relationships' in the mind. In this respect, childhood is considered to be the most formative period of a person's life, although internal object relationships can be changed in adult life by, say, psycho-therapy or other powerful life experiences.

The term 'object' is taken in this theory to refer *both* to people, or parts of people, in the external world and to the internal psychic 'objects' or representations in the mind that result from these relationships.

This book describes the ways in which these object relationships are explored using the therapeutic techniques of psychodrama. In the warm-up to the psychodrama we have already met, indirectly, two internal objects of members of the group: George's father (who gave him the toy soldier) and Thelma's mother (who threw away her rag doll). These objects, or mental representations of the other person, exist in the mind in relationship with aspects of the individual's self-representation. Access to (or memory of) these object relationships in the therapeutic setting was gained through the symbolism associated with the memories of the toys.

In this book I present a model of the inner world which draws upon the theoretical developments of various psychoanalysts, while not following any one exclusively. Indeed, there is a continuing debate between theorists on these issues which has not always resulted in clarity. The psychoanalysts Joseph Sandler and Anne-Marie Sandler, in a paper 'On the development of object relationships and affects', state that:

> The topic is not an easy one to discuss because the psychoanalytic theory of object relationships is far from satisfactory, and our theory of affect is, at best, in a state of healthy and constructive chaos.
>
> (Sandler and Sandler 1978:285)

J.L. MORENO AND PSYCHOANALYTIC THEORY

The focus of this book is on the applications of psychoanalytic theories to the therapeutic techniques of psychodrama. It might, however, be useful to consider Moreno's position further, as his attitude to psychoanalysis has had a profound effect on the development of psychodrama. Moreover, important aspects of his philosophy remain crucial to my practice as a psychodramatist.

Moreno's antagonism to Freud, which clearly had both a philosophical and a personal basis, prevented him from using the significant developments in psychoanalytic theory that were provided by Freud's successors. These attitudes have tended to continue among some psychodramatists, especially in English-speaking countries, delaying the benefits that psychoanalytic theories might bring to psychodrama (see Blatner and Blatner 1988). However, psychodramatists in France, Brazil, Argentina, Mexico, and several other countries have long worked on a creative integration of Freud and Moreno.

It is also possible that many more psychoanalytic therapists might have experienced the therapeutic power and excitement of psychodrama had Moreno been a less difficult (although charismatic) individual. The style of Moreno's published works has not helped either. His books tend to be rambling, disorganised, and at times rather naive, problems that have no doubt put off many potential readers from other therapeutic schools.

In his autobiography Moreno was very direct about one of his problems with Freud. He wrote:

> I realized later that my quarrel was not ... with Freud's psychoanalytic system. My quarrel was with [his] behaviour as therapeutic 'actor'. I did not think that a great healer or therapist would look and act the way ... Freud did. I visualized the healer as a spontaneous, creative, protagonist in the midst of the group.
>
> 'Autobiography' (Moreno 1989:62)

Moreno believed in the reciprocity of the encounter between healer and healed, a relationship that should be full of potential creativity and spontaneity. He disliked the classical medical model followed by Freud in which the doctor placed his patient

> on a couch in a passive, reclining position; the analyst placed himself [at the] back of the patient so as not to be seen and to avoid interaction. . . . The patient reports what is going through his mind. The transference of the patient upon the analyst was not permitted to extend and become a real, two way encounter . . . by this life itself was banned from the chamber, and the treatment process became a form of shadowboxing.
>
> *The Psychodrama of Sigmund Freud* (Moreno 1967:11)

Moreno was interested in the 'encounters' that occur between individuals. I doubt that he would have tolerated the use of the word *object* to describe real people. I certainly have great reservations about the term. How could anyone describe my mother or father as objects? There is, however, some logic in the word's use and I will continue to use it in this book.

Moreno described more of his objections to the analytic system of Freud. He wrote:

> The psychoanalytic system has in common with other analytic systems which followed in its steps, the tendency to associate the origins of life with *calamity*. The key concept of the Freudian system is the libido, *but Freud instead of associating sex with spontaneity associated it with anxiety, insecurity, abreaction, frustrations and substitution*. His system shows strong inclinations towards the negative. . . . It was not the sexual actor and his warm up towards orgasm, it was not sexual intercourse and the interaction of two in its positive unfoldment, but rather the miscarriage of sex, its deviations and displacements, its pathology rather than its normality, to which he gave attention.
>
> (Moreno 1967:9)

This quote comes from Moreno's account of another of his famous confrontations, this time in 1931 with the American Freudian psychoanalyst Dr A. Brill. Moreno objected to Brill's use of psychoanalytic theory to analyse a dead man, Abraham Lincoln, who could not of course respond to his 'analyst'.

Moreno preferred to look to people's strengths, to help them discover their own ways to ease problems through processes that increased spontaneity. He was also concerned about what he saw as Freud's rigid determinism. He quoted from Freud's *The Psychopathology of Everyday Life*:

> There is nothing arbitrary or undetermined in the psychic life.
> [and]
> From our analysis we need not contest the right of feeling the conviction that there is a free will. If we distinguish conscious from unconscious

motivation, we are then informed by the feeling of conviction that the conscious motivation does not extend over all our motor resolutions. . . . What is thus left free from one side receives its motive from the other side, from the unconscious, and the determinism in the psychic realm is thus carried out uninterrupted.

(Freud 1901, quoted by Moreno 1946, 1977:102)

Moreno did not like this belief in predetermination in which the forces that control human interactions are conceived of as coming from either a genetic inheritance or (more powerfully) childhood.

> The desire to find determinants for every experience and for these determinants further determinants further back, and for these determinants still more remote ones and so forth, leads to an endless pursuit after causes. They deprive the present moment in which the experience has its locus of all reality.
>
> *Psychodrama Volume 1* (Moreno 1946, 1977:102)

He preferred to consider the individual's capacity for spontaneity, which occurred through the presence of what he termed the 's-factor', a force in man which does not follow the laws of the conservation of energy, unlike Freud's concept of the libido which belongs to the worlds of physics, chemistry, and medicine. Spontaneity is considered further in Chapter 6. Psychoanalytic theory and clinical practice have matured and developed over the years, and it must be stressed that Moreno's attacks were directed at his perceptions of the early classical techniques and theories of Freud and his followers.

The meeting of Jacob Levy Moreno and Sigmund Freud

Moreno's description of his one brief meeting with Freud, when he was in his early 20s and Freud was 56, provides more information about the historical background to the differences between psychodrama and psychoanalysis. The encounter occurred after one of the much older man's lectures on the analysis of a telepathic dream. Moreno reported that Freud asked the young Moreno what he was doing:

> Well, Dr Freud, I start where you leave off. You meet people in the artificial setting of your office. I meet them on the streets and in their homes, in their natural surroundings. You analyze their dreams. I give them the courage to dream again. You analyze and tear them apart. I let them act out their conflicting roles and help them to put the parts together again.
>
> (Moreno 1989:61)

Moreno admitted that he hoped to win over the famous older man to his ideas, although Freud had no hope (should he have wished to) of influencing the impetuous young Moreno for:

Except for my biological 'sonhood', I was never able to be a 'son' to anyone. In my early life, I tried and succeeded in becoming a 'father' very early. Although youthful, I was just as unyielding as Freud. We were both 'fathers', rulers – in my case, in expectancy. It was as if the unknown chieftain of an African tribe met the king of England. Just the same, it was one father against another. At the time Freud's kingdom was larger than mine, but we were both on the same planet.

(Moreno 1989:62)

It is interesting to note that there is no entry for Moreno, Buber, or psychodrama in the index to the full standard twenty-three-volume edition of Freud's works.

PSYCHODRAMA AND OBJECT RELATIONS THEORY

Antony Williams, in his book on strategic psychodrama *The Passionate Technique*, suggested that Moreno, although he never denied the importance of the past or of the unconscious, was more interested, in his attempts to understand and resolve problems in relationships, in the here-and-now (or horizontal) encounters between two people than in their long past childhood experiences (Williams 1989).

HERE and *NOW*

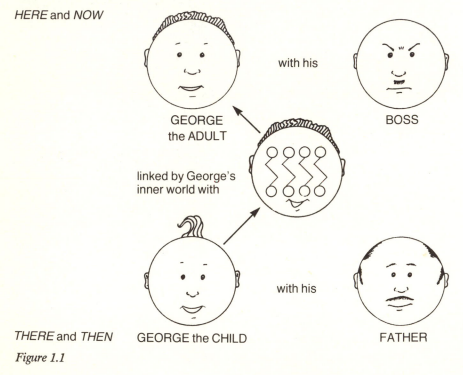

with his

GEORGE
the ADULT

BOSS

linked by George's
inner world with

with his

THERE and *THEN* GEORGE the CHILD FATHER

Figure 1.1

On the other hand, according to Williams, Zerka Moreno favours what he calls the 'vertical' approach. This concentrates on past and primal experiences and could be described as regressive in that it looks backwards to life events in childhood in an attempt to explain problems in the present. In this respect Zerka Moreno has much in common with the psychoanalysts and their interests in the past.

As a psychotherapist and a psychodramatist I am interested in how inner objects, laid down as part of the psyche in childhood, influence (and at times control) a person's life. This is not to say that I (or Zerka Moreno or psychoanalysts) see all problems as having their origins in the past, a point that I shall return to in Chapter 2.

Object relations theory provides a meta-psychology that explains how early (childhood) experiences and relationships affect relationships in the present: two horizontal (there-and-then and here-and-now) systems linked by the inner world created by the vertical psychological system of the individual. See Figure 1.1 on the previous page.

Many psychodrama sessions move from scenes from the present to dramas in childhood. This ability to integrate the encounter (horizontal) and the regressive (vertical) views of psychic function is one of the therapeutic strengths of the technique of psychodrama.

The chapters that follow will demonstrate how I use my understanding of object relations theory to facilitate my therapeutic work as a psychodramatist. While I do not consider it a 'weak and idle theme', I do ask that you

Gentles, do not reprehend;
If you pardon, we will mend.
And, as I'm an honest Puck,
If we have unearned luck
Now to 'scape the serpent's tongue,
We will make amends ere long.

A Midsummer-Night's Dream, V. i. 436–41

2 The director's assessment
Systems within systems

The group

The group needed a protagonist for this evening's session. Paul asked himself if he should mention some of the group dynamics that were so obvious in the coffee room. But this could lead to a 'group-centred' rather than a 'protagonist-centred' session. Paul's style was to work with protagonists unless group dynamics became so florid that they could not be ignored. He felt no need to address group issues directly this evening. A further warm-up exercise seemed called for.

'What about a guided phantasy?'

The group seemed pleased with the suggestion. They liked this warm-up. Paul felt relieved. The group were still with him, more alive than at the start of the evening.

'Well, make yourselves comfortable.'

The group settled down on the cushions and closed their eyes.

'You're walking down a country lane, there are trees on either side of you. What can you see over the hedges?'

The phantasy encouraged group members to create their own world in the mind.

'What's the weather like? Hot or cold? Wet or dry?'

Paul continued to lead his group along the byways of the imagination.

'You have now reached a fork in the road. Spend some time looking down each possible way forward. Down one path you see a group of familiar houses from your past. What do you see down the other path?'

People were encouraged, within the safety of the guided phantasy, to recall places. On going into a house they were told that they would find a pile of objects from their life – past and present.

'Choose an object. Pick it up. This is psychodrama. You can pick up the largest things.'

The phantasy continued with each person being asked to bring back to the group one object from the house.

'You're now back in the group room.'

Slowly they opened their eyes and looked around.

'Get into threes and talk about your objects.'

The group were used to this and quickly formed small groups to talk and ask questions. After a few minutes Paul brought the group together and information was shared about the objects. Some people had a sense of satisfaction, some talked in a rather dry way about their guided phantasy and object. George was very worked up.

'I remember that toy soldier so well, my father gave him to me on one of his rare visits.'

The group knew that George's parents were divorced. His shoulders slumped and he started to cry. Paul asked him.

'Are you ready to do some work this evening?'

'Yes.'

Paul looked around the group. There seemed to be general agreement that George was ready to be the protagonist.

'Does anyone else wish to work this evening?'

No one seemed ready, everyone appeared to support George.

'Well then, let's start.'

Paul and George moved away from the group which settled itself at one end of the room.

'For some reason the soldier reminded me of the troubles I've been having with my boss, Fred, at work. I used to get on well with him, but lately we seem to disagree about everything. He's the head of our unit and spends much of his time out working on committees. I know how important they are. The government doesn't like our sort of unit and we might lose our funding. Then I'd be out of a job but I feel he should be putting more work into the unit. I sometimes feel that he uses these problems as a way of avoiding our clients.'

As George talked it was obvious that he was very warmed up to the issues but Paul felt he needed to know more.

'How upset are you getting?'

'Well I've not been sleeping at all well; in fact, I've been waking early every morning for the last few weeks.'

Paul was worried that George might have been depressed.

'How's your appetite been?'

'Not that good, but Maria [George's wife] is not being very sympathetic. She says I never listen to her and spend too long at work. She says that I should understand Fred's position. It's all right for her, she's got a safe job. She talks to my mother about my moods, I don't like that. My mother says I'm just like my dad, moody, angry, and difficult. She says it runs in the family genes!'

'Hold on, George. You've told us a great deal just now. Things are clearly very difficult for you at present. But what would you like to start with this evening?'

'Well, I suppose my difficulties with Fred. He got me really uptight this afternoon. That's why I was almost late for the group.'

'OK. This is psychodrama, so let's look at what occurred at work today. Don't tell us; show us what happened.'

The initial dialogue between protagonist and director was over. A contract to work on a problem had been set ('troubles with the boss at work'), additional information had been given (rows with his wife, hints of problems with his *parents), and George had said something about his mental state (poor sleep, loss of appetite and weight). Paul had much to think about. He was already forming some tentative ideas about George's situation. But this was psychodrama. Further exploration must occur on the stage, through the drama.*

'Should we start with you meeting with Fred this afternoon?'

'Yes.'

Paul knew that he would ask a member of the group to play Fred; to become a auxiliary ego in George's psychodrama. However, first he needed to help George enter the scene in his mind. The drama needed a physical setting.

'Then set up the room!'

Continued on page 30.

THE DIRECTOR'S DILEMMA

Paul's aim that evening was to find one individual whose problems could be explored and helped using the therapeutic techniques developed by J.L. Moreno. George was chosen by the group to be the protagonist.

But how is the director to understand the problems presented to him in a session? George, like many protagonists, was anxious, and he had poured out to the group a wide range of problems in his life: he had difficulties in his interpersonal relationships, he was not getting on at all well with his boss, Fred, and they were often at loggerheads. He added that he had rows with his wife at home.

He also had practical problems: his social work unit was under pressure from its parent organisation who were having trouble with funding from central government. He also mentioned other things about his life: he was not sleeping very well and felt tense and miserable at times.

What should the director do?

In the initial stages of a psychodrama the director may be flooded with his protagonist's problems. Many questions passed through this director's mind.

Is the problem really Fred? If so, how can the situation be assisted in George's psychodrama?

Perhaps someone should be providing consultation and help to the social work team?

Is the protagonist hinting at serious marital trouble? Should he really be having marital therapy?

How big a role does government policy and the threat of the loss of his job have on George's state of mind?

How depressed is the protagonist? Should he see his general practitioner or even a psychiatrist? What's the link between George's moods and those of his father? Is the link genetic?

What's this all about? What's the association between the toy soldier and

Fred? Is there a link with father?
How am I going to manage this session? Where should we start?

In a practical sense Paul's options were limited. He was directing a classical, protagonist-centred psychodrama group (Holmes in Holmes and Karp 1991) and his protagonist had decided to start the drama with a scene involving his boss.

Paul guessed that by starting to explore George's problems in a scene with Fred the drama would move back in time during the session to his protagonist's relationship with his father. After all, it was George's memories of his father in the warm-up which led to his becoming the protagonist. The assumption that Paul made was one common to many psychotherapists since Freud: that the difficulties of patients are related to processes in the inner world and the unconscious, and that the problems have their roots in childhood.

However, a psychodramatist, like any psychotherapist, has wider responsibilities. The other possible causes of the protagonist's problems must at least be considered and perhaps discussed. The psychodrama group was not the only possible intervention that might have helped George with his difficulties, after all, it would not directly affect the situations at work or at home.

That is not to say that the techniques of psychodrama could not be useful, for they can be applied to face to face encounters in family or marital therapy sessions, and to consultations to professional teams (Williams 1989, Zerka Moreno in Holmes and Karp 1991, Holmes 1992).

The director must also make an assessment of the protagonist's mental health. All psychotherapists should have some knowledge of psychiatric conditions, such as severe depression (see Karp 1991) and psychosis, and information about where further help, often medical, may be obtained.

These issues and possibilities should not be forgotten by the psychodrama director as he assesses and decides (often with the group's help) who should become the protagonist. A very disturbed individual may need help from a psychiatrist before he or she is ready to become the protagonist in the group, while sometimes it might be appropriate to suggest that a group member also seeks marital or family therapy.

Professional assessments

Paul might have responded thus to his inner voices:

We cannot undertake family therapy tonight as I've got only George in the group. I'm not a politician or a social worker, nor am I George's doctor. I'm a psychodramatist. Let's get on with what I'm offered in the session. Let's begin to explore George's inner world and discover more about his relationship with his father. I assume that it's this that is causing him trouble with his boss who is clearly a father figure. Let's forget all these other issues and get on with the psychodrama.

If Paul had made this decision he would not have been facing all the implications of his questions about George's predicament. Such avoidance of an overall assessment of a patient's or client's needs may put them at risk, as serious problems, outside the remit of psychodrama, might be missed.

This sort of behaviour is also the source of constant debate, and indeed friction, between workers involved in the provision of mental health care:

The psychiatrist, a doctor, believes that the lay psychotherapist ignores the signs of organic depression which can be helped (or even cured) by drugs.

The psychotherapist or psychodramatist 'knows' that the doctors never have enough time really to talk to their patients.

The social worker might focus on the marital tensions feeling that medication only hides the real problems.

And the political activist is convinced that only social or political interventions can really resolve the problems of the world, believing that therapy only 'papers over the cracks'.

These apparently disparate views can, and indeed must, be reconciled if a fuller understanding of a protagonist's dilemmas is to be reached. Only with a more complex and sophisticated assessment can the director know how to handle the psychodrama and be certain that the protagonist requires no additional help outside the group. How, then, is the psychotherapist to make sense of all this information?

I suggest that a reconciliation of these conflicting views of mental distress is possible if the *systemic* relationships between the different models are considered.

SYSTEMS

The Concise Oxford Dictionary (1990) defines a system as:

A complex whole: a set of connected things or parts; an organized body of material or immaterial things.

Theories have been developed to describe the workings of systems in both the physical and social sciences (von Bertalanffy 1968). A basic tenet of a general systems theory may be given as the belief that:

The whole is qualitatively different from a group of parts because the properties of the whole derive from the properties of the *relationships* between the parts interacting. The parts mutually define each other.

(Gorell Barnes 1984)

Thus, in a system 'the whole is greater than the sum of the parts'. For example, there can be no doubt that a whole, working wrist-watch (which is a system) is greater than exactly the same collection of parts after a bus has run over them. Then it is just a mess. Likewise, a psychodrama group or a family group (both systems) are different and greater than a mere collection of individuals.

Every part of a system has an effect on all other parts. In systems causes and effects are circular (A affects B and C, B affects C and A, C affects A and B)

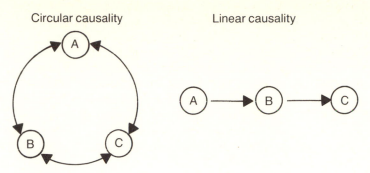

Figure 2.1

rather than linear (A affects B which affects C and so on). These relationships are illustrated in Figure 2.1.

The parts of a system must interrelate with information passing between the parts linking them into a functioning whole. The links in the nervous system are the nerve impulses and neurotransmitters and in social systems, the human interactions (elaborate exchanges in many modalities) between people in, say, a marriage or office. This process of communication requires the energy necessary for the system's survival.

In a psychotherapy group communication may be conscious, whether verbal or non-verbal interactions (e.g. body language, facial expressions). It may also involve unconscious processes. These include those described as tele (by Moreno) and transference (by Freud). Communication may also involve more overtly organic processes such as smells and pheromones (the chemicals which play a part in sexual attraction) (Stoddart 1990).

Systems can be 'closed' in that there is no contact with other systems. In time, in such systems, the energy required to maintain the order and communication between the parts will run out. The system will then cease to be 'greater than the sum of the parts'. A radio with a flat battery is in such a state.

Systems can also be 'open' in that they relate to other systems across their boundaries, energy and information constantly flowing in and out. The human body and a psychodrama group are examples of 'open' systems.

SYSTEMS WITHIN SYSTEMS: WHEELS WITHIN WHEELS

Family therapists have been very active in using the concepts of general systems theory. Indeed, in the field of mental health care, any other approach, such as individual psychotherapy, may well be labelled by some practitioners as 'non-systemic'.

However, most aspects of an individual's existence and problems can be conceptualised in systemic terms. In addition to the obvious organic systems of the body, systems theory has been applied to the understanding of

```
        The System                          Example
   THE INTERNATIONAL NEXUS          USA < > EUROPE < > JAPAN
                                                 ∧
                                                 ∨
   NATIONAL POLITICS               LABOUR < > CONSERVATIVE
                                                 ∧
                                                 ∨
   THE COMMUNITY                        LOCAL COUNCILS
                                                 ∧
                                                 ∨
              SCHOOLS < > SOCIAL SERVICES < > POLICE
                                                 ∧
                                                 ∨
   THE FAMILY        FATHER < > DAUGHTER < > MOTHER < > SON

   THE INDIVIDUAL                             ∧
                                              ∨
   THE METAPHORIC "INNER
   WORLD"                          EGO < > SUPER EGO < > ID
                                                 ∧
                                                 ∨
   THE ORGANIC "INNER WORLD"          THE NERVOUS SYSTEM
                                                 ∧
                                                 ∨
                                   ENZYMES < > HORMONES
                                                 ∧
                                                 ∨
                                    MOLECULES < > GENES
                                                 ∧
                                                 ∨
                                           ATOMS
```

Figure 2.2
Source: adapted from Holmes (1989b)

psychoanalytic groups (Ashbach and Schermer 1987) and organisations (De Board 1978). I have applied it to the complex processes involved in the assessment of disturbed adolescents (Holmes 1989b).

George was part of many systems: his nervous system, his family, his marriage, his office, and the political world in which he lived. Each of these systems can be understood and perhaps 'changed' or 'treated' on its own without reference to the other systems. However, I suggest that all the systems relevant to George have a complex relationship with each other which could be conceived of as being hierarchical.

At the top would be that system that involves the largest number of people: this might be called *the international political nexus* involving all the people on this earth. At the other extreme would be the system of the tiniest parts of any individual, *the atomic structure*. This hierarchy is shown in Figure 2.2.

An analysis of systems in general and of George's systems in particular

An analysis of any individual's situation should take account of all these highly complex interlocking systems for it is not only those apparently nearest to the individual (the inner world, the family, work) which will exert effects on his day-to-day life.

Let us consider George's situation in the light of the systems of which he is part. His difficulties were complex and it was clear that his problems might be conceptualised as existing in several of his constituent systems.

The inner world: organic–somatic systems

A reductionist understanding of the hierarchy would see everything as being controlled by the basic or fundamental molecular and atomic systems. These then influence the more complex systems of genes, hormones, enzymes which in turn together form the body's higher physical systems (such as the nervous, endocrine, and cardiovascular systems) which together produce the complete working body.

Systems theory can be used to describe these interactions. Nerve cells lock together in highly complex networks, information from one cell, transferred by electro-chemical impulses and neurotransmitters, influencing many other cells (Katz 1966). Indeed, the output of a cell, via feedback loops, may have an influence on the activity of the very cell producing the initial impulse.

The nervous system interacts with other bodily systems in which information is transferred by other means (e.g. hormones or the level of sugar in the blood). It seems certain that many aspects of the individual's psychological state are influenced or controlled by these organic systems. To give a simple example: we feel tired and irritable when the level of sugar in the blood falls; eating a nice sweet cake will not only raise our blood sugar, it may also improve our mood and cheer us up.

Conversely, psychological factors can clearly alter the body's physical functions; for example, when we are in emotional states of fear or excitement our pulse rate and blood pressure may well increase. Medication, given to alter psychological states such as depression, works on the organic or physical systems of the body, altering the transfer of information around the nervous system by changing levels of the neurotransmitters which convey information (nerve impulses) from nerve cell to nerve cell (see, for example, Hippias *et al.* 1986).

These organic, somatic systems are, as Freud suspected, now known to be the bedrock of human psychological functioning and are integrated with the psychological systems of the mind (see Kernberg 1976 for a psychoanalytic account of this topic, or Buck 1988 for details of the psychophysiology). While they influence the mind, these organic systems are themselves influenced by psychological and indeed social events.

George was showing one of the classical symptoms of organic (biological) depression: poor sleep with early morning waking. This problem is often associated with other symptoms such as weight and appetite loss, tearfulness, loss of sexual drive, and suicidal thoughts (or at worst attempts). Some psychiatrists believe that such depression is mainly organic in origin; certainly such moods tend to run in families and there is now good evidence for the involvement of genetic factors (Forrest *et al.* 1978).

These biological symptoms can also result from social or psychological pressures. However, even in these circumstances, an organic remedy, such as antidepressant medication, can be invaluable and indeed at times life saving.

So should George have seen a doctor? Would he have benefited from antidepressants?

No easy answers can be given; the psychodrama director had to use his clinical experience and judgement. I believe, however, that, even *if* medication was eventually prescribed by a doctor, interpersonal therapy (such as psychodrama) would *also* have been necessary. I've seen too many distressed people just given drugs and no time to talk. Pills are not magic solutions.

This evening George had come to the group. He was ready for his psychodrama and the group was supportive. Paul saw no reason not to provide George with psychodramatic therapy or to suggest he went to see his doctor. Had George been more distressed and depressed, a combined approach (psychodrama plus medication from a doctor) might have been appropriate.

The inner world: psychological systems

Without the organic nervous system there can be no mind. This was clearly Freud's position. It is in the brain that the complex psychological structures of the mind exist. These too form systems with the parts in dynamic relationship with each other.

The rules for intrapsychic interaction and the methods by which information is transmitted are very different from those in the organic nervous system. The means available for scientific investigation are different too, for the human psyche cannot be put in a test tube or on a slide in a microscope. Indeed, Freud's internal psychic system, or those described by object relations theory, are no more than metaphors devised in an attempt to describe the workings of the human mind.

Freud, in his topographic model of the mind (Freud 1923), described the individual's inner psychic world as consisting of parts (ego, id, and super-ego) in dynamic relationship with each other and with the outside world. My adaptation of Freud's revised diagram of this model is illustrated in Figure 2.3.

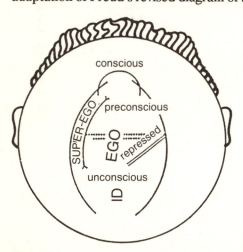

Figure 2.3
Source: adapted from Freud (1933)

There are no physical counterparts to the psychological concepts described by Freud, although it now seems likely that the functions of the id with its drives and instincts, which Freud believed to be constitutional and inherited (Freud 1915), can be associated with those parts of the brain below the cortex, perhaps especially the hypothalamus (Kernberg 1976; Buck 1988).

Progress in neurophysiology, endocrinology, and anatomy in the last hundred years has told us much about the workings of the brain linking the organic and psychological systems; however, many of the basic enigmas remain. Some of this progress is described in the book *Neuronal Man* (Changeux 1985).

George had a father who was an absent figure in his childhood. This became clear in the early stages of this psychodrama. He also had recurrent difficulties with 'father figures' at work. It seemed that he tended to act out his inner world in everyday life, causing distress and problems both to himself and to others.

Such dynamics are the stuff of psychodrama. Subsequent chapters will describe how George was given help in the group.

The outer world: the family

Most people are members of families; interacting nexus of biologically or legally related individuals capable of successful function or of dysfunction and pathology. The individual (with his or her own internal physical and psychological systems) influences the family; the family influences the individual.

In systems theory the question 'Is it marital disharmony that produces delinquent teenagers or difficult adolescents who stimulate rows between their parents?' is irrelevant. Change in one part (or member) of the family system inevitably produces changes, to a greater or lesser extent, in all the other parts (or individuals). While the person who demonstrates the greatest change may become the 'patient', for the systemic family therapist the problems lie within the dysfunctional family and not in the individual.

Treatment may be provided for the family and its 'patients' using various therapeutic techniques (for reviews see, for example, Watzlawick 1974, Skynner 1976; Gorell Barnes 1984).

Therapy with George's family of origin would have been difficult as he was adult. His day-to-day family now consisted of his wife, Maria. Hints were given during the warm-up of tensions in his marriage. These might be eased as a result of the work George did on his own difficulties in the group. However, therapy for the marital system might also have been useful. Perhaps this possibility might have been mentioned to George if he had continued to talk about problems at home.

Social systems

Moving further up the hierarchy, the members of the family relate to the wider systems: to the extended family, the local community, and, for a child, the school system.

Offices and social services departments are highly complex institutions consisting of many separate parts (social workers, secretaries, managers, clients, etc.) all of whom exist in dynamic interaction with each other. Such systems can be understood using the same theoretical models applied to nerve cells or families. Changes in one 'part', say the office secretary or a demanding, disturbed client, will have powerful influences on the whole social services office and on its wider network (see De Board 1978).

Poor George had major problems in his social work office. Intervention in this system could involve a consultation with the staff team. Such help might reduce staff tensions and help them cope better with the pressures on them from both clients and politicians (see, for examples, Holmes 1989a; Williams 1991).

George was a part of another system in the community: the psychodrama group. Paul noted before the session started that there were issues and tensions developing between members of his group. George's late arrival annoyed Joyce who began to nag him.

Should these problems have increased, Paul might have decided to focus on these issues. S.H. Foulkes and W.R. Bion provided psychoanalytic models for the understanding of group dynamics which are discussed in Chapter 11.

This evening Paul decided to focus on his protagonist, believing that the issues of the group would resolve themselves. As the personal intrapsychic system of one member of the group changed, shifts would have to occur in the group system as well.

Political systems

The individual also exists in the local parochial systems (involving education committees, school managers, town councils) which exert a powerful influence on their population. These systems must themselves be understood in the wider context of national government and politics which are the product of complex historical factors such as the class struggle, past imperialism and its modern consequences, and changes in economic relationships between individuals and between countries.

It seems probable that, as one political party adopts certain policies, the other parties respond by becoming, say, more or less extreme in their policies. A move by the Right may produce a counter-move by the Left. Again there is a system of interlocking activities.

This hierarchy of systems can be extended further into the international sphere in which activities, on a political front, between the great powers will have consequences on a country's political scene, its economy, and ultimately the entire population. Indeed, changes in the earth's climate (caused, for example, by a reduction in the ozone layer) are brought about, in part, by political and economic factors and may, in turn, produce significant economic and social changes. These will, in time, no doubt have a profound influence on most individuals on this planet.

George, his family, his clients, and indeed most of the rest of the country were under pressure from the consequences of government policy. While this small group could have no direct effect on these large systems, the issues raised could be explored in a sociodrama. This might help group members understand their own roles and responsibilities better.

Moreno too was interested in the integration of different ways of viewing man. With a not untypical grandiosity he wrote about 'cosmic man'.

> Now we come to the fourth universal – the COSMOS. Early in the twentieth century, during my youth, two philosophies of human relations were particularly popular. One was the philosophy that everything in the universe is all packed in the single individual, in the individual psyche. This was particularly emphasized by Sigmund Freud, who thought that the group was an epi-phenomenon. For Freud, everything was epi, only the individual counted. The other philosophy was that of Karl Marx. For Marx, everything ended with the social man, or more specifically, the socio-economic. It was as if that were all there were to the world. Very early in my career I came to the position that there is another area, a larger world beyond the psychodynamics and sociodynamics of human society – 'cosmodynamics'. Man is a 'cosmic man', not only a social man or an individual man. When I first said this, about fifty years ago, it sounded a little bit like highly exaggerated mysticism. Today it is almost common sense. Man is a cosmic being.
>
> (Moreno 1966 in Fox 1987:10)

And I would add that man is *also* a biological, psychic, family, social, and political being. Moreno's 'cosmic being' integrates many systems.

Communications within the hierarchy of systems

There is a good understanding of how information is transferred around any one system in the hierarchy; for example, electro-chemical impulses in the nervous system and words, body language and behaviour in families, and the methods of diplomacy in international affairs. The nature of interactions between levels in the hierarchy of systems is less well described.

Clearly, an individual with a 'biological' depression will have a marked effect on their family; such an individual may also have an effect on the wider community (for example, the local housing estate or their place of work), but no direct influence at all, as a single person, on national government.

However, when individuals aggregate together, as in a political party, or as in a pressure group for a particular minority or cause (for example, single parents, the homeless, or those with mental illness), more forceful and coherent influences can be brought to bear on local or even central government.

The biological systems of the individual are also influenced by the other systems in the hierarchy. Loss or other social pressure may result in depression which can be conceived of as a symptom of the psychological system of the individual's inner world or a malfunction of a biological system. It has been demonstrated, for example, that women who lost their mothers in childhood are much more likely to become clinically depressed as adults (Brown and Harris 1978; Harris *et al.* 1990).

The biological changes in the body's function and metabolism associated with depression (loss of appetite and weight, sleep disturbance and hormonal shifts) are often precipitated by external losses or bereavements.

FORMULATING SYSTEMS

The manner in which each system within the hierarchy of systems is formulated will, in part, depend on one's own preferences, predilections, and prejudices. For example, some people would consider the intrapsychic system formulated by psychoanalysts (and described in this book) as fanciful, misguided, and useless, favouring perhaps the conceptual models of the behaviour therapists.

A reductionist view gives priority to fundamental or basic systems; medicine and much of psychiatry place emphasis on the organic and biochemical systems of the body.

It must also be noted that the form and rules that govern certain systems, for example, the family, may vary in significant ways between cultures and classes (Hodes 1990).

I believe, however, that it is more sensible not to give priority to any particular system in our attempts to understand people.

An example of the analysis of systems: children in schools

The relationships within, say, a school, between the head-teacher, the staff, and the education authority, might work smoothly. In such schools the children are happy and usually learn well (see, for example, Rutter *et al.* 1979). If, however, the institutional system of the school is dysfunctional, with, say, a depressed head, a highly disruptive pupil or an education committee that will not provide adequate funds to the school, then the education of every child is affected.

It is usually the more 'fragile' members of the community who become overtly disturbed: the child whose parents fight all the time, the lonely teacher, the boy with learning difficulties. Such individuals might be considered to be 'ill' or 'problems' or they might be seen as 'symptoms' of the failing system.

They have been affected by the school system but they will also in turn perhaps have effects not only on others within the institution (other staff and pupils) but also on the systems outside the institution (e.g. the education office, their families, the families of staff).

Conversely, the situation within a school is highly dependent on the wider educational and political systems within which it exists. Changes of local or government policies or funding will alter priorities and relationships within the school, either improving that system (perhaps by better funding or improvements in morale) or adding to its chaos.

For example, the adolescent who refuses to go to school or is disruptive in the class-room might be described as being 'maladjusted' or, alternatively, he could be considered to be but a 'symptom' of dysfunction in one or more systems:

His physical inner world. He might be suffering from the effects of an organic depressive illness.

His psychological inner world. He might be mourning the death of a grandparent.

His family. His father might have a mistress.

His school. The teachers might be disaffected and underpaid.

The local authority which cannot manage the school.

The government which has reduced funding to education.

These issues, in relation to the assessment of adolescents, are considered in more detail elsewhere (Holmes 1989b).

MAKING PRACTICAL SENSE OF SYSTEMS

I believe that, as a general principle, the hierarchy of systems must be given thought when the psychodramatist, or any professional, tries to understand a patient or client. I suggest, pragmatically, that two issues need consideration:

1 The identification of the *priority system* (or systems);
2 an awareness of what sorts of *help are available*.

The priority system

Although, as argued above, all the systems surrounding an individual interact, more marked disturbance might be observed in one specific system. Such an observation, made as a result of an assessment process, might help in the decision between possible therapeutic interventions.

If, for example, the individual is found to be deeply depressed, and perhaps psychotic, psychodrama in a weekly evening group may be inappropriate. Admission to a hospital might be required to protect the person's life. Additionally, a trial of antidepressant medication might be considered. In my experience when someone is very depressed (with considerable dysfunction in their biological systems) they cannot, at times, use interpersonal therapies until the depression has lifted a little. The use of medication does not of course preclude the use of interventions at other systemic levels at the same time.

If the individual is under marked external stress, such as the closure of his place of work, racial harassment from neighbours, or severe financial worries, the most potent intervention might be to attempt to improve these problems, antidepressants, psychodrama, or family therapy being only palliative to the major (social) systemic disturbances.

In many cases, however, there will be no easy way to decide on the most appropriate intervention. Change at each level will help in its own way.

I would suggest that it is helpful if an attempt is made to understand the individual in terms of their own personal history, the present family dynamics, and the factors in their immediate social environment.

An individual who is living in a reasonably well-functioning family and social environment, but who is very distressed, might benefit more from personal therapy. If, however, the distress appears to be related to major factors in the family or in society, while individual help (in a group or one-to-one therapy) might well help the person to cope with the stresses, it would not be the most effective way to reduce the pressures. For that, intervention in another system by another professional (e.g. a social worker or a politician) is required.

What becomes apparent when the hierarchy of systems is considered is that there is *no totally correct intervention*. A logical argument can be made for intervention in almost any one of the different systems. Indeed, it is fundamental to this model, that, since the systems of the hierarchy are themselves systemically linked, an alteration at one level, say following a psychodrama session, will produce changes (small or large) at other systemic levels.

Some professionals will always opt for interventions at one level: doctors who seek a physical/organic cause for emotional disturbance will often be happier with the concomitant use of medication. The political or social activist will seek to reduce distress by attempts at changing society.

Available help

The model proposed in this chapter argues that there is no absolutely right or wrong choice of intervention. So can the psychodramatist just press ahead and provide psychodramatic treatment and ignore the other possibilities?

I would argue that this is a narrow and potentially dangerous point of view. A competent professional must know when a situation, or a protagonist's state, is beyond their form of intervention alone. They must be able and willing to consider other forms of help. The ability to judge such situations comes both from a full and detailed training and from the accumulation of professional experience.

However, there are many situations in which only certain skills are available (at a certain time, place, or cost) to assist someone in distress. It may be counter-productive to insist on individual psychotherapy for a client when only medically orientated psychiatry or a supportive group is available. In these circumstances it would be more professional to offer the styles of help that can be provided.

Thus the position of a therapist can be complex and rather invidious. What should they do for the client? Are they offering psychodrama because they wish to fill the spaces in their group? Indeed, what sort of help *might* best help the client with his difficulties and distress? The choice of intervention can be said to depend, in part, on the professional skills and inclinations of the person from whom a distressed individual first seeks help.

I believe that much potential creativity and productivity is lost by different professionals not accepting that they *all* might have something to offer the world.

MAKING SENSE OF GEORGE

How does all this theory help the psychodrama director? I believe that it assists both director and protagonist by putting the problems into context. Psychodrama may not be the only way to help someone. It is for these reasons that psychodramatists in training need to learn something of the medical (psychiatric) model of mental health and of the social and political causes of individual and social distress.

It is also why all psychotherapists need continuing skilled supervision, so that a more objective observer can help prevent a too determined dependence on one therapeutic approach. Paul's contract with the group was to provide sessions of protagonist-centred psychodrama. If the group wanted a session of sociodrama this could be discussed and arranged.

George was miserable, his marriage was under stress, he came from a troubled family, and his job was under threat. There were problems in several systems, any one of which could be the focus for intervention. George was clearly anxious and warmed up to work that evening. And it was a psychodrama group. Paul decided to help George with both his life problems and his anxiety using the techniques and methods created by Moreno, who also had views about the variety of ways in which interpersonal difficulties may be understood. So that evening Paul directed a psychodrama, having given due (but passing) attention to the other ways in which George might have been helped. What were the links between George's childhood and his present difficulties? Perhaps psychodrama will help us understand.

3 Repetitions and the transference

The group

George moved around the stage in a purposeful way setting up the room in his office. Even though he was a new member in the group he had seen others set up the scenes for their dramas.

'This is the door, the room is big, but very tatty. We really need some new furniture but there is no money.'

'Where's the window?'

George pointed to the side of the stage.

'What can you see through it?'

'Well, the houses opposite. And our garden. It must have been a nice garden when this was a private house.'

The stage had become transformed in his mind into the room at work. He was in the room in the session.

'What furniture do we need for this scene?'

'Not much, just the two armchairs. This is our staff room. It's really the only place the whole team meets to chat.'

'Get the armchairs then.'

George selected two hardbacked chairs.

'Will they do? They don't look very comfortable,' said Paul.

'Well, the room doesn't feel comfortable. There are too many tensions.'

'Great, so this is the room. Now just tell us three things about Fred.'

'Well he's a fair bit older than I am. He's been a social worker for many years.'

'Good. He's older than you. Tell us another thing.'

'He's full of excuses, never gets things done when he promises. That makes me very angry. He'll never talk about our work, he always goes on about other things. I hate that.'

'One more characteristic please.'

Paul wanted to get a member of the group into the role of Fred. He needed to stop George just talking about this man. It would be better for him to enact their relationship in the psychodrama.

'He likes the women. He's a bit of a lad.'

'Thanks, George. Who in the group could play Fred for you this evening?'

'Victor.'

Victor agreed to take this auxiliary role and came onto the stage area.

'How does the scene start? Show us.'

'Well, I come into the room and see Fred, for once, sitting in the staff room [Victor as 'Fred' slumps onto one of the chairs] and he's smoking as usual. He knows that the team decided to ban smoking in this room. God he makes me angry.'

'Did you tell him?'

'No.'

'Show us what happened.'

'Hi Fred, how's things? I've just been to see Mrs Simmons, you know the woman with three kids whose husband's just run out on her.'

'Oh. Have you been to see the new film at the Odeon? It's great. Saw it last night.'

George looked at the floor. 'Fred' continued to chatter on about the film. George was obviously stuck. He wanted to talk about work with his boss, but could not get his attention. Nor could he confront him. He just looked helpless and frustrated.

'Is this what often happens at work?'

'Yes, either Fred's not here, or he doesn't listen to me. It makes me feel very hopeless and useless.'

Paul remembered that earlier in the session George had told the group that his wife complained that he didn't listen to her at home. He decided to say nothing at that moment.

'It seems that you feel very stuck with Fred. You can't get his attention. Nor can you confront him. Have you been in situations like this before?'

'Yes, with my first boss, before I trained. He never took me seriously. He never gave me enough supervision, saying that it was good for me to have some professional freedom. What I wanted was his support. I felt he never gave me it. That made me very angry. I left that job as soon as I could.'

'Any other situations?'

The warm-up with the toy soldier, a gift from the absent father, came into Paul's mind.

'Well, people sometimes say that I don't listen. Maria often does, but then she's very demanding. I couldn't listen to her all the time. It would drive me mad!'

'It seems that we have two possible scenes now. One with a boss, the other with your wife.'

Paul had decided not to bring up George's problems with his father. Remembering the tears in the warm-up, he felt that George might find this relationship too painful to explore at this point in the session. As the director Paul had to follow his protagonist and 'go with his resistances'.

'Let's look at my first job.'

'Great, tell us a bit about the situation. What was your boss called?'

'Peter.'

'OK. Can you be Peter for a moment? Move over here. So, Peter, you're a social worker and George's boss. Tell us a bit about him. What's he like to work with?'

George, now playing Peter in role reversal, began to tell Paul and the group something about George.

Continued on page 50.

REPETITIONS

How was Paul to make sense of his protagonist's problems? George's memories in the warm-up of the wooden soldier in his red tunic, given him by his father when he was a small boy, had led him on to talk about his problems at work. He had indicated that he had had similar difficulties with both Fred and a previous boss, Peter. It seemed that the repetitive patterns in his relationships caused him concern. Paul wondered what the link was between this toy and George's relationships in the present.

Such repetitions are common in life, and a constant cause of concern and distress to many people. We all tend, at times, to make assumptions such as: all bosses are the same or all lovers will in the end desert us. We respond with the same feelings and behaviour towards different people. We refuse (or are unable) to appreciate the reality of others, forcing them (through our behaviour) into roles of our own making. Sometimes we are conscious of the repetitive process: 'This fellow reminds me of my first boy-friend.' Feelings and thoughts such as this imply a degree of contact with reality. However, with time, things change (for most people), and reality imposes itself more firmly. The new man is increasingly seen for what he is, which may be better or worse than expected, but none the less different, a unique individual. This may be the start of a new relationship.

However, at times and particularly for some people, such reality testing remains impaired. They cannot 'see' that they have married a man exactly like their father. The unconscious, buried in the inner world, continues to dominate both feelings and behaviour. A confusion continues between the 'internal father' from the past (an inner object) and the new man in the external world of the present.

Intimate relationships (which of course need not be sexual or romantic) are usually marked by more intense, passionate feelings which may resemble those of situations from childhood. Issues of dependency, authority, love are involved and it becomes more difficult to separate the influences from the unconscious inner world from present reality. Our partners, lovers, or bosses may take on the roles once occupied by our parents.

Indeed the very reasons we find certain people so attractive that we 'fall in love at first sight' relate to the reverberations between our present experiences and the formative early relationships with our parents. Such interactions may also account for why we choose to work with certain people. Just as not all our early experiences are positive and loving so not all our relationships in adult life are easy, especially not when they are dominated by our inner world.

In such situations there is a tendency for the individual to regress, to feel and respond with an intensity more appropriate to childhood. It was the regressive quality of George's feelings towards Fred that, in part, upset and confused him.

Such responses can be the basis of some of the more intimate and passionate moments of a relationship. However, they can also make life very difficult. After all, most of us like to be seen and related to as ourselves and not treated as if we were someone else, perhaps unknown to us.

This tendency to repeat situations, an inability to avoid well-known pitfalls in life, and feeling distress and misery about being 'stuck in a rut' are among the reasons that cause people to seek help from therapists. It is as if their world is viewed through the distorting window of the unconscious.

The psychoanalyst Joyce McDougall considers the process of repetition in theatrical terms, thus, although not explicitly, making links with psychodrama.

> Each secret-theater self is thus engaged in repeatedly playing roles from the past, using techniques discovered in childhood and reproducing, with uncanny precision, the same tragedies and comedies, with the same outcomes and an identical quota of pain and pleasure. What were once attempts at self-cure in the face of mental pain and conflict are now symptoms that the adult *I* produces, following forgotten childhood solutions.
>
> *Theatres of the Mind* (McDougall 1986: 7)

This process of repetition involves, according to psychoanalysts, a phenomenon called the 'transference'. Were George's problems due to his past and his childhood? Were they due to the phenomenon of transference?

HISTORY OF THE CONCEPT OF THE TRANSFERENCE

In 1895 Sigmund Freud, together with another Viennese physician Joseph Breuer, published an account of the hysterical illness of a young woman, Anna O., in which for the first time psychological difficulties in the therapeutic setting were ascribed to the phenomenon of 'transference'.

Anna's much loved father had fallen seriously ill in 1880, and she had nursed him with devotion until his death the following year. During the period of her father's illness Anna developed a variety of hysterical symptoms including paralysis of parts of both arms, disturbances of her vision, and hallucinations full of death's heads and skeletons. She was also at times unable to speak her native language, German, although she continued to be able to communicate in English. Her complaints were overwhelming and she took to her bed for several months.

Breuer had used hypnosis to help his young patient to talk about what was distressing her, a process that 'she aptly described ... speaking seriously, as a "talking cure", while she referred to it jokingly as "chimney-sweeping"' (*Studies on Hysteria*, Freud and Breuer 1895: 83).

Over a period of months the treatment began to relieve her of the distressing symptoms. In May 1882 Anna decided that she wished the treatment to stop in June of that year.

At the beginning of June, accordingly, she entered into the 'talking cure' with the greatest energy. On the last day – by the help of re-arranging the room so as to resemble her father's sickroom – she reproduced the terrifying hallucinations . . . which constituted the root of her whole illness.

(Freud and Breuer 1895: 95)

Is this perhaps an early account of the use of a psychodramatic method? Breuer clearly recreated with Anna, in the session, the sickroom (in another town) where she had been so distressed while nursing her dying father. The dramatic enactment seems to have been the last stage of her treatment, which appears to have been a success since thereafter she 'enjoyed complete health'.

More recent studies have suggested that Anna O. did not, as Freud and Breuer suggested in their paper, manage the rest of her life without psychological difficulties (Wood 1990). However, the lack of a complete cure of a difficult patient should not be seen as invalidating Freud's early and highly creative work, for Anna O.'s treatment led on to the creation of psychoanalysis.

Things were not so simple, though, for Breuer for, according to Freud, young Miss O. had developed a significant erotic attachment to her physician (accounts of which were not given in Freud and Breuer's original paper). Her feelings for Breuer perhaps repeated or replaced those she had had towards her late father.

The situation became so difficult for Dr Breuer (who perhaps took Anna O.'s advances at face value and was terrified) that he withdrew from psychotherapeutic work altogether (Stafford-Clark 1965), feeling that the method was unethical for a medical practitioner (Hinshelwood 1989). In 1908 he wrote of psychoanalysis: 'So far as I personally am concerned, I have since that time had no active dealings with the subject' (preface to the 2nd edition of *Studies in Hysteria*, P.F.L. 3: 49).

Moreno's description of these events is interesting and demonstrates his awareness of the early psychoanalytic literature.

It was the acting out of the patient towards Doctor Breuer, of Breuer towards the patient, of Breuer's wife towards Breuer, of Breuer towards Freud and finally, of Freud towards himself in a number of scenes which a psychodramatic session could have easily objectified; it was more than the usual transference in an office. It was 'carried over' beyond the therapeutic situation into life itself, producing the vicious chain which involved the four persons. The patient lost her analyst (Breuer), Freud lost his friend and psychoanalysis lost its first leader. The only one who may have gained something was Frau Breuer: she gave birth to a baby.

(Moreno 1959: 93)

Freud, in his consulting room, observed a similar tendency in his work with hysterical patients. He noted that:

the patient is frightened at finding that she is transferring on to the figure of the physician the distressing ideas which arise from the content of the analysis. This is a frequent, and indeed in some analyses a regular, occurrence. Transference on to the physician takes place through a false connection.

(Freud and Breuer 1895: 390)

(This is the first use of the word 'transference' in this context.)
He later asked:

What are transferences? They are new editions or facsimiles of the impulses and phantasies which are aroused and made conscious during the progress of analysis; but they have this peculiarity, which is characteristic for their species, that they replace some earlier person by the person of the physician. To put it another way: a whole series of psychological experiences are revived, not as belonging to the past, but as applying to the person of the physician at the present moment. Some of these transferences have a content which differs from that of the model in no respect whatever except for the substitution. These then – to keep to the same metaphor – are merely new impressions or reprints. Others are more ingeniously constructed; their content has been subjected to a moderating influence ... by cleverly taking advantage of some real peculiarity in the physician's person or circumstances and attaching themselves to that. These, then, will no longer be new impressions but revised editions.
Fragment of an Analysis of a Case of Hysteria (Freud 1905a: 157–8)

Freud initially saw these reactions as serious obstacles to the treatment process which had to be overcome before therapeutic work could continue. Indeed, transference phenomena had so disrupted Joseph Breuer's work with Anna O. as to threaten his marriage and cause him to stop psychotherapeutic work with hysterical patients. They are indeed powerful forces.

By 1909 Freud had discovered that the analysis of the transference feelings experienced by the patient towards the therapist, far from hindering treatment, may play 'a decisive part in bringing conviction not only to the patient but also to the physician'. The patients were thus helped, by the process of analysis, to come to terms with their inner world, created in the past, that was causing them difficulties in the present. As the theories and techniques of psychoanalysis developed, the analysis of the transference(s) between patient and therapist became a crucial aspect of the treatment process.

[T]ransference, which, whether affectional or hostile, seemed in every case to constitute the greatest threat to the treatment, becomes its best tool, by whose help the most secret compartments of mental life can be opened.
Introductory Lectures (Freud 1916–17: 496)

Indeed:

The development of the technique of psychoanalysis has been determined essentially by the evolution of our knowledge about the nature of transference.
The Technique and Practice of Psychoanalysis (Greenson 1967: 151)

Some psychoanalysts, in particular the Kleinian school, consider every free association from the patient in the consulting room (verbal or non-verbal) to be related to the transference (Hinshelwood 1989: 466). Melanie Klein developed the view that most of what is expressed in the psychoanalytic relationship is a repetition of the experiences of the earliest years of life. Kleinians attach little significance to accounts of the everyday reality of the patient, focusing their interpretative efforts on that which occurs in the therapeutic relationship (Segal 1964).

Other psychoanalysts pay much more attention to the present reality of their patients, but still use the term transference to describe the full richness of the patient's responses in the consulting room (see Racker 1968: 133).

THE TRANSFERENCE AND EVERYDAY LIFE

However, George was not talking about feelings and thoughts held about his psychotherapist but about the troubles he was having with colleagues in the real world at work. Is it reasonable to equate his problems with his bosses with the phenomenon of transference first described by Breuer and Freud?

Psychoanalysts have disagreed about what can be called transference. Some take a narrow view, believing that the term can be applied only to experiences in the psychoanalytic consulting room, while others have adopted a much wider definition, accepting that the phenomenon is much more general and occurs in many situations and circumstances in real life outside the psychoanalyst's consulting room. The American psychoanalyst Ralph Greenson wrote:

> Transference occurs in analysis and outside of analysis, in neurotics, psychotics, and in healthy people. All human relations contain a mixture of realistic and transference reactions.
>
> (1967: 152)

> [It] is the experience of feeling, drives, attitudes, fantasies and defenses toward a person in the present which do not benefit that person but are a repetition of reactions originating in regard to significant persons of early childhood, unconsciously displaced onto figures in the present.
>
> (1967: 171)

To this list of 'feelings, drives, attitudes, fantasies and defenses' I would add 'and behaviour' because it is often actions that demonstrate what fears, hopes, and phantasies one person has about another. Our inner worlds are full of material, much of which is usually kept secret from the world at large and, of course, at times from ourselves. Who knows what thoughts and wishes fill the mind (conscious and unconscious) of the man sitting opposite us on the No. 24 bus to Pimlico. It is only when such phantasies become *actions* (taken to include words, deeds, and subtle manipulations) that an individual's inner world influences those around.

Freud saw the need to repeat disturbed patterns of behaviour as driven by a compulsion: the basic drive or instinct seeking release, often through neurotic behaviour. It is as if the route or psychic pathway for the expression of the drive was laid down in childhood, although the individual has the strong impression that the repeated 'situation is fully determined by the circumstances of the moment' (Laplanche and Pontalis 1973: 78). Freud's drive theory is considered in more detail in Chapter 4.

The 'driven' aspects of such behaviour may have links to Moreno's concept of 'act hunger' in which a protagonist, in a psychodrama, has a forceful need to enact a particular scene or event.

It would, of course, be a mistake to see all behaviour or interpersonal difficulties as being the consequences of transference. Sandler *et al.* (1973) stress that it is important to distinguish between general tendencies in behaviour such as 'demandingness', 'provocativeness', or 'intolerance to authority' expressed towards the world at large and quite specific feelings, attitudes, and behaviour directed towards an individual who is related to *as if* he was a person from the other's past. Both sorts of behaviour may originate from childhood experiences, but only the latter, they suggest, can be described as transference.

Our behaviour towards people can be considered a complex mixture of factors from the present (both internal and external), cognition, and forces from our inner world and our past. Internal factors might include the state of physical health, hormone levels, or the degree of physiological arousal. External factors might include being stuck in a traffic jam or our bosses at work having a hang-over. Some of the various influences that might impinge on the individual were discussed in Chapter 2.

However, I believe that, to varying degrees, all behaviour is influenced by aspects of our inner unconscious world of object relationships and thus by aspects of the transference. The most powerful influences from the past in our development are (usually) our parents, so it is aspects of our relationships with these figures that may emerge in the present.

ROLES AND THE UNCONSCIOUS

Moreno also believed that the way we react to people or situations is

> created by past experiences and the cultural patterns of the society in which the individual lives, and may be satisfied by the specific type of his productivity. Every role is a fusion of private and collective elements. Every role has two sides, a private and a collective side.
> 'The role concept, a bridge between psychiatry and sociology'
> (Moreno 1961 in Fox 1987: 62)

Thus the psychodramatic concept of the role has links with the psychoanalytic concept of an inner world, those aspects of a role 'created by past experiences' which Moreno described as 'private' relating to that psychic function called an 'internal object relationship' laid down in childhood.

Thus, when George was in role at work as a social worker and Fred's junior, his behaviour was influenced by a fusion of the roles of 'son with his father' (the private component based in childhood) and the role of a junior to a senior colleague (the social, cultural, or collective element).

For Moreno the roles we adopt in life (which define our behaviour) have three dimensions.

Social roles expressing the social dimensions;
psychosomatic roles, expressing the physiological dimension; and
psychodramatic roles expressing the psychological dimension of the self.

The psychosomatic roles include those of 'sleeper' or 'eater', and the psychodramatic roles may occur in a session or in life in general.

Moreno continued:

> But the individual craves to embody far more roles than those he is allowed to act out in life. . . . Every individual is filled with different roles in which he wants to become active and that are present in him at different stages of development. It is from the active pressure which these multiple individual units exert upon the manifest official role that a feeling of anxiety is often produced.
>
> (Moreno 1961 in Fox 1987: 63)

In Moreno's terms, the transferential relationship of patient to therapist (say that of son with father) is an enactment of one of the roles present in the patient's 'role repertoire' (albeit a role that is used only in certain circumstances). In reality the patient's reactions to the therapist are almost always coloured by the reality roles of patient and doctor. Such a relationship is rarely, if ever, totally dominated by the transference.

In psychoanalytic therapy the patient will, at different times, experience various transferences to the therapist. The pressure to enact (in the consulting room) these different roles is governed (in a regressive way) by early experiences and is an aspect of a repetition compulsion. The origins of these object relationships are considered in the next chapter.

OF THERAPEUTIC MADNESS

The British psychoanalyst John Klauber described the transference as 'therapeutic madness' or

> perhaps illusion would be a more suitable word than madness, especially if you accept a tentative definition of illusion as a false belief accompanied by uncertainty as to whether to give it credence. An illusion is produced by the breakthrough of unconscious emotion without consciousness surrendering

to it completely. An illusion is a waking dream but seems somewhat less convincing.

Illusion and Spontaneity in Psychoanalysis (Klauber *et al.* 1987: 6)

It is important to distinguish between the concepts of illusion and delusion. We are all, at times, unable to differentiate clearly that which comes from our unconscious inner world from the objective reality around us. George, for example, attributed to Fred certain qualities derived from his experiences with his father, but he never thought that Fred *was* his father. Some individuals, however, lose the illusory 'as if' quality that is crucial for sanity. They become psychotic and their strange beliefs are then described as delusions.

A psychotic transference is possible in the consulting room in which the crucial 'as if' quality of the therapeutic illusion vanishes and the patient believes that his therapist really *is* his father. Such a situation is alarming for both therapist and patient and is real madness (see Sandler *et al.* 1973).

The behaviour and feelings associated with the transference are aspects of roles learnt and internalised in childhood, roles that are often denied expression by social conventions in adult life, but which emerge in certain perhaps more emotional situations such as intimate or stressful relationships and in psychotherapy. This sort of reaction is called 'regression' by some therapists, but, for Moreno, 'regressive behaviour is not a true regression but a form of role playing' (Moreno 1961 in Fox 1989: 63) in which the adult adopts roles more appropriate to childhood.

George had developed a certain childlike quality in his interactions with Fred in the office. However, he only enacted aspects of the role of a 'son with his father', he had not become a real child to Fred. In Moreno's terms a true regression may occur only in an interaction with the original parent.

REPETITIONS AND TRANSFERENCE IN PSYCHODRAMA

These internal roles or objects also emerge through the dramatic process of psychodrama.

Elaine Goldman and Delcy Morrison, in their book *Psychodrama: Experience and Process*, describe a typical session as moving 'from the periphery to the core', early scenes exploring the protagonist's problems in the present, the drama then moving to earlier scenes in his life that seem to have links with the problems in the present.

Their 'Psychodramatic Spiral' is a graphic way of illustrating the links of the present and early childhood, links that would also emerge (and be explored) through the transference in psychoanalysis. See Figure 3.1.

As Moreno pointed out, our adult roles are a fusion of aspects associated with the socio-cultural and the private or personal experiences of our lives. In a psychodrama these links, which involve symbolism, are explored in different scenes as the drama probes further into the past.

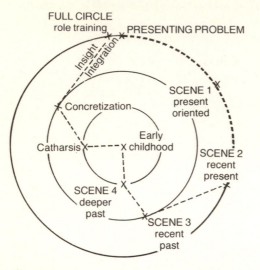

Figure 3.1
Source: reproduced with permission from Goldman and Morrison (1984)

Paul felt, from what he knew of his protagonist and from his clinical experience, that George needed to explore unconscious aspects of his relationship with Fred; to untangle the symbolic linking of the social or cultural relationship boss–junior with the more private and emotional relationship father–son. This would be a task of this psychodrama.

Role clusters

A process of association also occurs between different private or unconscious components of the roles we adopt. There appears to be in the psyche a clustering of object relationships. In infancy the clusters form through the association of relationships with similar affects (positive or negative). This process is described in more detail in the next chapter. Later in life the clusters appear to involve more complex symbolic links. George's psychodrama involved three men: Fred, Peter, and his father. These figures might be said to belong to the 'father cluster'.

Many other such clusters or associations exist within the psyche. For example, those experiences of the child (internalised as object relationships) associated with external authority and society's morality form a psychic cluster that Freud called the 'super-ego', which exists in relationship with both other clusters in the psyche and indirectly with the external world.

In a full psychodrama, as described by Goldman and Morrison (1984), a number of scenes will be directed, each involving the protagonist and a series of 'others' often from the same internal cluster (e.g. fathers or mothers or carers, etc.). It is a task of psychotherapy to unravel the confusions of our own roles in the world, created as these roles are by a clustering of different object relationships.

THE REPRESSION OF OBJECT RELATIONSHIPS

But why was George so unaware of the reasons for his problems at work? To explain this a further crucial element, repression, must be added to the definition of transference:

> Transference is the unconscious reliving of the *repressed* life of infancy in present-day relationships, both in treatment and in real life.
> *Personality Structure and Human Interaction* (Guntrip 1961: 57; my italics)

As the different aspects of the inner world of the child slowly begin to integrate, conflicts develop between incompatible object relationships. When George was a child the two self-representations in his inner world 'I love my mother' and 'I hate my mother for sending my father away' were in opposition. Any attempt at the integration of these two images into a single self cluster would have created marked psychic tension and his immature psyche was able to cope with only so much stress and anxiety. Therefore, one of these object relationships had to be pushed aside. One way to achieve this was to make it unconscious by the process of repression. The conscious psyche was then no longer bothered by this troublesome object relationship.

It is by this process that an unconscious realm is created filled with repressed object relationships. (Repression is discussed in chapters 5 and 8.)

The developing role cluster of the super-ego is a further force leading to the repression of internal object relationships. As children we learn that certain forms of behaviour or actions are unacceptable; certain our phantasies, wishes, and impulses have to be controlled. Initially children respond to such controls only when the parent is present. We *know* that we must not do something we might wish to do when told not to. This control is conscious, but soon these external authority figures also become part of the internal world, the super-ego, which begins to control in their absence behaviour of which our parents might disapprove. Such self-control also involves mechanisms of social learning and cognition.

Thus the child comes to believe that certain feelings and thoughts are not approved of. They are then repressed or buried deeper in the psyche, becoming unconscious. Should they start to emerge again anxiety will recur. The super-ego (the internalised social or parental disapproval) acts to prevent this and to censor those that approach consciousness.

However, this buried material may still reappear in dreams (which Freud called the royal road to the unconscious) and through certain actions (for example, slips of the tongue), and through behaviour such as George's difficulties at work. These expressions of unconscious, repressed wishes, impulses, and phantasies, that were pushed below the psychic surface in childhood, re-emerge as patterns of behaviour through the enactment of certain roles which may be experienced as ego-dystonic, that is alien to the ego or the subject's ideals or conception of himself (Rycroft 1968: 40).

Object relationships from the unconscious come back to haunt the individual in adult life and may cause them or society problems and distress. They may also surface in the somewhat unnatural situations of psychotherapy, in psychoanalysis or psychodrama. For some people it is only in the safe, anxiety-containing or holding situations such as psychotherapy (Josephine Klein 1987) or psychodrama (Holmes 1983) that the original anxiety can once more be experienced and accepted. This may allow the lost object relationships or roles to re-enter consciousness and the effective role repertoire.

Repression, used to reduce anxiety, tends to remove certain roles from the available role repertoire, as the repressed material consists of troublesome object relationships and their associated roles and affects. Such a situation may be of advantage to the individual: George was not overtly angry with his wife, he did not re-experience, through a repetition, his rage towards the mother he loved and needed. However, the active range of an individual's potential is of course also thus limited; George found being assertive, the positive face of anger, a problem at times.

GEORGE AND THE TRANSFERENCE

George experienced Fred's preoccupation with committee work outside their unit as a 'desertion' about which he felt very hurt and angry. He saw Peter's wish to give him some professional freedom as another 'desertion', one so painful that he resigned his job.

Now, in a psychodrama, we have only the protagonist's view of how his world was. Perhaps both Fred and Peter were inadequate, rather evasive bosses. We will never know. However, George had told the group that he had concerns about his relationship with Fred. Perhaps he was seeking a better way to cope with this awful superior. But enquiries by the director elicited the information that George had had this sort of experience before. Perhaps he was describing some sort of repetitive problem in which he 'transferred' feelings and expectations on to his superiors.

Relationships require two people. George may have initiated an interaction with Fred: 'Hello Fred, so you've decided to come into the office today!'

Perhaps Fred wondered what George was on about. He had just spent two days at head office attempting to negotiate the survival of the unit and he was looking forward to being welcomed back to his professional base. But as soon as he came in, George was on to him. He thought: 'This is too much!', as he retreated to his own office. George's view of the world was thus vindicated. Fred *was* an absent boss. 'I was really hoping to talk to him about my work.' Too late . . . Fred was in retreat.

Let us assume for that moment that George was also in individual psychotherapy (in my experience psychoanalysis and psychodrama can work well together for the same individual).

In psychoanalytic therapy George would have been offered the opportunity of understanding and perhaps resolving his tendency to repeat patterns of behaviour through the relationship with his therapist. It might be expected that he would initially have felt positive about the relationship: 'Roland, my therapist, is a nice guy, well qualified, he knows what he's doing. I'm really enjoying our sessions together. It's great to have space to talk about things.'

However, as time passed, George began to feel critical of his therapist, a negative transference becoming more obvious. The therapist, being a classical psychoanalyst, had told George next to nothing about himself. Thus George, having little reality to fall back on in the consulting room, began to experience his therapist like that most important man in his life, his father. 'Roland really doesn't care about me. Oh, he is always there, but I know that his mind is elsewhere. And some of his interpretations are so stupid!'

The first break in sessions for the holidays produced outrage, reflecting his father's departure from home years before. 'How dare he go away! Our sessions are just becoming useful, and he goes away on holiday. I bet that he's going with his children. I'm not sure that I'll cope without him. I need him too.'

Such is the process of analytic psychotherapy. The therapist becomes an individual onto whom much is 'transferred' by the patient. Positive and negative feelings are experienced in the consulting room. Treatment occurs as these transferences are analysed and 'worked through', the reality of the therapist slowly emerging as the patient begins to develop conscious awareness and control over the 'inner world' that governs his life.

David Malan illustrates the relationships between past and present with what he has called the Triangle of Persons (Figure 3.2). He described how relationships in the distant past affect relationships in present-day life with 'others' (say bosses or wife). This is the other–parent (O/P) link. The past also modifies the relationships with a therapist: the therapist–parent (T/P) link. In his book Malan uses the word 'transference' for the 'T' in this diagram as he sees this process occurring only in the consulting room (Malan 1979: 80).

George, in his individual psychotherapy, was having feelings and phantasies towards his therapist that mirrored those he has had towards his boss, Fred. Thus there was also an other–therapist (O/T) link which completed the triangle. Indeed, if Roland could not help George 'work through' his transference, therapy might have terminated with George acting out by leaving in a huff because 'My therapist never understood me, and he had too many holidays! He was never there. I don't really need him!'

Clearly both these relationships in George's adult life, with their associated feelings, roles, and behaviour have their roots in his anger and frustration with his absent, unreliable father in childhood.

So, perhaps we can attribute George's difficulties with Fred to

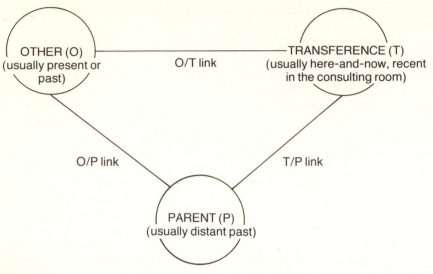

Figure 3.2
Source: adapted from Malan (1979)

transference, his anger and frustration with his father emerging in his day-to-day life yet again.

In the psychodrama George's relationships with his father were externalised not through his transference to Paul, his director, but through the enrolment of an auxiliary ego from the group. George chose Victor to play Fred in the session. This then was the relationship which was explored through the therapeutic process.

According to Greenson's definition (1967), 'all human relationships contain a mixture of realistic and transference reactions'; the difficulty is knowing in what proportion reality and transference are mixed.

George's dilemma was that angry, negative, destructive feelings emerged in his relationships with his bosses. However, as a child, he experienced many other types of relationship, with his mother, and indeed perhaps also with his father. These relationships too formed part of his 'inner world' and would also (according to the theories of transference) influence his relationships with the world. They may have contributed to the strengths of his marriage, and to his abilities as a caring respected social worker. If he had been in individual therapy they would also have emerged as different 'transferences' felt towards his psychotherapist.

A model of the psychological inner world which explains how the distant childhood past influences the present will be described in the following chapters.

MORENO: TRANSFERENCE VERSUS TELE

Moreno believed in the process of transference, but he considered it to be a phenomenon which 'plays a definite but limited part in inter-personal relations' (Moreno 1946: 229). He believed that psychoanalysts failed to acknowledge sufficiently that the psychoanalytic process involves two people in a relationship in the here-and-now, and that they *both* bring aspects of themselves to their interaction.

However, psychoanalysis, led by Freud himself, did soon become much more aware and concerned about what the therapist brings to the professional relationship. The concept of the 'countertransference', the therapist's emotional response to the patient and the treatment situation, will be considered further in Chapter 7.

Moreno, writing about the systems of relationships that the individual is part of (their 'social atom'), preferred to consider the unconscious links between people to be due to what he described as 'tele' rather than to transference. Tele is:

> The process which attracts individuals to one another or which repels them, that flow of feeling of which the social atom and the networks are composed.
>
> 'Sociometry' (Moreno 1937 in Fox 1987: 26)

He considered tele to be the general interpersonal process by which we all relate to others. Zerka Moreno says that 'tele is responsible for mutuality between persons, over and beyond their projections, and is responsible for interpersonal group cohesion'. J.L. Moreno gave an example of tele in the doctor–patient relationship.

> When a patient is attracted to a psychiatrist, two processes can take place in the patient. The one process is the development of fantasies (unconscious) which he projects onto the psychiatrist, surrounding him with a certain glamour. At the same time, another process takes place in him – that part of his ego which is not carried away by auto-suggestion feels itself into the physician. It sizes up the man across the desk and estimates intuitively what kind of man he is. These feelings into the actualities of this man, physical, mental or otherwise, partly based on information, are tele relations.
>
> (Moreno 1946 and 1977: 230)

And it must be assumed that the physician is, likewise, 'getting to know' the patient, a knowledge based in part on concrete information (say a letter of referral to the doctor or the clothes the patient is wearing), partly on tele. The doctor's feelings are, of course, to some extent influenced by his own transferences to the person sitting opposite him.

Moreno's views on the concept of the transference may be considered extraordinary by analytic psychotherapists for he wrote that:

the transference process itself was in many respects an expression of dream work, not of the patient this time, but of the psychiatrist.

The tele relation can be considered the general inter-personal process of which transference is a special psychopathological outgrowth. In consequence, underlying every transference process projected by a patient are also complex tele relationships.

(Moreno 1946 and 1977: 231)

So George, in his relationships with Fred and Peter, used tele as part of his way of knowing them. Since he was not mad, his facility of reality testing was at least adequate and his power of tele will have told him much about these men.

His difficulties with these men, I believe, arose from his early relationship with his father, but in part only since we must remember that Fred and Peter too had complex personalities with their own histories and childhood experiences which may have contributed to the problems with George.

HOW CAN YOU SPOT THE TRANSFERENCE?

The relationship between psychotherapist and patient in individual therapy can be considered to consist of three elements:

1 Those (not reality-based) aspects of the relationship derived from the patient's inner world (transference);
2 those similar aspects based on the therapist's inner world (countertransference);
3 additionally, as a rule, if the patient is not too deeply disturbed, a reality-based here-and-now relationship. Psychoanalysts call this the therapeutic or treatment alliance. It is an adult-to-adult contract and, in Moreno's terms, it is an encounter involving tele.

Therapeutic progress in individual psychoanalytic therapy is made, in part, through the analysis of the patient's transference reactions to the therapist (it must be stressed that this process is not the only thing that happens in this type of therapy). It is thus crucial for the therapist to have some idea about which of the patient's reactions are the result of the transference.

Part of this knowledge is derived from the therapist's self-awareness, having some sense of what he brings to the relationship from his countertransference.

Greenson (1967) describes some of the features of a patient's reactions to the therapist that might indicate transference, though he stresses that the presence of these qualities is not absolute evidence of the phenomenon.

Inappropriateness

As with all these characteristics, there is a degree of subjectivity in their assessment. The anger (or indeed rage) of the patient towards the therapist might be based on reality (Greenson gives the example of the therapist answering the phone during a session); however, the response might be very inappropriate, in which case transference is to be suspected.

Intensity

George described intense feelings towards his boss, Fred. He was himself concerned about a degree of inappropriateness in his reaction. The director was aware of this.

Ambivalence

Greenson describes how transference feelings towards the therapist are often marked by powerfully ambivalent and changeable responses; love and affection for the therapist exist with a degree of hate (often hidden). Certainly hate and rage coexist with a love and need that help get the patient to the session. If sexual attraction or longings develop there is usually also a sense of repulsion and guilt (that again may be covert).

George demonstrated a marked degree of ambivalence towards Fred, feeling fury towards him for what he experienced as desertion and dereliction of duty and at the same time responding to his boss in a needy and almost clinging way.

Capriciousness

Greenson describes how 'transference feelings are often inconstant, erratic and whimsical. This is particularly true early in analysis' (1967: 160).

I believe that this feature is much more typical of the transference in individual psychoanalytic therapy. Every individual relates to several people in childhood (and in many different ways to each person). Thus, in theory, many different 'transference' relationships are possible. In one-to-one psychotherapy the therapist is the only person onto whom *all* these potential transference relationships are focused. In psychodrama different group members acting as auxiliary egos in the drama are available to take on these different roles or transference reactions.

Yes, George was capable of several different types of transference reactions. However, the beauty of the psychodramatic technique allows separation onto different auxiliary egos. This brings about a useful degree of clarity which is not always (in my experience as both patient and therapist) available in individual analytic therapy.

Tenacity

Transference reactions in analysis may become prolonged and rigid, the patient holding the same somewhat inappropriate feelings about the therapist with great tenacity for months or years.

This long duration does not mean that the analytic work is stalemated, because during such periods other behavioural characteristics of the patient may change and new insights and memories may appear.

(Greenson 1967: 161)

George had shown great tenacity in the way he appeared to cling to his habit of reacting to his bosses as if they were fathers to him.

Greenson suggests that these five traits are characteristic of a repetition of previous relationships through the transference.

This holds true not only when such responses occur in regard to the analyst, but also when they arise in regard to other people. Reactions which are out of character or out of place are transference phenomena.

(Greenson 1967: 162)

THE TRANSFERENCE AND PSYCHODRAMA

The concept of transference is, after all, a construct, an idea originally developed by psychoanalysts in an attempt to explain human behaviour in the consulting room. I believe that the concept has a direct use for a psychodramatist as he attempts to make sense of the complex morass of human relationships that become apparent in a session.

An understanding of the concept of transference helps in the directing of psychodramas, providing an understanding of the protagonist's relationships with the director, and the group, and his world in general, coloured as they are by the repressed inner world.

An awareness of the features of the transference described by Greenson helps the director in his developing understanding of the protagonist. When he observes them in a protagonist in relationship with himself, other group members, or other roles played by auxiliary egos he might suspect that a hidden role or object relationship needs to be explored on the external psychodramatic stage.

This is often done by moving to another scene, usually from earlier in the protagonist's life in which the earlier and more fundamental object relationships of the role clusters are involved, usually parents (Goldman and Morrison 1984). Transference responses are not limited to the protagonist and may manifest themselves in four ways in a session.

1 In the protagonist's relationship with the director/therapist. This form resembles the transference in individual psychoanalysis.
2 In the protagonist's relationships with other group members.
3 Aspects of other group members' relationships with each other and with the director.
4 In the director's reactions to the protagonist and the group.

TO FINISH

Figure 3.3
Source: reproduced by permission of Yaffa Character Licensing

Psychodrama clearly differs in many ways from psychoanalysis. Moreno pointed out that:

> in the psychodramatic situation the chief therapist or analyst, if you wish, has associated therapists, so called auxiliary egos. He is now far less involved in the potential interactions. The auxiliary egos, moreover, are not just other analysts or observers like himself, but represent intimate roles and figures of the patient, past and present.
>
> (Moreno 1959 and 1975: 96)

I believe that those forces that drive the phenomenon of transference are related to the psychological processes that are involved in the protagonist's creation and use of auxiliary egos in a psychodrama.

In the next chapter we will look at how early experiences become part of the individual's world from which they may emerge as repetitive behaviour patterns.

4 The inner object world

The group

Paul now interviewed 'Peter'.

'Tell us a bit about yourself.'

George, as 'Peter', told the group that he was a middle-aged married social worker, head of a small team in a busy area office.

'And what sort of young man was George?'

'Oh, rather strange. Not very assertive, quiet. A bit of a loner really. I never really knew what to make of him. And he left the job very suddenly. Just gave in his notice one morning. I never really knew why. I gather that he did eventually train as a social worker.'

'Thank you Peter. Now reverse back.'

George moved and once more became himself.

'Who could play Peter?'

'David,' said George.

'Could you set the scene quickly.'

Paul suspected that the meeting between George and Peter would be brief and he did not want to waste time on a detailed scene setting.

'So Peter and George are talking together.'

George and David as 'Peter' started to talk about social work issues.

'Reverse. George be "Peter". I feel that Peter has some things to say to George.'

The scene began to become more intense. 'Peter' (now played by George) did indeed have things to say.

'I never know what you want. You hang around the office looking fed up, but you never say anything. Then some days you just don't come in at all. You say you're out seeing clients in their homes. I suppose you are. But you really should drop into the office every day.'

'Reverse.'

George reverted to himself, David became 'Peter'.

'Well, you never give me much supervision. I'm new to this job and I really need much more help. You're always too busy with other things.'

'Reverse.'

'But George, if only you were more direct. You sulk around the office. I never

know what you want. You seem fed up and angry, but I never know what about. Certainly you never told me that you wanted more supervision and help from me.'

'Reverse.'

'Peter' had little speaking to do as George was now playing both roles, almost as if he was having a dialogue with himself. This continued for some time before Paul asked, 'What do you want out of this meeting with Peter?'

'I want to tell him to give me more time! And that I'm very angry with him!' George said this to Paul.

'Don't tell me. Tell Peter. Now!'

'Peter I'm really fed up with you.'

This statement was made by George in a very lack-lustre way. There was no feeling or energy in the statement.

'Reverse!'

Then David as George repeated the complaints in the same passive manner.

'But you always whine on George. You're never satisfied. I give you as much time as the others. And you know I'm a very busy man, I've many other duties in this office.'

'Reverse.'

'Oh, I suppose you're right. I ask too much.'

George, the protagonist, once more lacked energy. It appeared that even in the safety of a psychodrama he could not confront people. Paul asked him, 'How old do you feel now, in this scene?'

'I don't know. Small, young, perhaps 7 or 8.'

Paul felt that the time was right to link George's bosses (Fred and Peter) with his father, mentioned in the warm-up.

'So was it like this with your father?'

'Yes. He was never around.'

'OK, let's finish with "Peter". Thank you, David.'

David left the stage, and Paul cleared the chairs off the stage helped by another group member.

'So, shall we go to a scene with your father?'

'Yes.'

In the warm-up the group had been asked to remember a toy from their childhood. George had initially found the exercise difficult, but had eventually role-reversed with, and become, a very upright military toy soldier his father had given him. Playing this toy had reminded him of his difficulties at work as an adult. Later, following a scene with a former supervisor he suddenly felt as if he was once more a little boy. He had remembered that this was how he felt with his father. He agreed with the director to explore the meetings between himself and his father.

'Where do you meet your father?'

'In the local coffee shop. When he did turn up to see me that is! My mother wouldn't have him in her house so we had to go somewhere to talk. He didn't have a car then . . .'

Paul felt that George was losing his energy and spontaneity as fears and anxiety began to return.

'OK George, show us this coffee shop. Set it up for us.'

George looked a little lost.

'It was all so long ago, I'm not sure I can remember.'

Paul felt that he needed to contain George's anxiety and resistance by some firm directing.

'Stand in the doorway of this coffee shop. What is its name?'

'Tea for Two. I never liked the name, or the sulky woman who served there. And the pot plants always looked half dead! What a dreary place it was.'

'So, set this scene. Where was the serving counter and the tables?'

George now seemed to be recalling more about the 'Tea for Two' café, memories perhaps he hadn't had for years. He quickly set the scene: the tables and chairs, the dying pot plants. You could almost smell the dusty atmosphere. Paul was delighted. His protagonist had refound his spontaneity. Clinically he was pleased too. He felt that George had much to sort out with his father. However, he remembered George telling the group how frustrated his wife could become with him. Paul noted the link between George's frustrations with his superiors and his wife's complaints about him.

Continued on page 82.

REPETITIONS – THE PAST RELIVED

Like Andy Capp's, George's behaviour had changed little since he was a young man.

As became clear in the psychodrama he repeated the same patterns of frustration and complaint with almost any 'father' figure he met in his adult life, a problem that could be attributed to the process of the transference (discussed in the previous chapter). What is it that drives these repetitive patterns in people's lives? Why is it that so many of us continue to be stuck in old ways of being?

Whatever controls these behaviour patterns must be firmly entrenched within our *inner world* because we carry it everywhere. We may change partners, jobs, or even countries without being able to alter our well-established mode of interaction. 'It' continues to emerge with great force, often against our conscious will, leading at times to the most troublesome circumstances.

George, when asked how old he felt in the scene with Peter, made an immediate association with his childhood; he said that he felt 7 or 8 years old. Paul suggested to him that his feelings might be linked to his relationship with his father. Using the psychodramatic method George had associated his problems at work with events in his past: situations linked by his inner world. Let us consider how this realm of the mind is created.

FREUD AND AN INFANT'S NEEDS

In order to put modern psychoanalytic theory in context let us once more consider Freud's views on the infant and its relationships with its surroundings. Freud was mostly (but not entirely) concerned with the 'closed system' of an individual's psyche or mind, which he saw as the psychological accompaniment of biological processes. He was much less concerned with the infant's relationships with others.

He believed that people have instincts or drives that have a biological origin (Freud 1915). He observed what he called the 'ego-instincts' (such as thirst or hunger). These are concerned with 'preservation, assertion, and the magnification of the individual' (Freud 1933) and influence the individual's relationship with external stimuli such as danger or the presence of food.

He also described other psychological instincts. These arise from the id which contains

> everything that is inherited, that is present at birth, that is laid down in the constitution – above all therefore, the instincts, which originate from the somatic organization and which find a psychical expression here [in the id] in forms unknown to us.
>
> (Freud 1940: 376)

One of these id instincts, Freud said, was linked to sex and the human need to procreate and continue the species. Since he saw a link between sex and love he called this instinct the libido (or Eros). It represents a force for life.

Later, in 1920, perhaps after his experiences of the horrors of the First World War, he decided humankind had a further id instinct or drive. This involved the psychic energy of aggression and the need to destroy. This death instinct, or a drive to destruction, was later called, apparently by the analyst Federn, 'thanatos' (from the Greek for death). According to Freud, this force in people attempts to return them to their previous inorganic, disorganised state. It is in opposition to the life force or libido.

The mechanisms of the psyche were, for Freud, those of the nineteenth-century sciences. Psychic energy, the drives or instincts, had a source, the id, and, like water arising from a spring, could be dammed, resulting in problems or symptoms as the pressure built up and sought release. Like hunger or thirst these psychological drives produce an internal disturbance that requires release through discharge or satisfaction.

These instincts seek 'objects' onto which to release their energy, much as the electrical energy of lightning in a thunderstorm will seek a church steeple or a tree. If they are held back they will force their own release, a situation that results in psychological problems or symptom formation. In the jargon of psychoanalysis they 'cathect' these 'objects', which may be a part of the infant itself or part of another:

> We can distinguish an instinct's source, object and aim. Its source is a state of excitement in the body, its aim is the removal of that excitement. . . . The aim can be achieved in the subject's own body: as a rule an external object is brought in.
>
> *New Introductory Lectures* (Freud 1933: 128)

The manner in which the basic instincts or drives are handled in childhood determines the subsequent development of the human personality.

Freud described, at different times, two rather inconsistent views about the ways in which, he felt, the newborn infant relates to the world (see Balint 1968).

He originally suggested that the baby needs, to gain the satisfaction of the release of its libido, an external *object* which is separate and outside the baby's body. The instinct gains release 'with the taking of nourishment. The sexual instinct has a sexual object outside the infant's own body in the shape of the mother's breast' (*Three Essays on the Theory of Sexuality*, Freud 1905b: 144). He later wrote that:

> Sucking at the mother's breast is the starting point of the whole of sexual life. . . . This sucking involves making the mother's breast the first object of the sexual instinct. I can give you no idea of the important bearing of this first object choice upon the choice of every later object.
>
> (Freud 1916–17: 356)

Freud, however, also postulated that the infant's earliest drives were directed towards parts of themselves (being less aware of those around them) rather than towards others. He called this the phase of 'primary narcissism' in which the infant interacts with its own body using its instincts in an 'auto-erotic' way. According to this theory, only later does the child begin to make relationships of psychological importance to it with others.

A NEW WORLD – THE EARLIEST PERIOD OF AN INFANT'S LIFE

Object relations theory, on the other hand, considers the infant to be an 'open system' in constant relationship to the external world. This activity results in the creation of an inner world which can be studied as it develops in childhood (see Stern's *The Interpersonal World of the Infant* 1985 or his *Diary of a Baby* 1991), or in the analytic consulting room or psychodrama theatre.

It is perhaps logical to start with the foetus's life and experiences in the womb. The psychoanalyst Michael Balint described this environment as:

> probably undifferentiated; on the one hand, there are as yet no objects in it; on the other hand, it has hardly any structure, in particular no sharp boundaries towards the individual; environment and the individual penetrate into each other, they exist together in a 'harmonious mix-up'.
>
> *The Basic Fault* (Balint 1968: 66)

It is clear from recent research that the foetus is not totally psychologically fused with the mother. Some experiences from the world outside do indeed seem to penetrate the uterus and affect the growing foetus (see Stern 1985: 92). However, the womb is still a relatively safe place from which the infant must emerge at birth into the big world outside. A world in which many others exist with whom the infant must relate. It is an environment full of new sounds, sights, smells, and other experiences, with new and exciting possibilities and dangers with which the baby must come to terms as it develops physically and psychologically.

RELATIONSHIPS, MOTIVATION, AND EMOTIONS

From the moment of birth the infant begins to relate to others. What is it that promotes these relationships with the world and what are the consequences for the inner world?

An infant is not a passive object; it moves, cries, and in time will smile, walk, and seek the company of others. It has motivational forces that are related to the basic needs that include food, sleep, and contact with others (and later in life sex): all fundamental aspects of any animal's physical survival. These systems involve inherited instincts and drives and produce complicated patterns of behaviour often involving objects or other people (see Buck 1988 for a review). It is the memory of these activities which forms the basis of a child's inner world of memories.

There are other inherited systems which act as a drive or motivation towards the organisation and integration of the memories laid down in the psyche. Such progress is crucial for the infant's survival because, like other higher animals, we are not simple programmed beings. Unlike ants we are able to learn and thus adapt ourselves to our environment.

Feelings or emotions are psychic phenomena associated with the motivational systems. They have a physiological basis, and can be described as 'drive derivatives' as they occur as a consequence of a drive's need for expression (Kernberg 1976: 29–30). An individual's emotional state depends on the neurophysiological responses occurring in the brain as the consequence of motivated behaviour (or other experiences).

Emotions provide information to the individual about the state of their drive or motivational systems. In computer terms they provide the psyche with a 'read-out' or 'feedback' about specific drive activities and the associated physiological consequences (Buck 1988).

Freud pointed out that anxiety (a feeling) acted as a signal to the psyche of the presence of danger, which he saw as being potentially external (perhaps a lion in the street) or internal (for example, conflict between the id's needs and the restraints of the super-ego and external reality).

Emotions also provide others, through the body's responses, with a 'read-out' about an individual's state. Such a 'read-out' is called communication. The facial expression and cries of a baby soon inform the mother that the baby is in a particular emotional state: a state that relates to a motivational system, for example, the need for food or physical comfort.

The rising level of sexual hormones in an adolescent boy stirs up the inherited drive for sex. The teenager will feel randy and excited (feedback to his psychological systems) and may also unconsciously communicate his desires to others, thus giving them information about the state of his drives. It is of course obvious that much communication between people about the state of the sexual drives is conscious.

Child George

Paul remembered that in a previous session George had described how, as a child, he had a need (or motivation) for physical comfort from his mother. This drove him to seek the warmth of her bed: an activity that involved verbal and non-verbal communication between mother and son. In the safety of his mother's arms he felt pleasure. Thus this emotion was the drive derivative of the motivation to seek physical security.

THE PHYSIOLOGICAL ASPECTS OF PSYCHIC DEVELOPMENT

We have our psychological roots in our organic inheritance with its internal physiological and biochemical mechanisms. However, from the moment of birth the infant is aware of its environment: it sees, it hears the voices of the parents, the doctors and the nurses, it feels the slap on the buttocks after delivery, and it has a sense of smell. The smallest child is involved in highly complex relationships with others (Stern 1985). For example, a tiny newborn infant can distinguish the special smell of its mother from all other mothers (MacFarlane 1975).

It is impossible to know exactly *how* the infant experiences the world. We do know that the physical structure of the brain is still immature and that the number of neurons will go on increasing in number for some time after birth. With this growth comes a developing sophistication and complexity in the functioning of the nervous system.

Many of the crucial developments are governed by the infant's inherited (genetic) potential. They occur regardless of the child's experiences in the external world. Blind and deaf children, who have never heard or seen the world, still develop many basic facial expressions which they use correctly in appropriate situations (Buck 1988).

However, physiologists have demonstrated that the anatomical, bio-chemical, and functional development of the brains of animals is by no means totally independent of life experiences (Buck 1988). Presumably, too, what occurs, or exists, around the baby has profound consequences on certain fundamental features of its developing brain.

For example, a kitten reared in a world without horizontal lines in its visual experience will *never* be able to respond (psychologically or physiologically) to a horizontal visual stimulus. As a consequence of the quality of its experiences as a kitten the necessary cells for such a response cannot function in the visual cortex of the adult cat (see Goldstein 1989).

For the human infant, too, experiences of the external world have an influence on the inner world, in a physiological sense. It has been said that individuals brought up in an environment full of the curves of round mud huts and trees and without the straight lines and angles of brick-built houses (as may have occurred in the past in parts of Africa) have trouble with perceptual tasks or illusions that involve straight lines and corners (Gregory 1966: 161).

It seems reasonable to assume that the developing psyche and personality are (to some extent) accompanied by similar neurophysiological processes in the brain in which the genetic disposition of the infant acts to bring order to its experiences of the world.

Although there remains a great gulf between the knowledge of human neurophysiology and anatomy and the amazingly complex functioning of the human psyche, as the years pass Freud's dream of relating the biological with the psychological is nearer fruition.

PSYCHOLOGICAL ASPECTS OF PSYCHIC DEVELOPMENT: BIRTH AND AFTER

At birth the umbilicus is cut to allow the infant a life physically separate from the mother. However, the psychological ties may last longer. Some psychoanalysts considered that the infant discovers only slowly that the other person (often mother) is not the same as itself (see J. Klein 1987). However, this conceptualisation seems to have been based, in part, on those disturbed children and adults who are for ever unclear about what belongs to themselves and what belongs to others, with boundaries that remain for ever blurred, leading to psychotic (and perhaps autistic) confusions. Most infants are, in fact, aware that they are separate from others in their world (Stern 1985: 105).

As infants (or adults) we *sense* the world (with eyes, nose, ears), a process that leads to activity in the neurons which is analysed by the nervous system to form *perceptions*. These physiological experiences may then be remembered, laid down as records in the mind together with the associated emotional responses. This, of course, is a process that continues throughout life (Buck 1988; Goldstein 1989): We hear (or sense) sound, we perceive music, we appreciate Mozart with pleasure.

We have five senses, and there is evidence that the final memory or representation of an experience is amodal, that it involves features from more than one sensory modality (Stern 1985: 51); that is, the mind automatically integrates into one perception information about the sight, sound, and smell of an experience.

It might be assumed that for the tiny infant almost every experience (in its narrow new world) is notable and memorable. However, its cognitive mechanisms are still immature and the analysis of the sensations into perceptions will be incomplete and simple. The infant's psyche will become filled with many new memories which will be associated with aspects of the physiological response appropriate to the feeling or affect experienced at the time.

Just as the nervous system co-ordinates the infant's developing motor skills such as sitting up and walking, it is the task of the infant's developing psyche to start to make sense of and integrate all this information.

A THEORY OF OBJECT RELATIONSHIPS

How do drives, emotions, and memory traces produce the complex inner world of individuals such as Andy Capp or George?

George's experiences of his relationship with his father when he gave him the toy soldier became part of his inner world. His senses gave him information about the meeting. He also had associated feelings, of unhappiness, anxiety, and anger with both his parents which became internal records or memories that were re-enacted in the psychodrama.

The infant's first memories are simpler than those internalised by George when he met his father. However, they are the basis of the developing inner world.

The American psychoanalyst Otto Kernberg has proposed an object relations theory explaining these psychic developments (Kernberg 1975, 1976, 1980). He described how the infant's relationships with the external world result in changes in its psyche. This process, which he called 'internalisation', becomes more complex with increasing age. He wrote:

> Introjections, identifications and ego identity are three levels of the process of internalisation: all three will be referred to comprehensively as identifications systems. All these processes of internalisation bring about psychic precipitates or *structures* for which we will use exactly the same term as for the respective *mechanisms*. Introjection, for example, will be considered to be both a process of the psychic apparatus and as a result of the process, a structure.
>
> *Object-Relations Theory and Clinical Psychoanalysis*
> (Kernberg 1976: 25; my italics)

Josephine Klein (1987) called the process 'learning' and the structural products in the psyche 'memory traces'. Certainly these terms more readily coincide with our everyday experience of the world.

Let us consider Kernberg's three levels or stages of internalisation: *introjections* (discussed below), *identifications*, and *ego identity* (see Chapter 5).

Kernberg's level 1: introjection

Kernberg suggests that the psychic memory traces, taken into the infant's psyche at this stage of internalisation, consist of three basic elements or components:

a object-images or object-representations,
b self-images or self-representations, and
c drive derivatives or dispositions to specific affective states.

(Kernberg 1976: 26)

The process of 'remembering' depends on the infant *sensing* and *perceiving* someone (or something) in the external world. The memory of an-other (or object) is then linked to a memory of the self (as experienced at the time of the interaction and subsequent perception) together with the affects or feelings existing in the infant at that point in time.

These early internal psychic structures consist of representations of *only* two objects in relationship, for at this stage the infant is mostly aware of only two things at any one point in time: itself and another.

The inner objects that result from the internalisation or memory of the self (in relationship with the other) could be called 'self-objects'. However, this term, in the form 'selfobject', has already been appropriated by Heinz Kohut (1977) for a different psychoanalytic concept. Therefore, in this book, I propose to call this inner object an 'I-object', a term that reflects the concerns of both Martin Buber, with his ideas about I–Thou relationships (Cooper 1990), and the psychoanalyst Joyce McDougall who referred to the *I* that is involved in, among other things, repetitions (McDougall 1966: 4 and 7). The reciprocal inner objects could be called 'thou-objects'. I will, however, continue to call them 'other-objects', as this term is more in line with modern usage in English.

Kernberg, like Freud, conceptualises the psyche as consisting of the two basic human drives, aggression and libido, which promote, and are an integral part of, human interactions. However, he stresses that they are not rigid, separate, genetically given forces, but reflect the nervous system's ability to have pleasurable and painful affects along the polarity 'good' to 'bad'.

Libido is the drive to have pleasurable experiences which result in the physiological responses associated with positive feelings or affects. Negative feelings (say of anger or frustration) are often associated with the aggressive drive. Kernberg believes that in the two basic drives 'the affective colouring of both the object-image and the self-image [are] under the influence of the drive representative present at the time of the interaction' (Kernberg 1976: 29).

Or, to put it another way, the object relationship remembered by the infant is linked with the mood pertaining at the time. If the instinct seeking release was 'libido' the mood (or affect) would be positive or pleasurable. If the drive was 'aggression' then the mood would be one of anger or distress. Thus a basic early memory trace, or triad of experience, has three parts, as illustrated in Figure 4.1.

Let's look at a simple example:

A hungry baby is sucking from its mother's breast, giving it the sensation of satisfaction and pleasure.

The image of the object (other-object or object representation) may be that of the breast (or indeed just the nipple) as the immature infant psyche cannot yet perceive that the breast is part of something larger, namely its mother. The image of the self (I-object or self-representation) is the mouth (or indeed perhaps just the lips); again the infant, due to its cognitive immaturity, may not yet be able to perceive as parts of an integrated whole (itself) the separate parts of its body. The affect is one of pleasure.

THE TRIAD OF EXPERIENCE

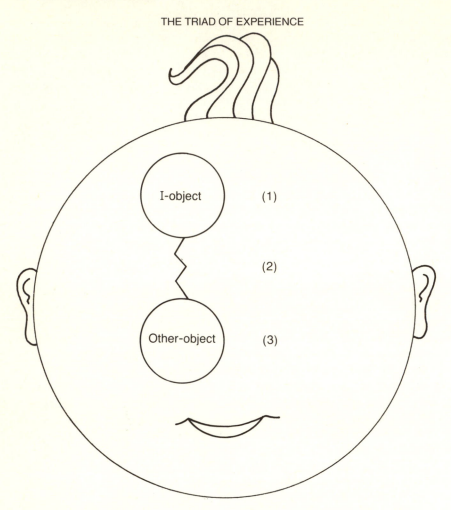

In the inner world the self-representation or I-object (1) is in relationship with the representation of an-other or other-object (3). The memory trace of this dyad is associated with the appropriate affectual colouring (2), creating a triad of experience.

Figure 4.1   The triad of experience

Kernberg suggests that in this initial phase of introjection, the infant does not possess the perceptive and cognitive abilities to recognise the role aspects of the relationship.

Obviously the 'other' (in this case the mother) also has her own internal world, but one that is more complex, sophisticated (and one hopes adult) than that of her baby. Unless the mother is deeply psychologically disturbed she will see her baby as a whole separate being, and she will also have a view of herself as a complex person with many integrated roles (mother, wife, friend, worker, and indeed child to her own parents).

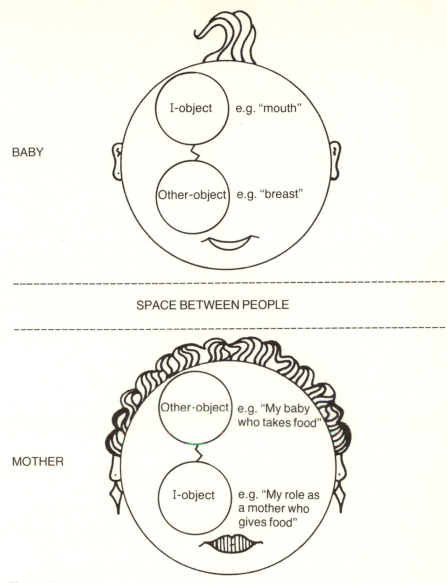

BABY

OTHER-OBJECT e.g. "breast"

I-object e.g. "mouth"

SPACE BETWEEN PEOPLE

MOTHER

Other-object e.g. "My baby who takes food"

I-object e.g. "My role as a mother who gives food"

Figure 4.2

This relationship laid down in the mind is shown diagrammatically in Figure 4.2. I have chosen to link the I-object with the other-object with a zig-zag line to illustrate the complexity of the object relationship, including as it does aspects of roles and affects or feelings.

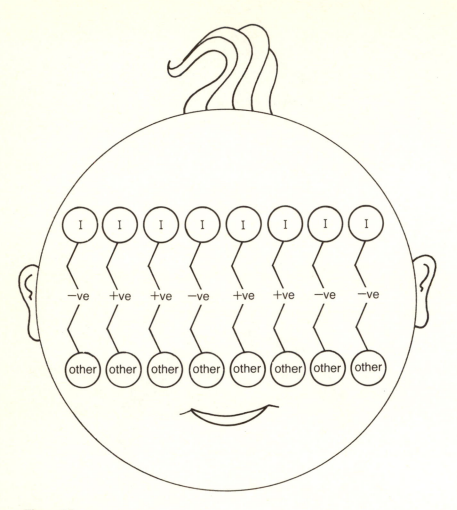

Figure 4.3
Note: For the sake of clarity the terms I-object and other-object have been
abbreviated to I and other.

M-other and self

As I have described, Balint and other psychoanalysts see the infant at birth as
not being psychologically separated from the m-other, a view that is central to
much psychoanalytic writing. For example, Kernberg suggested that, for the
tiniest infant, the situation is not quite like that illustrated in Figure 4.2 for:

in the earliest introjections the object and self-image are not yet
differentiated from each other, and the definition of introjection suggested
really corresponds to a somewhat later stage in which successive

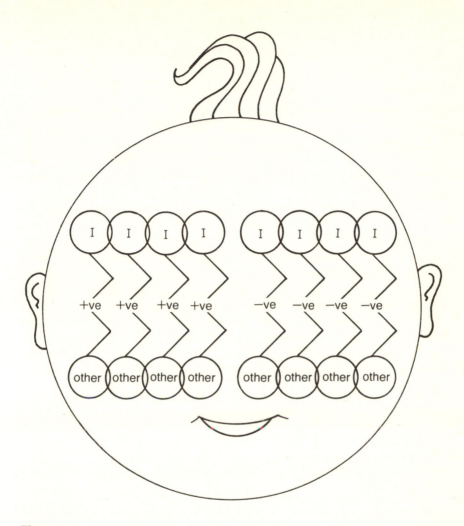

Figure 4.4

differentiations, refusions and redifferentiations of the self- and object-images have finally crystallized into clearly delimited components.

(Kernberg 1976: 29)

This view is not supported by recent work in developmental psychology (Stern 1985). However, whatever the exact details of the infant's earliest experiences of self and other, it soon begins to accumulate many separate and unintegrated object relationships each with its associated mood or affect.

Put diagrammatically, the inner world of the infant begins to look like

Figure 4.3, a floating mass of unorganised object relationships. Kernberg, no doubt having had a good scientific training, describes these object relationships as having either a 'positive or negative valence'. (The 'valency' of an ion or molecule depends on whether it has a positive or negative electric charge.)

Order begins to grow from chaos

The drives, in their various ways, act to promote the survival of the individual and the species. They are also, according to Kernberg, the organisational forces in the psyche. Their ability to add affective colour to the object relationships is crucial in the process, an early function of the infant's ego, that sorts out the initially random memory traces resulting from the infant's experiences.

The drives come to represent two poles or extremes (pleasure and pain) of the possible affective states associated with the memory traces in the infant's psyche. According to Kernberg, initial organisation is by valency, negative and positive. Order is brought from chaos by the association within the psyche of various object relationships with the same affectional valency. Positive (or 'good') memory traces become associated with one pole (libido) and traces associated with negative (or 'bad') feelings with the other. Thus the process of integration within the psyche begins and is well under way by the time the baby is three months old (Kernberg 1976).

Stern does not accept that such a clear-cut separation into 'good' and 'bad' exists in the infant's psyche. However, he wrote that:

> In spite of this critique [of Kernberg's views], I do believe that infants will group interpersonal experiences into various pleasurable and unpleasurable categories, that is, into hedonic clusters. The forming of hedonic clusters of experience, however, is different from dichotomizing or splitting all interpersonal experience along hedonic lines.
>
> (Stern 1985: 253)

Melanie Klein also saw the infant's psyche as having 'good' and 'bad' realms, but she saw this separation or 'splitting' as an active psychologically defensive act, keeping 'good' and 'bad' apart. I will return to this point later.

So, in the inner world there begins to be a degree of fusion or integration of both the I-object and the other-objects or representations. Diagrammatically the psyche begins to look like Figure 4.4 on p. 63.

5   Relationships and roles

Roles?

What would you be to me,
Mother or child?
Or is there someone else?
You seem not to know
I cannot tell.

This morning I watched unnoticed,
Fighting fear as I saw
The iron-rigid stance,
The tight, locked-up lips,
The tense, martyred movements
And hot, angry eyes.

Just for a moment I saw
Another mother at her hated task.
(Are dish-water hands
Always so vengeful?)
My little, lonely child
Loved, but was unloved
In that stiff, armoured back,
In that war-weary silence,
In those resenting steps
And go-away gaze.

Yet within hours you came
Looking lost and bereft,
Baby-wet eyes pleading
For the mother in me
To hold and cherish,
To comfort and love
Your forgivable child.

I saw her again then
Child-bride at her sink,
Softer and sadder,
Too young for her task.
Salt-streaked cheeks
And quivering lips
Needing maternal reassurance
And feeding forgiveness
At a too-young breast.

What would I be to you,
Child to the mother
Or mother to child?
Or is there someone else,
Searching through time-locked roles
For release into self?

'ME' 30/3/90

SO WHY MAKE RELATIONSHIPS?

The poet ME described the pain that may occur in relationships, especially when there is confusion over roles.

But other people are essential for our survival. George needed his mother, he had from his birth. He also needed his father, and had started his relationship with him when he was only hours old. Like all children, his contacts with others were crucial for his physical and emotional survival. But his parents hated each other and were constantly fighting. These events caused him anxiety and pain.

Before we go on to consider the next stages of the process of internalisation as described by Kernberg, let us pause a moment and consider psychoanalytic views about what drives the infant, then the child, and finally the adult into making any contacts with the great world around it, for without such contact no internal 'object relationships' will ever develop.

Freud associated the process of relating with the instinctual need for the expression or release of the drives from the id which for their satisfaction, or pleasure, must cathect an object.

The British psychotherapist Ronald Fairbairn saw the libido, however, as primarily object seeking (Fairbairn 1952: 176). The basic drive in the individual (and thus the infant) is to find an 'object', or, in more common language, *someone else*. In the infant this drive is clearly related to survival, as it needs someone (usually mother) to provide food, warmth, comfort, and safety. In adults this 'object'-seeking drive is related to finding other people for, among other things, close relationships, sex, and procreation.

I am personally sympathetic to this view, finding it more compatible with an ethnological view of 'man the animal'. Konrad Lorenz described how a fundamental instinct of an animal is to bond to a mother figure. For infant ducks this bonding occurs to the first object heard to quack, be this a 'a fat white Pekin duck, or a still fatter man' (Lorenz 1952; see also Bowlby 1969). Lorenz was 'mother' to the ducklings and they followed him.

In 1963 Fairbairn summarised his theoretical views. His first seven points were:

1 An ego is present from birth.
2 Libido is a function of the ego.
3 There is no death instinct; and aggression is a reaction to frustration or deprivation.
4 Since libido is a function of the ego and aggression is a reaction to frustration or deprivation, there is no such thing as the 'id'.
5 The ego, and therefore libido, is fundamentally object-seeking.
6 The earliest and original form of anxiety, as experienced by the child, is separation-anxiety.
7 Internalization of the object is a defensive measure originally adopted by the child to deal with his original object (the mother and her breast) in so far as it is unsatisfying.

> 'Synopsis of an object-relations theory of the personality'
> (Fairbairn 1963: 224)

Negative feelings or affects are not the result of the death instinct, but of libidinal attachment to bad objects (Fairbairn 1952: 78).

I am, however, less convinced by Fairbairn's view that the first objects (people) internalised are 'bad objects'; a process which, he postulates, occurs so the infant can cope with a frustrating or bad external object (say the mother). Fairbairn wrote:

> the internalisation of bad objects represents an attempt on the part of the child to make objects in his environment 'good' by taking upon himself the burden of their apparent 'badness', and thus to make his environment tolerable. This defensive attempt to establish outer security is purchased at the price of inner insecurity.
>
> *Psychoanalytic Studies of the Personality* (Fairbairn 1952: 164)

In the model described in this book the infant internalises *all* experiences, in the form of pairs of inner objects with the associated positive or negative affects, which are based on the neurophysiological response of the infant at the time the relationship was occurring.

George's need for others in infancy (J. Klein 1987) was the first step towards the creation of his inner world, filled with object relationships coloured by both positive and negative affects.

Kernberg's level 2: identification

> Indentify: associate (... oneself) inseparably or very closely (with a party, policy, etc.) ... establish the identity of ...
>
> (*Concise Oxford Dictionary* 1990)

As time passes the infant's nervous system continues to grow and mature, and along with these physical and neurophysiological changes the structure and functioning of the psyche (or ego) becomes more complex and sophisticated.

Kernberg suggested that by the end of the first year of life, as its perceptive and cognitive abilities develop, the baby is able to:

> recognise the role aspects of interpersonal interaction. Role implies the presence of a socially recognized function that is being carried out by the object or by both participants in the interaction.

> (Kernberg 1976: 30)

In this more advanced form of internalisation the infant becomes aware of and learns about those roles it takes in response to the reciprocal roles of others. Indeed they become part of the inner world.

We thus return to our example of the mother feeding her child: for the young child the mother has the role of the 'feeder' or 'giver', while the baby itself has the role of 'the fed' or 'taker'. The roles associated with feeding are likely to be internalised with a positive affective colouring, although a bad experience for the baby while feeding may result in an internalisation associated with a negative affect.

Other possible roles, such as 'the smacked' and the reciprocal role of 'the beater', are associated with negative feelings such as despair, fury, and pain.

As with introjections, these more complex and richer identifications tend to remain associated with others of like affective status. Thus the dyads of, say, feeder–fed, kisser–kissed, comforter–comforted become associated together in the mind, forming indeed a rather idealised inner image of both 'self' (fed/kissed/comforted) and 'other' (feeder/kisser/comforter). Likewise those object relationships associated with negative feelings also remain associated.

Moreno too was very concerned about roles which he defined as:

> the actual and tangible forms which the self takes. We thus define the role as the functioning form the individual assumes in the specific moment he reacts to a specific situation in which other persons or objects are involved. The symbolic representation of this functioning form, perceived by others, is called the role. The form is created by past experiences and the cultural patterns of the society in which he lives. . . . Every role is a fusion of private and collective elements. Every role has two sides, a private and collective side.

> (Moreno 1961 in Fox 1987: 62)

Moreno thus adds to the personal and developmental (but still socially determined) aspects of the 'role' described by Kernberg another element: society's view of a role, say that of 'mother' or 'doctor', a view that contains historical, cultural, and political elements. This results in time, in the child or adult, in the creation of sophisticated internal roles that integrate the personal and private with the public.

In time there is a degree of fusion of objects (and their associated roles). If

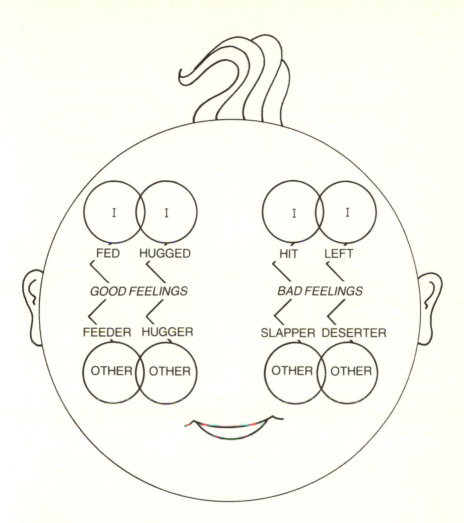

Figure 5.1

for the moment we consider only the child's relationship with its mother, four possible integrated inner objects exist. There are inner 'good' and 'bad' *I*-objects and the reciprocal inner 'good' and 'bad' (m)other-objects. It must be stressed that all four are part of the inner world of the infant. All are aspects of its developing psyche. To continue with our diagrams, the inner world of identifications looks rather like Figure 5.1.

These identifications integrate various objects and roles by the affectual colouring. However, it is apparent that eventually the psyche also integrates roles by other qualities, such as 'maleness' or 'maternal features'. The resulting associations of roles have theoretical links with the concepts of 'role clusters' described in psychodrama.

The super-ego, according to psychoanalytic theory, develops rather later in the child's life. It may also be considered to be a role cluster, being an association of the memory traces of object relationships involved with the external prohibitions of parents and, later, society.

Kernberg went on to point out that:

> Since identifications imply the internalisation of roles ... behavioural manifestations of the individual, which express one or both of the reciprocal roles of the respective interaction, become a predominant result of identification.... The child learns his own, at first more passively experienced roles as part of his self-image component of the identification. He also learns mother's roles (as part of mother's object-image) and may at some time re-enact those roles.
>
> (Kernberg 1976: 31)

Thus the child will at times play at being 'mother', feeding his dolls and teddy bear. At other times he will punish them and, perhaps, 'send them to bed without food'. If he has been beaten or shouted at, he may assault his toys.

It is as if the 'self' who actually engages in behaviour (or games), at any one point in time, can become one of (again in a simplified form) the four basic poles of the internalised objects. This is shown in Figure 5.2.

In fact it seems probable that in the state in which the 'self' feels itself to be like an internalised other-object an intermediate step in the psyche has occurred in which the self-representation introjects, or identifies with, aspects of the internal representation in its psyche of others. This is the reverse of what Sandler (1988: 16) described as stage one projective identification (see Chapter 8), and thus may be seen as a form of introjective identification. These processes occur within the inner world and do not (at this point) involve people or objects *outside* the mind. They thus occur in phantasy.

Life is experienced as all 'good' or all 'bad'. People are not experienced as whole or integrated. Indeed relationships between self and other may still be conceived of as being between parts of people (e.g. breasts, mouths, hands). The self (or the other: breast, mother, father, etc.) is either great, idealised, and all-providing, or the self (or the other) is awful and denigrated.

George too had internalised roles, but, as he had moved beyond these early stages in his psychic development, his roles were more complex, and involved interactions of different sub-roles. In everyday life he considered himself to be a male social worker; however, conceptually this role could be separated into its original components, a task that could be undertaken in a psychodrama. His maleness resulted from a role identification with his father, while the roles of feeder and supplier, which he enacted in his job as a caring social worker, were linked to internal object relationships involving his mother.

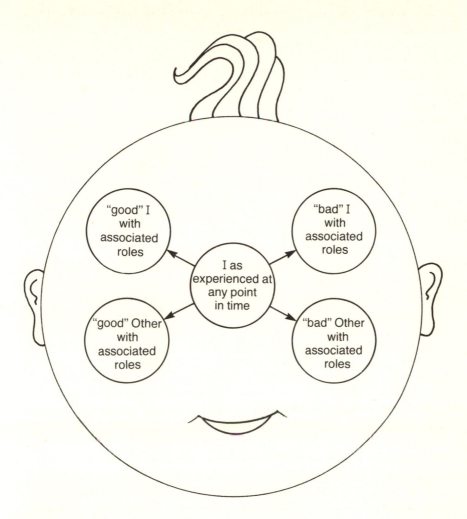

Figure 5.2

Melanie Klein and the paranoid-schizoid position

Klein's theories of early human development are complex, and different in important ways from the ideas developed in this book. However, there are important similarities (which is not surprising as Klein was one of the first object relations theorists). Her views are well reviewed in the books by Hanna Segal (1964 and 1973, 1979) and Hinshelwood (1989).

Klein's writings seem to propose an inner world in which the inner objects exist, floating free on their own rather than in dyads (with associated affects), as described in this book. The outcome, in terms of psychic structure, in Klein's view is similar even if the mechanisms whereby the inner world develops in an infant are rather different.

Her model of early psychic development depends heavily on her belief in the two basic instincts and drives. For her the inner world in the infant was a place where active psychological 'phantasies' (of love and destruction) control and order mental life from the start.

Melanie Klein too described the inner world of the infant as consisting of inner objects kept apart from each other. However, for her, this situation was the result of a splitting process in the psyche associated with the mechanism of projection. She called this phase of development (which she dated as the first few months of life) the 'paranoid-schizoid position'.

For Klein the defensive process of projection was of crucial importance in infancy; aspects of the 'death instinct' are projected onto the external object which is then perceived as 'bad'. The libido may also be projected so the object (say the mother's breast) is then perceived as 'good'.

These external objects (now coloured by projected affects) can then be internalised to become parts of the infant's psyche (internal objects). The resulting objects, such as the 'internal breast', remain actively split or separated within the child's psyche, as a defence against the overwhelming anxiety that would occur if the 'good' psychic object were to be damaged by the sadistic destructive impulses (the 'death' instinct or aggressive drive) associated with the 'bad' internal objects.

In this early phase of life the immature ego must defend against the anxieties that could not be tolerated if an attempt were made to integrate 'good' and 'bad' internal objects. Klein's view was that 'sufficient ego exists at birth to experience anxiety, use defence mechanisms and form primitive object-relations in phantasy and reality' (*Introduction to the Work of Melanie Klein*, Segal 1973: 24). Klein believed that:

> the ego is incapable of splitting the object – internal and external – without a corresponding splitting taking place within the ego . . . [these] processes . . . are of course bound up with the infant's phantasy life; and the anxieties which stimulate the mechanisms of splitting are also of a phantastic nature. It is in phantasy that the infant splits the object and the self, but the effect of this phantasy is a very real one, because it leads to feelings and relations (and later on, thought-process) being in fact cut off from one another.
>
> 'Notes on some schizoid mechanisms' (Klein 1946 and 1975: 6)

However, it has been pointed out that:

> Unfortunately in their formulations the [Kleinians] appear to have attributed profound psychological knowledge to the infant by confounding psychological and biological behaviour. As a consequence they endow the infant with psychological intentionality and complex cognition in the first

weeks of life. In our view, the infant is, for a considerable time, the passive experience of its own activities, feelings and sensations.

(Sandler and Sandler 1978: 285fn.)

Of being unintegrated: a world of good and bad

Thus, in Kernberg's phase of 'identifications' the inner world of the very young child consists of objects (those of self and others) linked in dyads with associated roles and affects. The images of self are not integrated nor are those of others. As a result the child does not have (by sane adult standards) a realistic view of the self or of the world of others.

Klein believed that by the sixth month of life this phase resolved or matured into what she called the 'depressive position'. This correlates with Kernberg's third state, that of ego identity which Kernberg suggests develops over the first year of life, to be followed by further modifications and integrations of the inner object world over the next couple of years – if indeed integration ever fully occurs, for in some traumatised and deprived children (lacking adequate parenting) these modifications of growth and integration occur in only a partial manner. Such individuals remain disturbed all their lives.

The psychologist and educator Barbara Dockar-Drysdale (1973: 33) described them, as children, as 'unintegrated'. They panic constantly, have disruptive and chaotic behaviour, and a very poor sense of self and of their own boundaries.

Such children grow into adults who live on the borderline of psychosis. At times their reality testing is adequate, at others the integrated sense of self and others collapses, reality testing becomes impaired, and psychosis occurs. Kernberg, other psychoanalysts, and some psychiatrists describe such people as having 'borderline personality disorders' (Kernberg 1975; American Psychiatric Association 1980; Pope *et al.* 1983). Perhaps 'unintegrated personalities' would more accurately describe their psychic problems. The problems of such individuals are considered in more detail in Chapter 8.

The psychological functioning of the normal child in the period of 'identification' (or Klein's paranoid-schizoid phase), the older 'unintegrated' child, or the 'borderline' adult are determined both by the structure of the inner world and by the associated psychological defences: projection, projective identification, and splitting.

Kernberg's level 3: ego identity

With time the increasing cognitive and perceptive skills and ego development of the child begin to allow for an increasing integration of inner objects. Kernberg said that this internal synthesis implies;

1 a consolidation of ego structures connected with a sense of the continuity of the self (the self being the organisation of the self-image components of introjections and identifications) . . .

2   a consistent, overall conception of the 'world of objects' derived from the organisation of the object-image components of introjections and identifications and a sense of consistency in one's own personal interactions...
3   a recognition of this consistency in interactions as characteristic of the individual by his interpersonal environment and, in turn, the perception by the individual of this recognition by the environment ('confirmation').

(Kernberg 1976: 32)

The child has developed a defined and more realistic view of who it is. It has an identity, a sense of 'absolute sameness' and an 'individuality' (*Concise Oxford Dictionary* 1990). To put it another way, our young child begins to recognise that the mother that feeds her is the *same* person as the one who may frustrate, deprive, or even hit him. Likewise the child discovers that the 'self' that loves and needs the mother is the *same* as the 'self' that hates and becomes furious with mother.

The British paediatrician and psychoanalyst D.W. Winnicott felt that this phase of development should be called the 'stage of concern' for:

At first the infant (from our point of view) is ruthless; there is no concern yet as to the results of instinctual love *.... It should be noted that the infant does not feel ruthless.... The stage is one that is pre-ruth.
* [D.W.W.'s footnote:] This love is originally a form of impulse, gesture, contact, relationship, and it affords the infant satisfaction of self-expression and release from instinctual tension.

Through Paediatrics to Psycho-analysis (D.W. Winnicott 1958: 265)

Ruth is now a little used word defined in Webster's Dictionary of 1864 as 'Sorrow for the misery of another; pity; tenderness'.

To stir up gentle ruth
Both for her noble blood, and for her tender youth.

(Spenser)

It should be noted that Winnicott believed in 'instinctual love' and saw aggression as evidence of life, not of a death instinct. He added, as a footnote:

Here please allow for a quite different thing, which I must omit; aggression that is non-inherent and that belongs to all sorts of chance adverse persecutions which are the lot of some babies but not the majority.

(Winnicott 1958: 265)

According to these theories the infant is not aware at first that the person it screams at, hits, and bites is also the one that it loves, cuddles, and needs so much. However, developmental psychologists have shown that a baby is capable of integration, certainly across sensory modalities, and perhaps also across time (Stern 1985).

As the ego matures and develops, Winnicott said:

At some time or other in the history of development of every normal human being there comes the change over from pre-ruth to ruth. No one will question this. The only thing is when does this happen, how, and under what conditions?

(Winnicott 1958: 265)

Winnicott attributed this development to the quality of the mother's relationship with her infant, for the 'good-enough' mother is able (without much thought) to know that the baby who, at times, hates and kicks her is the same child who loves and smiles at her. She can understand its complex, but initially non-verbal, communications, and view her relationship with her child with more objectivity. As an adult, she remembers her experiences and is able to integrate her impressions of her offspring over time even if the child cannot yet manage this.

The child will, with the help of what Winnicott called the 'facilitating environment' (1965), mature so that (to return to our simple diagrams) its inner world begins to look like Figure 5.3.

All these aspects lie within the infant's own inner world. The more integrated inner-object 'mother' refers at first to only one person in the external world. However (as with the affects), the psyche will tend to link together similar inner-objects in their dyad relationships. As a consequence the child will tend to associate 'mother figures' in the external world in the same way the 'mother-objects' have become associated in the internal world. The child will by now also have many more 'other' internal-objects, including perhaps 'father', 'brothers', and 'uncles'.

This clustering of inner other-objects with symbolic and role-related associations accounts for George's troubles with father figures in adult life.

So the inner world is in fact increasingly complex and might look a bit more like Figure 5.4.

The internalised aspects of 'other' produce what Sandler described as the 'representational world' (Sandler and Rosenblatt 1962). This is an internal model in the psyche of the external world. It consists of a more mature integration of the other-objects or representations. It is used by the individual to predict the world's behaviour (always a useful thing to be able to do).

THE ARRIVAL OF THE UNCONSCIOUS

In the earliest months of an infant's life all its internal object relationships or memory traces remain, potentially, accessible to consciousness. As I have described, they are eventually organised by affectual colouring, so that the psyche keeps 'good' from 'bad'. As integration increases anxiety arises, caused by attempts to bring together conflicting object relationships. This can be reduced by the use of the defence mechanisms of splitting, projection, and projective identification (see Chapter 8).

The implication of this model of the psyche is that in these early months

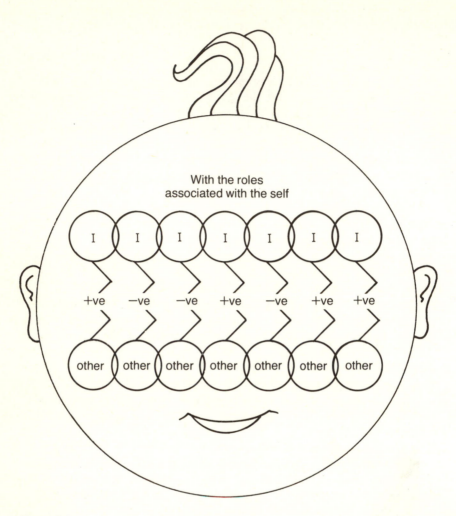

With the roles
associated with the self

Figure 5.3

there is no unconscious. The infant's sense of self at any point in time moves between the various possible (but separate) *I* or self-representations. It is only later, when the object relationships in the mind begin to become integrated, that repression starts to gain prominence as a defence against anxiety.

Repression results in the loss from conscious availability of whole object relationships with the associated affects. It is at this stage of psychic development (in this model) that the unconscious develops as a part of the psyche. Thus the unconscious, rather than being the source of the drives of libido and thanatos (the id in Freud's topology), is the unconscious realm of

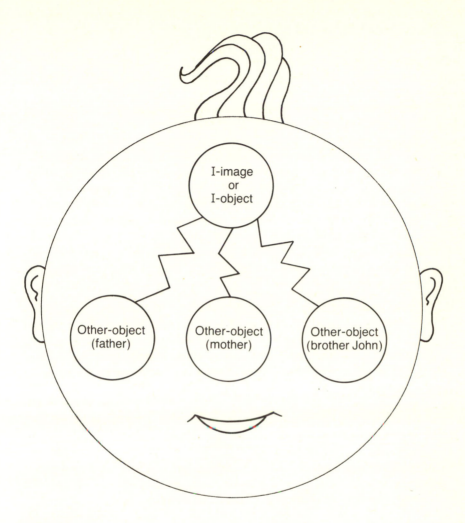

Figure 5.4

the mind to which have been banished those object relationships that cause
the more conscious areas of the psyche distress, anxiety, and pain (Kernberg
1976: 69).

PHANTASIES, DREAMS, AND THE WORLD OF THE UNCONSCIOUS

As adults we are well aware of our conscious fantasies or day-dreams. Note
how most of these involve aspects of *oneself* (sometimes projected or
displaced onto others) and an *object*, be this a person or a thing, in

relationship. Such phantasies are also explicit in the play of children, a point that both Melanie Klein and Moreno observed. Other, more deeply buried phantasies emerge in the rich world of dreams.

An internal object relationship could also be described as a phantasy. It represents an internal drama in the mind, with an object, and a subject, together with roles and feelings. For example: baby chokes while feeding at mother's breast and feels upset and angry.

It is in dreams that aspects of these buried relationships become conscious, altered by the mechanisms of dream-work: condensation, displacement, and symbolisation (see Rycroft 1968: 37). It is when these aspects of the psyche are conscious, and thus amenable to thought (cognition), that change is possible.

To describe to others a phantasy (once it has become conscious) we often use words, either spoken or written, but the earliest internalisations are clearly non-verbal and 'the phantasies are experienced as sensations, later they take the form of plastic images and dramatic representations' ('The nature and function of phantasy', Isaacs 1948: 96).

These early inner object relationships were laid down (or remembered) long before the infant has any use for or understanding of words and language. Susan Isaacs wrote:

> The primary phantasies, the representatives of the earliest impulses of desire and aggressiveness, are expressed in and dealt with by mental processes far removed from words and conscious relational thinking. At a later period they may under certain conditions (sometimes in children's spontaneous play, sometimes only in analysis) become capable of being expressed in words.
>
> There is a wealth of evidence to show that phantasies are active in the mind long before language has developed, even that in the adult they continue to operate alongside and independently of words. Meanings, like feelings, are far older than speech. . . .
>
> In childhood and in adult life, we live and feel, we phantasise and act far beyond our verbal meanings. E.g. some of our dreams show us what worlds of drama we can live through in visual terms alone.
>
> (Isaacs 1948: 84)

Susan Isaacs continued by pointing out that many activities, including dance, music, painting, and sculpture are experienced non-verbally, as are many other aspects of human interactions (for example, facial expressions, tones of voice, or gesture).

> These things, perceived and imagined and felt about, are the stuff of experience. Words are a means of *referring* to experience, actual or phantasied, but are not identical with it, not a substitute for it. Words may evoke feelings and images and actions, and point to situations; they do so by virtue of being signs of experience, not of being themselves the main material of experience.
>
> (Isaacs 1948: 84–5)

Dreams and certain aspects of repetitive behaviour suggest that within the integrated representations of self and others there lurk what Kernberg described as 'nonmetabolised object relationships' (1976: 29) which have not become solid parts of the ego identity or of the representational world. Normally these rogue (and usually primitive) object relationships are kept repressed, remaining buried within the integrated aspects of the ego identity.

However, from time to time, they may surface to influence behaviour (which can become quite disturbed as it then may be controlled by infantile object relationships). With the help of psychotherapy these phantasies can enter consciousness in a more controlled and helpful manner.

In George's psychodrama the externalisation of his inner world involved object relationships (by then integrated) from the phase of concern (or ruth) in his development. However, for some protagonists, this therapeutic method also allows for the dramatic exploration of these original, primitive dyads (as well as the more integrated internal views of self and others with their component roles).

The child, now having concern for its angry attacks on the person it loves, will begin to feel distress and guilt. It was these feelings (in adults sometimes associated with the clinical state of depression) that led Melanie Klein to call this normal period of development the 'depressive position'. The child struggles with its ambivalence about its love and hate, and about its power to hurt (or even, in phantasy, destroy) a loved person.

Some thoughts on terms and definitions

Winnicott (1958: 264–5) pointed out that most young children do not become depressed (a term that implies illness) at this time, hence his wish to use the more positive term 'the stage of concern or ruth'. He accepted, however, that for many reasons Klein's term might gain prominence (as indeed it has in some circles)

Psychological and psychoanalytic terms (or jargon) are often the cause of much confusion and indeed dissension. Many are ugly and rather brutal, seeming inappropriate to the wonders and mysteries of the growth of the human psyche. How can the mother, or indeed the breast or penis, be thought of as just an 'object'?

Additional problems arise when different authors coin new terms for concepts only slightly different (if different at all) from the ideas of others to describe the richness of the early psychological development of a child.

Josephine Klein (1987) makes a plea for plain simple English in the discussion of these matters and I would tend to agree with her. However, the history of the theories of the development and functioning of the human psyche cannot be ignored totally so I have continued to use the accepted and established technical terms.

WHEN DO WE INTEGRATE?

The timing of these events still remains a matter for conjecture, although as knowledge gained from the process of 'infant observation' (developed by the child psychotherapists) increases some more fixed guidelines might appear. However, I would suspect that, along with all the infant's other milestones (walking, talking, etc.), there is a great deal of variation between children.

Table 5.1 summarises some of the terms used and the timing of the stages of psychic development described in this book.

Table 5.1

	Kernberg	Winnicott	Klein
Birth			
The stage of a partially integrated inner world	Introjections	The pre-ruth stage	The paranoid-schizoid position
	Identifications		
A more integrated inner world	Ego identity	Stage of concern or ruth	The depressive position
Two to three years of age			

The next few years of the child's life

The model I have presented leaves our child with an integrated inner world and fairly realistic relationships with those in the outer world around it. We have now just about reached the level of psychic development achieved by George.

However, psychic maturation does not stop here. Other processes occur, including the development of the 'super-ego' and 'ego ideal', which add further sophistication to the individual's psyche. These topics are touched on in this book, but are much more fully described by authors such as Kernberg, Fairbairn, Guntrip, and Winnicott.

Psychic growth in adult life

It is clear that the process of identification, leading to changes in the ego identity, may continue. Some people we interact with as adults can become, rather than just memories, part of the psychic structure and thus our personalities. Indeed the intensive process of psychoanalysis (with the patient having sessions up to five times a week) encourages the patient to identify with the analyst.

This can be of the greatest help for those individuals whose inner worlds are in a great muddle and lack (due to trauma and deprivation in early childhood) appropriate internal other-objects or integration (see Kernberg 1984; J. Klein 1987). However, even in a less intense way, we all tend to internalise, and then integrate with our existing inner objects, aspects of people we relate closely to and respect.

AND WHAT ABOUT GEORGE?

It may seem to you that George has been somewhat forgotten in the last two chapters. In the next chapters we will return to him and consider how his inner world was externalised on the psychodrama stage.

6 The inner world and the drama of psychotherapy

The group

The scene was set in the café 'Tea for Two'; there were tables and chairs. Only George's father was missing.

'George, who in the group could play your father?'

'Victor.'

George was very quick and decisive in his choice.

The scene started easily. Victor, as George's father, seemed able to play the role without difficulty. Indeed Paul felt no need to check out with his protagonist if this 'father' felt right to him. The interaction between father and son was developing fluently.

They made small talk. Nothing dangerous, and certainly no mention of 'that woman who divorced George's father'.

'Here you are, son, a toy soldier I bought on my last trip to London. I hope you like him.'

Victor was a good auxiliary ego, and used what he had learnt about George in the warm-up to this psychodrama session.

'Thanks dad, he's super, I'll put him on the shelf in my bedroom along with the plane you gave me last year. When are you going to come and see me again?'

'Reverse.'

Victor could not answer this question; George, now role-reversed as his father had to answer.

'Oh, I don't know. Things are very busy at work you know, I'm never sure when I'll be able to get the time off.'

'Reverse.'

Victor repeated the last part of 'father's' comments.

'Things are very busy at work, I don't know when I'll be able to find the time.'

George looked crestfallen but said nothing directly.

'Where did you buy the soldier? I think he's great. I think that I'd like to make a collection of them.'

'Why not. I bought him at Arding and Hobbs in Clapham. They had others too, all different, a whole battalion of them. I'm going up to London again in a couple of weeks, I'll get you another one then.'

'*That would be great! Do you mean it?*'

'*Reverse.*'

Paul wished to learn more about George's father, and he felt that it might help George too, with his difficulties in life, if he could identify more with his 'inner father'. This process was assisted by the role reversal.

'*Of course I do, Georgie. I know that I don't always come to see you when I promise, but I do try. Life's not been easy for me since your mother left me. You know that. Don't you?*'

'*Yes, but I do wish you and mum had got on better.*'

George continued the drama, still playing his father.

'*Well it wasn't easy for either of us you know. Your mother could be a very difficult woman, and I never lived up to her expectations. Though, God knows I tried hard enough at first.*'

Paul and the group were learning more about George's childhood.

'*Reverse.*'

'*I never knew that, mum always blamed you for all the troubles.*'

'*Reverse.*'

George began to continue the scene moving from his role (and position on the stage) to his father's role and position. He added, as his father.

'*I was always so worried that, when your mother and I had fights, you could hear us from your bedroom.*'

Continued on page 97.

DRAMA

That drama is considered to be a process in the external world is obvious (for example, Webster's Dictionary (1864) gives this as one definition of drama: 'A series of real events that are invested with a dramatic unity or force'), but it is also a feature of another realm, that of the unconscious. Psychotherapy provides a theatre or forum for a meeting of the two.

There are private dramas in the internal world of every individual which reflect the complex object relationships which are such a fundamental part of someone's identity. These dramas are often unconscious, the only sign of their existence being emotional states such as anxiety or depression. They may, however, surface during those silent dialogues between two aspects of the self.

'I really don't want to go to work today, I'd much rather sit at home in the sun. . . . No one would miss me!'

'Yes they would! And don't forget that I'm being paid. I'd only feel guilty in the sun.'

'No I wouldn't, I had a great day off last month!'

As Freud noted, they also surface powerfully at night in our dreams (the royal road to the unconscious) and nightmares. These dramas appear too in the material of day-dreams when, unlike in some of the other forms of expression of the unconscious, a degree of conscious control is possible. The activity of the inner world also emerges through 'slips' of the tongue or behaviour, a concept that has helped make Freud known to a wide public (Freud 1901).

The deepest levels of the mind: primary processes

These internal dramas start becoming part of the inner world in infancy (and indeed perhaps before birth). The earliest memory traces (which encode interpersonal dramas in the mind) are not integrated and involve only parts or aspects of self and other. They also involve sensations and actions remembered (non-verbally) before the child's development of language (Isaacs 1948). Even in the sanest adult these objects relationships lurk as non-metabolised and unintegrated aspects of the psyche.

It might be expected that when these early object relationships surface in adult life they first do so through non-verbal feelings and actions. It is only with time that names (for example, anger, hate, fear) can be attached to certain feelings and responses.

These unconscious activities in the mind, originating in a child's early experiences, have been called 'primary processes' which, according to psychoanalysts, lack a sense of time, co-ordination of impulse, contradiction, and negation. These features account, in part, for the surreal aspects of dreams (Laplanche and Pontalis 1967).

INTERNAL AND EXTERNAL WORLDS MEET

The drama of everyday life

The dramas enacted in George's staff room were usually low key, and rather Pinteresque. However, from time to time the scene exploded as George and Fred argued with one another. Their interactions were a rich mixture of reality-based encounters and the unconscious expression of their inner worlds.

George tended to use the psychological process of projective identification (a process that will be described in more detail in the next chapter), projecting aspects of his inner world onto others. This mechanism is a feature of everyday life (Moses 1988: 143–4), adding its own colour to reality-based dramas or encounters.

We all may become linked in relationships that are influenced, and perhaps controlled, by aspects of the inner world of at least one of us. The projection or externalisation of some figure from the past involves the individual in the manipulation or provocation of the other person in an attempt to induce the other to behave in a way that facilitates the repetition of childish patterns of behaviour. George 'manipulated' his bosses by his complaining but passive stance.

However, for this projective process to be successful the other person must respond, both emotionally and in actions. Some people let themselves be used in this way while others avoid it by not behaving in the appropriate and necessary manner. Sandler (1976: 44) described how the individual 'scans' the people available in the environment and then enters into a trial relationship to see if the other person will respond in the way required by the internal object relationship that is seeking expression or externalisation.

Perhaps only Fred, in George's office, responded with the appropriate frustration and guilt in the role of 'father–boss'. Other colleagues may have been unable or unwilling to enact George's internal drama of father and son with him. Moreno noted that roles have a public and social aspects, as well as those which are private or internal. It was the socially determined boss–junior aspect of the relationship in the office that facilitated the enactment of the father–son drama between George and Fred.

The drama of psychodrama

I would suggest that in the magical setting of the psychodrama stage the protagonist experiences the same 'therapeutic madness' as does the patient through the transference in psychoanalysis. Even the sanest protagonist will suspend disbelief and talk to his 'father' or 'mother' with a complete sense of emotional reality and conviction. His parent is there, on the stage, real, alive, and, in a literal sense, tangible. They can be touched and can respond. They are 'real' even if the auxiliary is the wrong age, shape, or even gender. Dramas from childhood can be, once more, enacted with great power and immediacy.

The protagonist at the same time, however, knows (unless psychotic) that the auxiliary is only transformed by the process of psychodrama. It is all only an illusion. George related to Victor 'as if' he was his father.

In the early scenes of a psychodrama, which are often moments from the present or near past in the protagonist's life, the 'others' in the drama (in the case of George his boss) have been perhaps fairly accurately observed, remembered, and are presented with a degree of objectivity. These individuals have not the power to become (in the full sense) inner objects and thus part of the protagonist's psychic identity.

However, many psychodramas (when they follow the model of Zerka Moreno or Elaine Goldman) go backwards in time, regressing to earlier scenes from life. Now the portrayal of people (often parents) is going to be less objective. The 'people' on the stage, played by auxiliary egos, are increasingly the externalisation of inner other-objects that are aspects of the protagonist's psychic identity.

The technique allows for different internal 'others' to be externalised in a clear and dramatic manner by the use of more than one auxiliary ego. Thus George's externalisation of his father was played by Victor, while later in the session his mother was played by Thelma.

The psychodramatic method also allows for the different aspects of the same internal objects, say 'good' and 'bad' father (both internalisations of the same external figure), to be externalised with great clarity by the use of two (or more) auxiliary egos to play the different aspects of the internal object(s).

A digression on language

It has always interested me that Moreno chose the term 'auxiliary ego' for the group member who assists the protagonist. He wrote:

> One of the basic instruments in constructing a patient's psychodramatic world is the auxiliary ego, which is the representation of absentee individuals, delusions, hallucinations, symbols, ideals, animals and objects. They make the protagonist's world real, concrete and tangible.
>
> (Moreno 1966 in Fox 1987: 9)

Again we can observe links between the concepts and language of psychodrama and psychoanalysis.

Drama of 'Tea for Two'

The episode in the 'Tea for Two' café had a certain dramatic force and apparent reality (as is often the case in psychodramas) when enacted in the session. When the drama slowed, or the auxiliary ego was uncertain how to respond, the director requested a role reversal which brought both more information and more energy to the scene, which was, after all, an externalisation of what George remembered, or had internalised, of his relationship with his father.

George and Victor were both playing roles, or parts, from George's inner world. As the drama developed it became easier for the protagonist to play both roles involved in the relationship with the result that the auxiliary ego was less active. The object relationship father–son internalised in George's childhood was externalised on the psychodramatic stage. *Both* roles were part of him. This fact, I believe, explains why protagonists so easily role-reverse with auxiliary egos, for in both roles they are playing aspects of themselves.

Zerka Moreno describes this role-reversal as perhaps the most powerful therapeutic tool in psychodrama (personal communication) and indeed the active taking of the role associated with the other-object is one of the unique therapeutic aspects of this method of treatment. Role-reversals also add crucially to the excitement and thus to the potency of psychodrama.

Playing his father in the scene in the café 'Tea for Two' brought back memories of painful and difficult times. George remembered things that he had forgotten for many years. The internal dynamic was dramatised through the use of an auxiliary ego to enact the 'other' pole of the internal dynamic dyad.

Through the use of 'role reversal' the protagonist can, in one session, experience a conscious adoption of *both* poles, that is, of 'self' or 'I' from the past and of the 'other'. George, by his taking on his father's role, was able rapidly to regain both emotional and cognitive information about his father's difficult and painful position, allowing him to feel more compassionate towards this man and thus towards crucial aspects of himself.

The drama in psychoanalysis

In psychoanalytic therapy the dramas of childhood are re-enacted in the consulting room. For example, the image of a parent is projected onto the therapist; the patient, falling back into the appropriate *I*-object position and role, feels like the 'child/son'. When this happens, the relationship is accompanied by the associated affects and sometimes behaviour.

The therapist becomes the focus of the projection and externalisation of many different internal object relationships of the patient. At different times he might be experienced, say, as either the mother *or* the father. Part of the skill of such a therapist is to be able to respond to various different projections according to the needs of the patient, and by keeping a rather neutral profile (and thus reducing the patient's reality testing in the sessions), to allow the patient to re-experience these early relationships.

However, the therapist and the patient never reverse roles; one remains sitting in his chair, the other often lying on a couch. The internal relationships between the *I*-object and the other-object are re-enacted in the drama of the transference. In the consulting room this involves the patient in the roles of 'self' or '*I*' in relationship with the 'other' (roles assumed by the analyst).

Therapeutic progress occurs, in part, when the therapist analyses and interprets the complex of different transferences. The exploration of the inner world takes skill (see Greenson 1967) and can be, in my experience, a slow process.

The techniques of psychoanalysis make this form of treatment less overtly dramatic than psychodrama, but the one-to-one relationship in the consulting room provides some patients with the intimacy and containment (or holding) they need. This is not always possible in the more exciting, but for some more terrifying, forum of psychodrama. Perhaps Roy, who left the group after only a few sessions, would have done better in individual psychotherapy.

THE REPRESSED RETURNS

Psychotherapy involves helping the repressed to surface from the depths of the unconscious. This allows the individual to gain some awareness and control over his internal conflicts.

In both forms of therapy discussed in this book the repressed is remembered through the *process* of the treatment; in psychodrama through the use of auxiliary egos and in psychoanalysis through the transference aspects of the relationship with the therapist. Psychoanalysis too is, in its way, at least psychologically active and dramatic, a point ignored by many ignorant of this form of therapy.

A question of reality

'How close was this scene in the café to what actually happened in George's childhood?'

I think the answer must be 'we don't know'. In this psychodrama the group saw the meeting with his father as George recalled it, a portrayal of events which was certainly very different from that which a video-recording would have shown. Had we asked George's father, or indeed the 'sulky waitress', what they remembered of the scene, both might give very different accounts. For the process of memory is coloured by many factors, especially emotional ones.

His father might have remembered having tea with a sullen difficult boy who was hard to please. The waitress (if she remembered them at all) might have described a father and son talking together 'while they waited for the wife/mother to finish her shopping'. Each participant, while sensing the same scene (with all five senses), will have perceived different things and remembered what (in some ways) suited their inner worlds and their emotional needs. Indeed, the waitress seems to have muddled what she 'saw' with what she 'guessed' about her customers. For her the assumptions she made have become part of her remembered 'reality'.

And George was then still a child with a developing inner world so every contact with his father will have produced memory traces of this relationship that became fundamental aspects of his personality which did not yet have the more fixed quality we associated with adults. Many aspects of 'George' will, of course, have been very well established by this age.

Initially the quality of 'father' would have existed as an other-object. Subsequently the process of introjective identification, in which the *I* identifies with a role (or object) initially internalised as an other-object, would have led to some structural alterations in his self-identity. He would have begun to feel that he, himself, had certain qualities of his father.

The memories of his relationship with his father (both in general and at that specific tea time) will have become a powerful factor in his inner world. These new memories will have become integrated with those other already existing internal object relationships associated with the grouping or role clusters of 'father' and the 'male me'.

The adult's memories of the scene in the café will not have become such an integral part of their psychic structures, although, as with George, their memories of the events will have interacted with already established internal structures and preconceptions. Those pre-existing internal psychic factors in the waitress may have accounted for her memory that the father and son were waiting for the wife/mother. Was she a mother for whom people wait? Or had she been a child who waited for her mother?

THE I-NESS OF GEORGE

With such a richness of internal objects we might well ask: 'Who was George?' Who did he consider himself to be (in terms of his inner objects), for it would be a mistake to consider that the inner world of any individual is simple. Indeed it is the inevitable internal complexities that make psychotherapy such a difficult and at times convoluted but rewarding activity.

As well as the internalisations of his father, George's inner world must also have included those aspects of his self-identity that derived from his relationship with his mother who hated his father, her ex-husband. So, to return to our diagrams, the relationships look like Figure 6.1.

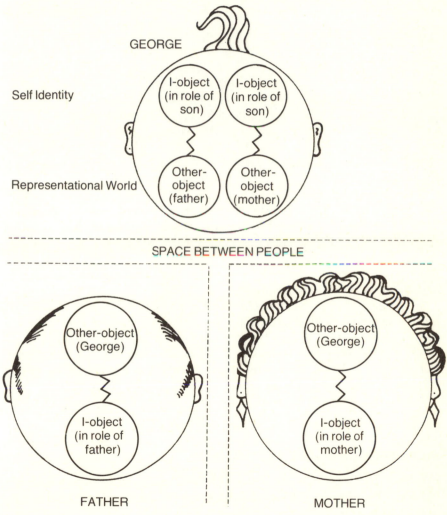

Figure 6.1

But who did George feel he *was* at any specific point in time? Clearly he had a choice of roles (as we all do). The psychoanalyst Joyce McDougall said that:

> Language informs us that the script writer is called *I*. Psychoanalysis has taught us that the scenarios were written years ago by a naive and childlike *I* struggling to survive in an adult world whose drama conventions are quite different from the child's. These psychic plays may be performed in the theatre of our own minds or that of our bodies, or may take place in the external world, sometimes using other people's minds and bodies. We are also capable of shifting our own psychic dramas from one stage to another in times of overwhelming stress. For the *I* is a multifaceted character.
>
> (McDougall 1986: 4)

Thus in adult life George had the possibility of being any one of several different *I*s. That is, at any one point in time, he may have experienced himself (or have *felt*) more identified with the *I*-object resulting from his relationship with his mother (the object relationship 'son with mother'). At other times his *I* will have been that of a son, in relationship with his father.

For George each of these aspects of his total self identity involved different aspects of the role cluster 'self or *I* as son'. However, each of these sub-roles was in relationship with different other-objects: either his father or his mother. Both these individuals existed within him as inner objects with whom his *I*-objects (or the script-writing *I*s) were in relationship.

For many people this clustering of roles leads to confusions both in their self-image and in their perceptions of others. It is as if there is 'cross talk' between two or more object relationships. Questions such as 'Am I a loving or hating son?' and 'Who am I really angry with?' will provide much material for psychotherapy, as the individual becomes more aware of the ways in which the richness of their muddled internal world causes them anxiety or distress, or is acted out in the external world.

It was also possible, at any point in time, for the *I* of George to have felt more identified with his internalised roles of father or mother. Perhaps, when in the role of father, George became distant and unreliable to those in his world who had the roles of 'children' (or dependent ones) to his 'father' role. For example, perhaps at times of stress, George was not always the caring responsible social worker to his clients that he would have liked to be. In these circumstances he might have acted towards them in a similar manner to the way in which his father had treated him when he was a dependent child.

SOME THOUGHTS ON ENACTMENT

Enactment, as a process, has been described as a feature of psychodrama (Blatner 1988, Kipper 1985), of family therapy (Minuchin and Fishman 1981), and psychoanalysis (Casement in Klauber *et al.* 1987).

The family therapist Salvador Minuchin wrote that enactment occurs:

when the therapist gets the family members to interact with each other, transacting some of the problems that they consider dysfunctional and negotiating disagreements, as in trying to establish control over a disobedient child, he unleashes sequences beyond the family's control. The accustomed rules take over, and transactional components manifest themselves with an intensity similar to those that manifest in these transactions outside of the therapy session.

Family Therapy Techniques (Minuchin and Fishman 1981: 78)

This is a here-and-now interaction of family members in the therapeutic session. As Minuchin so graphically described, in this process of enactment the 'therapist asks the family to dance in his presence' (Minuchin and Fishman 1981).

Such a situation involves people relating together in their shared reality. It has the same reality-based psychological significance for the participants as those interactions that Moreno described as 'encounters'. Two people meeting in their common shared space in which they, as far as possible, treat each other as real and equal. The relationship can be thought of as symmetrical, and in Moreno's terms their communication is modulated by tele, involving the reciprocity of attraction, rejection, excitation, or indifference (Moreno 1966 in Fox 1987: 4).

The British analyst Patrick Casement used the term enactment in the psychoanalytic consulting room (Casement in Klauber *et al.* 1987: 80) to describe the drama that occurs between patient and analyst in the transference. In this situation the then-and-there (say, George and his father) is enacted in the here-and-now between patient and analyst.

Thus the psychological processes involved in the enactments of the family therapists can be seen as different to those which occur in the psychoanalyst's enactments in the transference. I would suggest that both dynamics may occur in the psychodrama theatre and that psychodramatists would call both these processes enactments.

Psychodramatists use the term enactment for the re-enactment in the theatre of personal conflicts (Kipper 1986: 66 and 214) following the dictum 'don't tell us, show us'. In such sessions members of the group, as auxiliary egos, assume the roles of important others for the protagonist.

Both J.L. Moreno (1969, 1975) and Zerka Moreno (in Holmes and Karp 1991) have written about another use of psychodramatic methods in which actual members of a family worked together in the session in attempts to resolve their difficulties. Moreno said to a married couple seeking help in his Therapeutic Theatre:

Don't report what happened, don't tell a story of what you said to each other, but re-live the situation as it actually occurred.

(Moreno 1969, 1975: 85)

In these sessions the families enacted aspects of their family life in the theatre. This of course results in a very different dynamic to that which occurred in George's session in which a member of the group, unrelated to him, played his father in perhaps a more classical form of psychodramatic enactment.

While I believe that many psychodramatists would describe both processes as enactments, the interactions in the family or marital meeting, resembled enactments as defined by family therapists, while I would suggest that the psychodramatic enactment in George's session was more similar, in its psychological significance, to the process of enactment in the transference as described by some psychoanalysts.

Thus it may be possible to differentiate two forms of psychodramatic enactment.

Psychodramatic enactments in an encounter

George's interactions with Joyce (before the session started) and later with Paul in the session could be described as encounters as they occurred in shared reality. George and Joyce were two real group members in the coffee room; later there was an encounter between a real director and his equally real protagonist.

Psychodramatic enactments from the inner world

George's enactment of the scene in the café between himself and his father clearly related to the externalisation of his inner world and was an enactment using the magic of therapeutic madness and illusion. The psychological significance was as if George reacted in the transference to his psychoanalyst.

It is interesting to note that in the family sessions described by J.L. Moreno and Zerka Moreno, while using psychodramatic enactments 'in encounters', both also used enactments from 'the inner world' when the directors introduced people into the dramas who were to be played by auxiliary egos in the session (J.L. Moreno 1969, 1975: 98 and Z. Moreno in Holmes and Karp 1991: 57).

Can we always separate the two types of enactment?

No, for, as has already been pointed out, many of our here-and-now relationships are coloured, if not dominated, by our unconscious world. Is it also possible that the dramatic interchange between George and his director, Paul, could be thought of as also a form of enactment? If so, what sort? Clearly they had a relationship in reality, so this could have been an 'enactment in an encounter'. Thus it would be possible to emphasise the transferential aspects of George's interactions with Paul, and of course Paul's role responsiveness to George's psychic needs. This might then be seen as an 'enactment from the inner world'. The director's own neurotic, unconsciously determined needs are also important and will be considered in the next chapter.

In any situation, in life or on the psychodrama stage, an encounter (an enactment in reality) can slip into an enactment dominated by the unconscious inner world of one or both of the participants. Thus George's reality-based interactions with Fred, his senior, imperceptibly became a relationship of 'son' and 'father'.

In our psychodrama George's father was played by another group member, Victor. It is, however, possible for a real parent and child to role-reverse. Moreno, writing about such a situation, said of a real father and son role-reversing with each other in a psychodrama that:

> each may be represented in the repressed part of the other's unconscious. Therefore by means of role reversal they may be able to bring out a great deal of what they have stored up in the course of years.
>
> (Moreno 1959: 52)

It seems that, in this paragraph, Moreno was describing the fact that a son stores up memories of his father in his unconscious and the father stores memories of his son. This is a clear statement of ideas more fully developed by the object relations theorists.

THE AUXILIARY EGO IN THE DRAMA: CREATIVITY, SPONTANEITY, AND ROLE TAKING

The auxiliary egos listen and respond to the psychological needs of the protagonist, providing them with the 'others' that are required to people their psychodramatic world. In our psychodrama Victor's enactment of the role of father was a creative combination of three factors.

1 He had the role of 'father' as one of his inner other-objects; it was in his role repertoire and he was thus able to identify *himself* with George's inner *father*. Although it was not a role he used in everyday life (having no children of his own) he had access to it and enjoyed playing a 'father'.
2 He was role responsive (Sandler 1976) to George's projections, a point that I will return to in the next chapter.
3 He also added to his dramatic interpretation of the role by creating something new, not directly based on his own inner 'father' or on George's projections of his inner 'father', for it must not be assumed that group members can play only parts that in some way respond to their 'inner world' or that of the protagonist.

As the psychodrama progressed the director had to check that Victor was playing George's 'father' (as a good auxiliary should) and not just external-ising onto the psychodrama stage his own inner 'father', and creating a new father alien to George.

Tele and the choice of an auxiliary ego

The fact that Victor had had a father made it easier for him to become
George's in the session. But why did George ask Victor to play his father
knowing that this man had no children? After all every man in the group had
a father. The process whereby a protagonist chooses his auxiliary egos, and the
resulting need for their creativity if the role is not part of their immediate role
repertoire, is complex.

Moreno was aware that choices made in life or in psychodrama groups are
never random. The links that people make with others are rich and powerful.
He believed that the selection process often did not involve 'transference'
(which he defined as 'the factor responsible for dissociation and
disintegration in social groups') or empathy, which he saw as a 'one-way'
feeling that helps someone understand another or an actor find his way into a
part. He felt that some other crucial factor was involved and tried to find

> a theoretical framework for my sociometric and psychodramatic discoveries.
> Neither transference nor empathy could explain in a satisfactory way the
> emergent cohesion of a social configuration or the 'double' experience in a
> psychodramatic situation. . . . I hypothecated [*sic*] therefore, that empathy
> and transference are parts of a more elementary and more inclusive
> process, *tele*. . . . I defined it as 'An objective social process functioning with
> transference as a psychopathological outgrowth and empathy as an esthetic
> outgrowth.'
>
> (Moreno 1934 and 1953: 311; my italics)

He said that it was tele that was 'responsible for the increased rate of
interaction between members of a group, "for the increased mutuality of
choices surpassing chance possibility" ' (Moreno 1934 and 1953: 312).

Thus George, in part using tele, felt a positive link with Victor. This helped
him to judge that he would feel positive about him playing his father, the most
important man in his life, in this psychodrama. Without this bond of positive
feelings and regard, the drama enacted in the session would not have had the
necessary degree of emotionality.

Spontaneity and the creation of roles

For Moreno, spontaneity was another factor crucial to the creation of new
roles and thus to the process of psychodrama. He wrote of it

> as a dramatic function [which] energises and unites the self. Spontaneity as
> a plastic function evokes adequate responses of the self to novel situations.
> Spontaneity as a creative function endeavors to create the self and an
> environment for it.
>
> (Moreno 1946 and 1977: 85)

According to Moreno, spontaneity in the individual can be developed or increased by training (Moreno 1940 in Fox 1987); that is, by interpersonal activity in the social sphere. The increase in the group's spontaneity is one of the functions of the warm-up phase of a session.

The concept of spontaneity (or the 's-factor') differs from that of the libido which, according to Freud, arises in the id, and does not vary in quantity in an individual. Moreno wrote:

> The individual is not endowed with a reservoir of spontaneity, in the sense of a given, stable volume or quantity. Spontaneity is (or is not) available in varying degrees of readiness, from zero to maximum, operating like a psychological catalyzer.
>
> (Moreno 1946 and 1977: 85)

Moreno did accept a degree of what he called 'functional operational determinism', which could influence a person's behaviour, for 'the total denial of determinism is just as sterile as its full acceptance' (Moreno 1946 and 1977: 103). This is another area of agreement between Moreno and psychoanalytic theory. He implied that such psychological forces come from the past.

> It is not necessary, indeed it is undesirable to give every moment in the development of a person the credit of spontaneity.
>
> (Moreno 1946 and 1977: 103)

Spontaneity, according to Moreno, is the force or factor that allows the individual not only to express the self, but also to create new works of art, new social and technological inventions and new social environments (Moreno 1977: 91) and new roles in a psychodrama. With a high level of s-factor an individual will appear more vivacious, vigorous, and infectious.

The level of spontaneity also determines how they respond to new situations. According to Moreno, in an individual without any s-factor there may be either 'no response' or 'an old response'; with the s-factor, a 'new response' is possible which may allow for creative solutions. Moreno argued that the developing child requires 'a plastic adaptation skill, a mobility and flexibility of the self, which is indispensable to a rapidly growing organism in a rapidly changing environment' (Moreno 1946 and 1977: 93). However, he warned that:

> when the functions of spontaneity are left undirected, contradicting tendencies develop within its own functions which bring about a disunity of the self and a dismemberment of the cultural environment.
>
> (Moreno 1946 and 1977: 101)

It seems to me that in these paragraphs the theories of Moreno and modern psychoanalysis approach each other. Both are concerned with the psychological concept of the 'self'. The misdirection of either Freud's 'libido' or Moreno's 's-factor' appears to cause problems for the individual.

TEA FOR TWO

George and Victor were able to recreate the scene in the café. However, at this point in the session, the drama focused on an approximation to past reality. It was an enactment of George's inner world. Later in this psychodrama (described in Chapter 10) George and his auxiliaries, using their creativity and spontaneity, were able to move the drama into scenes that had never happened (and perhaps never would). The psychodrama then entered surplus reality, creating a new emotional and cognitive experience for George. A new world was created and entered, the drama no longer being simply an enactment of George's inner world.

7 The countertransference

The group

George looked rather worried.

'I know that Dad. I really hated it when you and mummy shouted at each other. I felt really scared. I thought you might hurt each other, or even hit me.'

'You know I love you. I would never hurt you. But I never got on with your mother. That wasn't your fault. I'm sorry that I can't see you as often as I would like. You know that my flat is too small for you to stay in with me.'

'Yes Dad, but it's nice to see you.'

Paul was beginning to feel a bit anxious and wondered where the scene was going. At this point it was a clear re-enactment of the rather difficult meetings of father and son. He decided to intervene:

'George. What do you want out of this scene?'

'It's just fine the way it is. Paul, why do you always interrupt?'

George fell out of role. No longer was he a 7-year-old with his father. He was an angry member of the group challenging the director. The flow of the psychodrama had been broken. The working relationship between Paul and George had been threatened.

'Please carry on with the scene.'

The request failed, the magic that creates the process of the drama had shifted. George's creativity and spontaneity were no longer in the scene with his father. The energy seemed to be in his relationship with Paul who was becoming aware that he had a problem in the session. He was aware that his comment had broken the flow. He had made a mistake. He should have let the scene continue. He was now feeling rather tense and angry with himself. But he had some awareness of what might be going on for George. His father too had also been rather an absent figure in his childhood. He had some idea about how 7-year-old George might have felt. He also wondered about the role of the mother in this father–son relationship.

Paul had to resolve the present situation if the psychodrama was to continue. He paused and looked around the group. Joan spoke up from the cushion in the corner of the room.

'Can I say something?'

Paul looked at her and nodded.

'I think you should have let the scene with George's father continue.'

'I agree, but now I've stopped the drama I'm not sure what to do next.'

Clearly George had some issues with Paul. And indeed Paul admitted that his intervention had been mistimed and rather tactless. George had enjoyed talking to his 'psychodramatic' father. At this point he seemed a little downcast and rather irritable. Paul was aware that he had some previous difficulties with George who had, on more than one occasion, challenged his role as group leader and director. Was the present situation a continuation of these difficulties? Had Paul been covertly attacking George when he interrupted the scene with his father? Was George continuing his attack on Paul's leadership? However, the intensity of George's response surprised him. Perhaps Paul's interruption had reminded George of someone else in his life.

'Let's stop this scene. We can come back to it later. George you know I feel that I made a mistake. I should not have interrupted your talk with your father. It seems that you enjoyed and valued it and are annoyed with me for stopping the scene.'

George relaxed a little and Paul felt that his apology (sincerely meant) was enough, at least for the time being, on the here-and-now relationship between himself and George.

Paul had a hunch that he decided to test out.

'I wonder if you felt that other people in your childhood used to get in the way of your seeing your dad?'

'Yes. My bloody mother. She threw dad out of the house. She wouldn't let him see me in our home so we had to go to that crummy café. The food was awful. Cold and boring. We never went anywhere nice together!'

Paul felt relief. Whatever the issues in real life between him and George (as two adult men) George's personal psychodrama was under way again. He was right. George did experience his intervention in the scene like his mother's intervention into his relationship with his father.

'Perhaps we need to meet your mother. It seems she had a very important role in your relationship with your father when you were a boy.'

'Yes, but I'm not sure I want to do anything with my mother tonight.'

'I feel we should. I know how painful you feel it might be, but it seems that you felt that she stopped you seeing much of your dad.'

'I don't know. I always thought it was my dad's fault. My mother always told me that he had other women. Perhaps he did.'

Paul had decided to challenge George's obvious resistance to looking at his mother's role in his relationship with his father.

'Let's meet your mother.'

Continued on page 112.

OF PATIENTS AND THERAPISTS

Moreno's view of the doctor–patient relationship differed from Freud's, who continued, in many ways, to be an orthodox physician following the rules of his training and profession.

In the medical model the doctor or therapist has a clearly distinct, and in many ways more powerful, role than the patient. Such a relationship resembles that of a parent and child and thus encourages the experiencing of transference responses.

Moreno talked of the relationship between therapist and patient as an encounter of two equals, both bringing aspects of their skills, weaknesses, and personal histories to the session. His views are encapsulated in a poem he wrote in 1914:

A meeting of two: eye to eye, face to face.
And when you are near I will tear your eyes out
and place them instead of mine,
and you will tear my eyes out
and will place them instead of yours,
and I will look at you with your eyes
and you will look at me with mine.

       from *Einladung zu einer Begegnung* (Invitation to an Encounter)
       (Moreno 1914, translation taken from Blatner and Blatner 1988: 19)

However, Freud, if not agreeing with Moreno's view about the equality (in the consulting room) of patient and physician, did acknowledge that the psychoanalyst could never be an impassive, emotionally unresponsive observer of the patient.

In this chapter I will consider the ways in which a psychotherapist (be he a psychoanalyst or a psychodramatist) must become involved, directly and emotionally, in the therapeutic maelstrom. An involvement that may be used to facilitate (or sometimes to hinder) the treatment.

THE DIRECTOR'S RELATIONSHIP WITH THE PROTAGONIST

The process of dynamic psychotherapy cannot just be the application of specific techniques or tactics to the patient's problems and symptoms, for there are personal as well as professional aspects to the therapist's relationship with his patient. In psychodrama, as in analytic psychotherapy, the therapist's own feelings, intuitions, and experiences play a crucial element in the process; indeed the relationship between patient and therapist is of paramount importance.

Paul's feelings while directing George's psychodrama

At the point we have reached in the session Paul was beginning to feel ill at ease. Something was unsettling him, he wasn't certain what. He had, like every psychotherapist, his own 'inner world' with its own richness, complexities, and history. He gave some thought to his own feelings and involvement in the psychodrama.

What feelings were stirred up in him watching his protagonist, George, relating well to his (psychodramatic) father in the session? Was his own history beginning to affect the process of the psychodrama session adversely? After all he too had had a rather distant father in his childhood.

To what extent was Paul reacting to the slight hostility and competitiveness that was developing between George and himself as this man began to challenge his leadership role in the group? Was he still upset and bothered by his discussion with his colleague, Tom, before the session started?

Paul was aware that he was feeling rather tense, angry, and a bit anxious. He needed to know why. His feelings at that moment in the session might have originated from various sources. Put simply, they included:

A *Feelings that occur in the director as a result of his transference reaction to the protagonist*
After all, therapists are only human. They too can confuse people in their present with important figures from their pasts. Perhaps Paul might have been responding to George, in a neurotic way, as if he were his own younger brother with whom he was in competition as a child.

B *The therapist's feelings that relate to the protagonist's transference to the director*
The ways in which the transference relationship 'manipulates' the feelings and actions of the other person are subtle and complex. Maybe Paul was being 'made' to feel 'as if' he were George's mother, anxious and a bit guilty about her care of her son and his lack of contact with his father.

C *Feelings that are appropriate to the here-and-now*
These include, for example, the normal anxiety and uncertainty that exists in anyone when they are having difficulties with a professional task. It is also of course normal to have feelings stirred up by someone else in an 'encounter'; for example, anger with a group member who arrives very late to a session. There might be good reasons in the here-and-now for Paul to feel a bit annoyed with George.

D *Feelings unrelated to the psychodrama session*
We all enter any situation with feelings related to other events in our everyday life. Some of these may continue to dominate our thoughts and feelings when we are engaged in a very different activity.

THE COUNTERTRANSFERENCE

The term countertransference was first used by Freud in 1910 to describe those feelings that arise in the psychoanalyst or therapist as a result of their contact with the patient. Like many technical terms associated with both psychoanalysis and psychodrama, it is rather clumsy and leaden.

Definitions of countertransference vary. Some authors use the term in a narrow and specific manner, relating only to the therapist's *own* neurotic difficulties as experienced in the session. Other psychoanalysts go to the other extreme and use it to describe almost every feeling or response the therapist has while working with a patient.

I tend to follow the latter position and use the term to describe most of the feelings and emotional reactions of the therapist in a session. I do, however, exclude those arising from situations entirely outside my contact with a psychodrama group (D in the above list).

Let us now consider in more detail the possible sources of the therapist's or director's feelings in a session.

A The therapist's personal transference involvement: the neurotic countertransference

Even in the earliest days of psychoanalysis it was apparent that psychotherapy was a challenging activity, requiring the full commitment and emotional participation of the therapist. I have already described how the dangers of this very involvement resulted in Joseph Breuer returning to the safer waters of medicine and physiology.

Freud initially, perhaps as a result of his medical training and Breuer's difficulties, advised the psychoanalyst to be 'opaque to his patients, and, like a mirror, [he] should show them nothing but what is shown to him' ('Recommendations to physicians practising psychoanalysis', Freud 1912: 118).

The psychotherapist cannot be a neutral passive presence in the therapeutic relationship, however hard he tries. The very nature of the involvement has its consequences. It is not possible to maintain the dispassionate objectivity that surgeons or general physicians often assume (perhaps wrongly) that they have towards their patients.

The process of psychotherapy (both in the topics discussed and the techniques used) tends to lead to intimacy between the helper and the helped and thus involves the emotions of the therapist more directly.

Freud was aware of this and of the resulting complexities of the relationship that develops in the psychoanalytic consulting room. He wrote:

> We have become aware of the 'countertransference', which arises in [the psychoanalyst] as a result of the patient's influence on his unconscious feelings, and we are most inclined to insist that he shall recognise this countertransference in himself and overcome it ... no psychoanalyst goes further than his own complexes and internal resistances permit.
>
> 'The future prospects of psychoanalytic therapy' (Freud 1910: 144–5)

So, as with the history of transference, countertransference was at first seen as a problem in the therapy that had to be overcome.

Freud suggested that the patient could come to represent someone from the analyst's past, the therapist being unable to separate his feelings and phantasies (derived from his inner world) about this important person from those more appropriate (in the here-and-now) to his relationship with the patient. Freud initially believed that this phenomenon in the analyst could cause serious resistances and blocks to treatment. It had to be analysed, understood, and overcome. This meant that the psychoanalyst required his own personal therapy if his patients were to be helped so that his *own* transference response in the consulting room could be resolved.

Difficulties in therapy could also arise if the patient's problems (say with aggression or with relationships with women) had parallels in the therapist. Then patient and analyst could collude, both demonstrating a 'resistance' to the exploration and resolution of these issues. Such a situation is obviously unproductive.

Moreno had similar concerns about the dangers of countertransference responses in psychodramas. He explained that:

> It is obvious, therefore, that if the transference and countertransference phenomena dominate the relationship among the auxiliary therapists [or auxiliary egos and group members] and towards the patients [or protagonists] the therapeutic progress will be greatly handicapped.
>
> (Moreno 1946 and 1977: xviii)

In 1951 the psychoanalyst Annie Reich pointed out that the analyst

> may like or dislike the patient. As far as these attitudes are conscious, they have not yet anything to do with countertransference. If these feelings increase in intensity, we can be fairly certain that the unconscious feelings of the analyst, his own transferences onto the patient, i.e. counter-transferences, are mixed in. . . . Countertransference thus comprises the effects of the analyst's own unconscious needs and conflicts on his understanding or technique. In such cases the patient represents for the analyst an object of the past on to whom past feelings and wishes are projected . . . this is countertransference in the proper sense.
>
> 'On countertransference' (Reich 1951: 25)

Annie Reich was clearly separating emotional responses in the analyst (that Moreno would have attributed to an encounter) from those caused by the therapist's own neurosis. The fact that a therapist may like or dislike a patient involves the process of tele. The therapist's emotions in the counter-transference (in Reich's sense) relate to his own inner world, and its roots in childhood: thus this response has been called the 'neurotic counter-transference'.

These developments of psychoanalytic theory in the early 1950s might have pleased Moreno who, in 1946, wrote of the psychoanalytic situation:

> there is only one who transfers whether positive or negative, the patient. There is only one role. The psychiatrist is considered as an objective agent, at least during treatment, free from emotional implications of his own, merely present to analyze the material which the patient presents before

him. But this only appears to be so. Perhaps because only the patient is analyzed.

(Moreno 1946 and 1977: 227)

In fact, in 1910, Freud had advocated that all physicians undertaking psychoanalysis with patients should engage in a continuous self-analysis, but he later recommended that all psychoanalysts undergo a personal analysis while in training so that they could gain insight and resolve unconscious conflicts. By 1937 he realised an initial analysis might not be enough and further advised that an analyst may need to be re-analysed every five years if he was to continue in productive practice.

That Moreno was in fact aware of these practices amongst psychoanalysts is clear. He wrote,

The prospective practitioner may have become free from transference in regard to that particular psychiatrist who analyzed him. But that does not mean that he has become free from transference in regard to any new individual he may meet in the future. He would have to gain the armor of a saint. His armor may crack any time a new patient walks in, and the kind of complexes the patient throws at him may make a great difference in his conduct.

(Moreno 1946 and 1977: 228)

I feel that Moreno failed to acknowledge that an individual gains 'insight' through the analysis of the transference in therapy, and thus is able to understand and alter their response to others, later, with whom they might have previously developed feelings and reactions determined by the transference. This is as true for therapists in training as it is for their patients.

The psychodramatist's neurotic countertransference

In a psychodrama the same range of emotions may arise in the director. The nature and intensity of the feelings might give the therapist some indication of their origin (as is the case in a patient's transference responses). Those reactions of low intensity (source C above) might derive from the reality of the therapist–protagonist relationship, an encounter modulated by tele. More intense responses (A above) might originate from the director's own transference relationship with his protagonist.

However, the separation of the source of the director's feelings is far from easy. It is, for example, possible to become very angry in a reality-based encounter. There is thus a need for psychodramatists to have their own therapy as part of their training. Moreno wrote that:

therefore the first recommendation which we made in the first days of psychodramatic work was that the psychiatrist who participates in the procedure – as well as the patient – has to be analyzed by *others* during the treatment.

(Moreno 1946 and 1977: 229) (JLM's italics)

Moreno was suggesting that the psychodrama director can be treated by the group and I have no doubt that this does happen. Indeed in this session Paul was helped to see that he had upset George by the comments from one of the group members. Psychodrama encourages such exchanges, an 'encounter of equals', which may certainly help people to understand themselves better.

Such interactions, however important, though, are not sufficient to allow for the full professional and personal development of the psychodrama director. For this, an experience of treatment is required, similar to the process that psychoanalysts call a 'training analysis'. I think that it is a moot point as to how much 'help' or 'therapy' the director of a psychodrama can receive from a group he is leading, although without doubt we all grow and learn through our role as therapists.

Psychodramatists in training and in practice need personal help or treatment in a group in which they are not the leader or therapist. As Freud pointed out eighty years ago, a therapist's ability to help others is limited by his ability to understand himself, a process that requires him to accept help for himself through personal therapy.

Regular supervision is also important. It assists even the most experienced practitioner's understanding and monitoring of their responses to their clients, increasing access to the full richness of the process.

Paul, George and their fathers

Paul felt supported in his perception of the session when Joan pointed out to him that something was going wrong in his encounter with his protagonist. While this comment seemed to help Paul continue the psychodrama, it did not really confront the psychological reasons that might explain why Paul had disrupted George's talk with his 'father'. Paul needed to take note of his own feelings and responses. Their very intensity warned him that perhaps his own objectivity was failing and that aspects of his neurotic countertransference were entering his directing.

Paul had his own therapy (both in psychoanalysis and through psychodrama); he thus had some insight into the sorts of issues that might be disturbing his relationship with his protagonist. He knew about his potential for rivalrous relationships with brother figures, and about his somewhat distant relationship with his father.

If Paul did confuse George with his own younger brother the psychodrama would run aground on the shoals of the director's own neurotic difficulties. There would be a risk that, whenever George was about to gain some satisfactions in the session, Paul's competitive envy would appear and he would unconsciously use his power as the director to disrupt the psychodrama.

This might have been what was happening when Paul stopped George from talking to his psychodramatic father. However, by using his self-knowledge Paul was able to understand and resolve his problems sufficiently to allow the session to continue.

B The protagonist's transference relationship with the director and auxiliary egos

However, George too sometimes related to others in a manner more appropriate to his childhood. As the session progressed the ways in which he confused other men with his father were becoming more obvious. He did this with Fred at work. There was similar behaviour, within the therapeutic framework of the psychodrama, towards Victor when this group member was playing his father.

It seemed possible that another of his inner object relationships was being externalised and enacted when he reacted to Paul with fury in the session. His response was powerful when he was interrupted in his talk with his psychodramatic father. The more relaxed director–protagonist relationship of the here-and-now contract (the therapeutic alliance) was replaced by an angry, petulant response which Paul reacted to with anxiety and guilt. Paul wondered if George had been furious with his mother when she stopped his contacts with his father. He felt he had some understanding of the dynamic and asked George: 'I wonder if you felt that other people in your childhood used to get in the way of your seeing your dad?'

With this question he was attempting to link George's difficulties in the session with his past. To this extent his comment resembled the sort of interpretative statements a psychoanalytic therapist might have made. George associated his feelings with times in his childhood when he was stopped from seeing his father. It felt to him 'as if' Paul was his mother. Paul was, in fact, indirectly interpreting George's transference to him.

C Feelings that are appropriate to the here-and-now

Moreno agreed that an 'interpersonal transference' develops between patient and therapist, but he felt that this process had to be distinguished from the tele relationship between two people which is

> not due to a symbolic transference, it has no neurotic motivations but is due to certain realities which this other person embodies and represents. . . . [It is] a complex of feelings which draws one person towards another and which is aroused by the real attributes of the other person.
>
> (Moreno 1946 and 1977: 229)

Moreno believed that there could be no therapeutic progress in a psychodrama session if transference or countertransference dominates and

> the auxiliary egos are troubled among themselves because of (1) unresolved problems of their own, (2) protest against the psychodramatic director, (3) poor portrayal of the roles assigned to them, (4) lack of faith and a negative attitude toward the method used, or (5) interpersonal conflicts among themselves, they create an atmosphere which reflects on the therapeutic situation. . . . The decisive factor for therapeutic progress is the tele.
>
> (Moreno 1946 and 1977: xviii)

There can be no doubt that in any relationship real factors, including tele, influence feelings. In psychodrama there is a need to increase the reality of the encounters between group members, while the opposite is required in psychoanalytic group therapy (see Chapter 11).

Indeed, one of the reasons that analytic psychotherapists remain relatively 'unknown' (or 'mirror'-like) to their patients is to diminish the feelings and thoughts that might develop in the here-and-now between the two people. An encounter, in Moreno's terms, must be avoided. For example, a patient may have the greatest difficulty being angry 'in the transference' with his therapist/ mother if he has recently learnt that in reality his therapist has suffered a personal bereavement. Should this information be divulged the patient might feel concern or compassion for the therapist, a response that would be appropriate in the circumstances. Such feelings are not produced by the transference.

A therapist who is often late for sessions might stir anger in the patient, as would be normal in anyone treated in this disrespectful way. This response in here-and-now reality could block the patient's ability to experience in the transference other more positive feelings towards the therapist. This is not to say that there might not be aspects of a transference reaction in the response. It is also possible that the therapist's behaviour is his unconscious response (being role responsive but unaware) to subtle attacks or manipulations from the patient. Life is rarely simple, and emotions cannot always be clearly attributed to just one source.

Reality issues in the session

So, the director's feelings may also arise from real issues between himself and the protagonist. Paul's leadership was being challenged by George who felt that he might run the group better. It is perhaps understandable that, in reality, Paul might have felt both threatened and somewhat angry. After all he was making a real effort to run the group well, in the evening, after a very full working day in his clinic.

I would include these feelings, stirred up by Paul's encounter with George, to the process of the countertransference. However, as I hope this chapter has made clear, this usage might not be accepted by all psychodynamic theorists.

D Feelings unassociated or unconnected with the therapeutic process

I find it useful to separate those feelings in the therapist that derive from all the aspects of therapeutic process from those that have nothing to do with the therapy.

Paul had had a minor disagreement with a colleague, before the psychodrama session. Tom, a social worker, knew little of psychodrama and had no links with the group. Their problem was unconnected with Paul's work as a psychodramatist. However, Paul started the session feeling somewhat ill at ease.

'Perhaps Tom was right? Perhaps I shouldn't have written that letter to Mrs

Smith?' These thoughts went round in Paul's head as the session began. They made him feel rather tense. He would have to try to sort out the problem tomorrow. As the group got under way Paul felt his mood easing, his attention moved away from his problems outside the session and towards his protagonist and his needs. However, there remained a small nagging doubt and worry about Tom's comments.

Paul began to feel anxious in the session when the relationship between him and George became a bit tricky. He once more felt uncomfortable. The feelings seemed similar to those he had felt at the start of the session when they were more clearly unconnected with the group. Perhaps his anxiety during the session also related just to his disagreement with Tom and had nothing to do with his protagonist, George. If that was the case his feelings should not be attributed to a countertransference reaction to his protagonist or his group.

However, it is more likely that there was an interaction of feelings and responses. His difficulty with Tom, unconnected with the group, perhaps mirrored his slight conflict with George. His 'mistake' in stopping George talking to his psychodramatic 'father' reminded him of the tensions and concerns outside the session.

THE MECHANISMS OF THE COUNTERTRANSFERENCE

The processes of countertransference are clearly of great importance in both individual psychotherapy and psychodrama. Paula Heimann wrote in 1950:

> My thesis is that the analyst's emotional response to his patient within the analytic situation represents one of the most important tools for his work. The analyst's countertransference is an instrument of research into the patient's unconscious.
>
> The analytic situation . . . is a *relationship* between two persons. What distinguishes this relationship from others, is not the presence of feelings in one partner, the patient, and their absence in the other, the analyst, but above all the degree of the feelings and the use made of them. . . . If an analyst tries to work without consulting his feelings his interpretations are poor.
>
> 'On counter-transference' (Heimann 1950: 81)

In his contribution to the debate on the processes that occur between patient and therapist, the Argentinian psychoanalyst Heinrich Racker expressed the view that the term 'transference' should be used to describe the total psychological attitude and emotional response of patient to therapist which consists of:

> both the transference disposition *and* the present real (and especially analytic) experiences, the transference in its diverse expressions being the result of these two factors.
>
> *Transference and Countertransference* (Racker 1968: 133)

Racker believed that the emotional responses in the psychoanalyst during a session are also a

> fusion of present and past, the continuous and intimate connection of reality and phantasy, of external and internal, conscious and unconscious, that demands a concept embracing the totality of the analyst's psychological response, and renders it advisable, at the same time, to keep for this totality of response the accustomed term 'countertransference'.
>
> (Racker 1968: 133)

The therapist's concordant and complementary identifications with the patient

Racker went on to consider the nature of the process whereby one individual (the therapist) gains understanding of the other (the patient). He suggested that the psychoanalyst, because of the task in hand, has a 'predisposition to identify' with the patient, a process, he says, which is the 'basis of comprehension'.

The same is true of the director or auxiliary ego as they work to understand the psychology of the protagonist they are seeking to help.

Racker believed that two forms of identification occur: concordant (or homologous) and complementary.

Concordant identification

Racker described how the individual who has a wish to understand the other

> may achieve this aim by identifying his ego with the patient's ego, or to put it more clearly ... by identifying each part of his personality with the corresponding psychological part in the patient – his id with the patient's id, his ego with ego, his superego with the superego, accepting these identifications in his consciousness.
>
> The concordant identification is based ... on the resonance of the exterior in the interior, on recognition of what belongs to another as one's own ('this part of you is I') and on the equation of what is one's own with what belongs to another ('this part of me is you').
>
> (Racker 1968: 134–5)

Chapter 4 described how the individual's inner world consists of object relationships of *I*-objects relating to other-objects, linked by a feeling (or affect) and roles. Concordant identification is a process whereby we all gain some understanding of other people in our lives. It involves putting oneself into the shoes (or at least the *I*-objects) of the other, relating one part of oneself with the same (or homologous) part of someone else. The process is in part conscious. 'I wonder what it would be like to be in his position?'

For much of the time, however, we do it without planning or much thinking. We identify with, and feel distress for, orphans seen on the television news. We can identify with being lost and without parents. We put ourselves, briefly and without forethought, in their position. We identify with their losses, sadness, and pain. I believe that this process relates to Moreno's concept of tele.

Paul's understanding of George may have been based on the fact that Paul became aware that 'If I were in that position of having a valued conversation stopped I might feel awful.'

Likewise, the director may consciously attempt to gain understanding of the protagonist by wondering, 'How would I feel if I were having this exciting meeting with my dad?'

It is through these techniques, which could be considered to be intrapsychic role-reversals, that we all gain some understanding of other people.

Complementary identification

This process is rather different in that the therapist identifies with the patient's 'other' inner-objects.

The patient in psychotherapy experiences his therapist as if he were, say, his 'father' and has feelings and perhaps behaves in a way more appropriate to his childhood. This of course is the transference. The therapist then identifies, not with the 'self' of the patient, but with his internal 'father' with whom the 'self' is in an internal relationship. It is through this identification that the therapist develops some of the feelings appropriate to the role of 'father'.

In psychodrama sessions a similar process occurs involving both identification (by the auxiliary ego) and projection (by the protagonist). The protagonist projects his internal 'other' object onto the group member who then, to a variable extent, responds to this projection. The group member playing the role of the 'father' identifies with this inner object of the protagonist.

This process involves both conscious and unconscious aspects. Victor and George both knew the dramatic nature of their 'father–son' relationship. Victor consciously took on the role of the father, but his ability to enact this part involved his unconscious use of his concordant and complementary identifications with the protagonist.

The uses of countertransference responses in a session

Psychoanalysts are now well aware of the therapeutic usefulness and importance of the countertransference in treatment. Let us consider, in more detail, how this process might be recognised and used in psychodrama.

What sort of feelings did George's transference relationship to Paul stir up in his director? Paul felt anxious and rather guilty. He could see no reason to feel quite so distressed at this point in the session.

How does the therapist (or for that matter anyone else) feel when they are related to 'as if' they are someone else? Often with confusion, as they become aware of feelings that intellectually or cognitively seem wrong or inappropriate to the situation. This sense of uncertainty can suggest that the other person (in this session George) might be, in some way, manipulating their feelings and behaviour.

How can the director and those members of the group acting as auxiliary egos use the feelings stirred up by their relationship with the protagonist? Their feelings give them information, if they choose to be aware of it, about the other person's modes of relating and thus hints about their internal object relationships.

And how can the director or group members use this information to help the process of psychodrama? In this session Paul asked a question that linked George's present and past. Victor used his feelings (countertransference) to (re)create George's father.

How did Paul reach the point when he felt that he could make the statement about people keeping George away from his father? I believe that, having used his own feelings (his countertransference) to gain understanding of his protagonist, he was able to separate himself emotionally from George. It was then easier for Paul, now being more objective, to form the hunch that George had been in this situation before in childhood and that he was unconsciously re-enacting it in the session.

George and Paul

The unconscious aspects of the relationship between protagonist and director can cause significant disruption to the process of protagonist-centred psychodrama if they are not understood and resolved.

In our psychodrama the protagonist's emotional focus shifted (due to Paul's clumsy intervention) from auxiliary to director. Now Paul experienced the effects of George's projections onto him. He was being treated 'as if' he was George's mother. For Paul sensed that George was no longer reacting to him as his director (with a contract in the working alliance). He felt (through his feelings in the countertransference) as if he was being treated as someone else. There was a sudden increase in the intensity of George's responses to him, and Paul began to feel distressed and guilty. 'I've hurt this man. I've deprived him of his father. I'm not a good-enough therapist/mother.'

Paul had identified with one of George's inner-objects and he knew that his intense feelings were a possible indication of a developing transference reaction towards him from his protagonist. He began to feel rather anxious and guilty as if he had committed a major offence against his protagonist. His self-awareness, and technical knowledge, suggested that his mistake in his directing did not warrant this strength of response. He asked himself: 'Who is George treating me as if I was?' From what he had learnt about George he guessed that it was the 'mother' who had deprived George of contact with his father. He used this intuition to move the psychodrama forwards.

George, it seems, reacted to his psychodrama director, Paul, with the anger he felt towards his caring, but controlling, mother when she interrupted his contact and relationship with his father in childhood. Paul isn't a woman, but his style of directing, which is both caring and at times controlling, linked with George's (natural) need to use and to depend on his director, seemed to remind George of his relationship with his mother.

This situation potentially threatened the psychodrama. For George, Paul had become unconsciously identified with his mother. Once Paul became aware of this he had several options:

1 Recalling his training as a psychoanalytic therapist, he could 'interpret' George's transference to him.
2 He could facilitate an 'encounter' in the session between George and the real Paul. 'Look George, why are you so angry with me at this moment. What have I done?'
3 He could ask George to do some of the work and say:
   'I wonder if you felt other people used to get in the way of your seeing your dad?'

Option one was not really possible as this was a psychodrama group. And experience in psychoanalytic therapy shows that, initially, the interpretation of the transference leads to the process being intensified. This would just have increased Paul's difficulties with George.

Option two was both psychodramatic and potentially effective. Paul decided to apologise to George (a statement made in a brief, here-and-now 'encounter'). This move appeared to be effective.

He then rapidly moved on to the third option in an attempt to discover who this inner object was in George's life. The next step was to enrol an auxiliary from the group into this role of 'mother'.

In the session George became rapidly aware that the problem was not just between himself and Paul. The interruption in his psychodrama reminded him of his mother getting in the way of his contact with his father.

This insight provided the director with more significant information about his protagonist and allowed the psychodrama to continue, by moving on into another scene crucial to George's dilemma.

8 Psychological defence mechanisms

The group

'Who could play your mother, George?'

George looked around the group; his shoulders became more hunched. He was finding it very difficult to choose. Paul moved closer to him and put a hand on his shoulder.

'Come on, George'

'All right. Joyce, will you play my mother?'

He sounded very tentative.

'Yes, I'd be pleased to.'

Joyce got up off her cushion and came onto the stage.

'George can you tell us three things about your mother to help Joyce play her.'

'Well, she's very loving . . . a good mother . . .'

'Yes.'

'And she's a good cook. I really like her apple pie. She can be a bit moody.'

'So, she's a loving good mother, a good cook, but a bit moody. Do you think you know enough to start playing her?'

'Yes.'

'So, where do we meet your mother? Can you remember a particular moment?'

'Yes, my parents were fighting. I was up in bed. I could hear them even though my door was closed.'

'Quickly, show us your house. What room were your parents in. Set it up and also your bedroom.'

George set the scenes, using chairs and cushions.

'Let's see you in bed. How old are you now?'

'Five, no 3 or 4. I know I've not gone to school yet. The bedroom has a small night-light. I used to be afraid of the dark. The door is shut.'

George snuggled down into the cushions that made his bed, as a group member lowered the level of the light in the group room.

'How are you feeling?'

'Small and lonely. I don't like it when my parents fight.'

'What are they saying?'

'My mother says she will throw my father out of the house. He's done it once *too often. Then I hear my father pleading, and then shouting. I wish I couldn't hear. I put my head under the pillow. It doesn't help!'*

Based on what George said, 'mother' and 'father' started the row. As the volume increased George huddled up more in his bed.

'*What do you want to tell them?'*

'*Nothing. I'm scared of my father. He gets so angry.'*

'*Do you get angry? Do you get out of bed?'*

'*Not until my father leaves the house. He's so angry and it's all my fault!'*

George seemed unable to leave his bed, so Paul indicated that the 'father' should leave the house. This was done by some final shouts and the crash of the front door (a chair hit hard on the floor of the group room).

'*OK, your father's gone. What do you do now?'*

George got out of bed, and crept down to his 'mother' who was weeping in the living room. George comforted her.

'*Poor Georgie, Daddy's gone.'*

George was silent.

'*Is there something you want to say to your mother?'*

George looked helpless and stuck.

'*Would a double help?'*

He nodded. Paul indicated that Peter, who had risen from his cushion could double George.

'*I'm so confused, Mummy,' said the double. George nodded in agreement.*

'*Why has Daddy gone?'*

'*Reverse.'*

George reversed with his 'mother', the double withdrew slightly.

'*I really can't tell you Georgie. You're too young.'*

They reversed again. The scene continued, but remained rather slow and stuck. The use of a double had not helped.

'*It seems to me George that you have both loving and angry feelings towards your mother. Should we try having two chairs, one for each aspect of your mother?'*

Two chairs were placed on the stage.

'*Which part of your mother is this chair? Reverse with your mother and tell us.'*

'*I'm the part that Georgie loves. We are never cross with each other. He's a very good boy.'*

Paul then asked George to change chairs.

'*I hate my son. I'd never have married if I hadn't been pregnant with him.'*

'*Reverse, become yourself again. Which part of your mother do you wish to talk to first?'*

'*The angry part. I've never spoken to that bit. Mummy and me always had such an easy relationship.'*

Joyce sat in the 'angry' chair.

'*You made me so angry at times. I really hated you. You drove Daddy out of the house. You made his life a misery. Are you surprised that he saw other women? Women who could be nice to him. Women who didn't always complain and nag. . . .'*

George was in full flight: many ideas, accusations thought for many years but not said out loud.

'Great, George! What do you need to say to the other part of your mother?'
Joyce changes chairs.

'Oh. I loved you, I needed you. You cared for me, and looked after me after daddy left us. You were such a great mum.'

George was able to relate to the separate parts of his mother, and, through the use of role-reversal, both parts expressed their views of George.

Continued on page 135.

THE INNER WORLD MAKES ITSELF KNOWN

The Desire and Pursuit of the Whole (Rolfe 1934 and 1986) was the title of the last book written by Frederick, Fr. Rolfe (a.k.a. Baron Corvo). In this strange autobiographical novel he described what he sought in life: the perfect friend. These words perhaps also sum up what the motivation is that drives people into psychotherapy.

Rolfe lived (1860 to 1913) a complicated and tormented life during which he wrote several mainly autobiographical and rather bizarre novels (including *Hadrian the Seventh* published in 1904). He was also an artist and made several abortive attempts to enter the Roman priesthood (hence his use of the title Fr.).

Rolfe fell foul of almost everyone he had any dealings with and responded to the world (and everyone in it) with an intense angry paranoia, constantly seeking friendship and security, but always losing it through his egocentric and impossible ways. There was a marked, and rather tragic, compulsion in the way he kept repeating the same disastrous patterns of behaviour (Symons 1934; Woolf 1974; Rolfe 1974b; Benkovitz 1977).

I believe that a modern psychiatrist or psychoanalyst would say that he had a borderline (or unintegrated) personality (Kernberg 1975; American Psychiatric Association 1980; Pope *et al.* 1983).

However, Fr. Rolfe was very different from, and much more disturbed than, George. An understanding of the psychological make-up of such individuals will help us to make sense of the earliest stages of the development of the psyche, as they use, in a developmental sense, the very primitive or immature defence mechanisms of early childhood which I describe later in this chapter. I am aware of Moreno's attack on the 'psychoanalysis' of the dead (Moreno 1967), but I think that there are some useful points to be made through discussing the tragic life of this man.

The title of his last novel sums up his aim in life, to be somehow whole, not to be in parts, and to have a relationship with another person. He failed in his aims. Unable to defend himself against his rages and inner conflicts, he died destitute in Venice still seeking but not accepting what was available to him.

George's problems were much less marked, his personality was more integrated and he tended to use the more mature defences of the neurotic individual. But he also experienced personal distress. His solution was to seek help in psychotherapy in an attempt to reconcile the contradictions and difficulties in his relationships with the world. He too had Desires and was in pursuit of the Whole: a sense of *self* without too many conflicts in easy relationship with *others*.

How to understand the problems

Fr. Rolfe and George had, in common with the rest of us, complex inner worlds, the product of their inherited genes, their personal histories, and cultural and social influences. These inner worlds made themselves known through the behaviour and feelings of these two men.

The ways in which their psychological problems are formulated will depend on the therapist's belief systems.

A classical Freudian would say that they both had the id impulses (the drives of love and aggression) that sought discharge, putting pressure on their egos which had to relate to the demands of the id, the super-ego, and external reality. Such internal conflicts may lead to anxiety and psychic distress.

Object relations theory, while accepting the existence of drives, puts more stress on the fact that both men were 'object', 'person', or 'other' seeking, and that the nature of the relationships they made with others will have depended, in part, on their inner 'object relationships' created as a result of their childhood experiences.

Certain new relationships could be made with impunity. Other relationships, perhaps driven by a repetition compulsion, would have had significant reverberations with internal reality. There would have been stress between conflicting inner object relationships with resulting psychic distress; for example, anxiety, panic, or depression.

THE PSYCHE DEFENDS ITSELF AGAINST PAIN

The psyche attempts to reduce these emotional responses through the use of its defence mechanisms.

Both the Freudian and the object relations theorists would be in agreement that not all aspects of the drives, or of the inner object relationships, can be easily thought about (which of course means in consciousness), let alone discharged or externalised in the real world.

Free expression could result in distressing repetitions or enactments of past dramas. Even controlling the impulse to act out (or externalise the drama) may not solve the problem. Anxiety and mental pain will increase as conflicting object relationships, and the associated representations of self and other, enter consciousness.

The defence mechanisms of Fr. Rolfe and George

The defence mechanisms that the psyche (or ego) uses in attempts to defend itself from this situation are created in infancy and childhood and can be considered along a developmental spectrum. Fr. Rolfe and George used the psychic defences appropriate to their very different levels of emotional growth.

Fr. Rolfe was an immature social and emotional failure, whose life was ruined by his inner turmoil, who gained fame (through his books) only after his death. He appeared to have had no realistic concern for others in his life.

George, however, was a hard-working, respected, and loved member of the community. Like many of us, he was a productive and caring member of society, not too disabled by his internal psychic conflicts.

THE EARLY YEARS OF NOT BEING INTEGRATED: THE DEFENCE MECHANISMS OF THOSE YET TO DEVELOP CONCERN FOR OTHERS

I have described how, according to my view of object relations theory, the inner world of the individual develops. In the early months there is an accumulation of memory traces, laid down as a result of experiences between the child and the environment. Slowly order is brought to the chaos, initially through the growth of clusters of object relationships grouped together by the associated valencies (see Kernberg 1976).

However, there is continuing controversy in psychoanalytic circles about the early life of the 'ego'. Freud's writings on the subject are complex and (as with much of Freud) not entirely consistent. This is understandable as he developed his ideas over almost fifty years. In his final formulations he believed that what he called the 'ego' developed during infancy as a consequence of life experiences. At birth very little of this 'ego' exists. Freud did, however, indicate that the tiny infant is capable of some defensive activity, even though he associated these processes with the ego. (For a review of these issues see Laplanche and Pontalis 1967 or Wollheim 1973.)

Melanie Klein's views were different. Hanna Segal stated that:

> In Melanie Klein's view, sufficient ego exists at birth to experience anxiety, use defence mechanisms and form primitive object-relations in phantasy and in reality.
>
> (Segal 1964 and 1973: 24)

Klein herself said:

> I would ... say that the early ego largely lacks cohesion, and a tendency towards integration alternates with a tendency towards disintegration, a falling to bits. I believe that these fluctuations are characteristic of the first few months of life.... We are, I think, justified in assuming that some of the functions we know from the later ego are there at the beginning. Prominent amongst these functions is that of dealing with anxiety.
>
> (Klein 1946 and 1975: 4)

The earliest defence mechanisms

However it is conceptualised, it is now generally accepted that the infant's psyche is able to use primitive defence mechanisms against psychic distress as well as undertaking the necessary developmental tasks of the mind.

These defence mechanisms are usually considered to be those of *splitting*, *projection*, and *projective identification*.

Splitting

Klein believed that the tiny infant's ego resorts to splitting, in an attempt to cope with the anxiety caused by the conflict between the death and life instincts (Segal 1964 and 1973: 25). In order to cope with the negative power of the death instinct the ego splits itself and projects outwards that part of itself containing the drive derivatives of this instinct. The external object (in Klein's theory the breast) is then experienced as persecutory or 'bad'.

There is also a splitting in the ego, and projection outwards of aspects of the libido. Thus, the ego's experience of its relationship with external objects is then one of a split, there being both a 'good' and 'bad' breast. The consequence of this projection is that the infant feels persecuted. Klein wrote: 'I believe that the ego is incapable of splitting the object – internal and external – without a corresponding splitting taking place within the ego' (Klein 1946 and 1975: 6).

Thus, for Melanie Klein and her followers, a unified, if fragile ego exists at birth, which early on uses splitting as an active defence against anxiety.

I describe another psychoanalytic view of these developments in the infant in Chapter 4. In this model the inner world, in its very earliest stages, is not integrated; that is, it is in parts (or fragments), positive and negative, good and bad, loving and hating feelings, that all exist separated and disorganised *because* that was the way these memory traces were laid down in the psyche.

The parts are not separate because of an active splitting process in which they are 'burst by explosion or pressure from within' to be 'deprived of or to lose unity' (*Pocket Oxford Dictionary* 1924), for they were not originally one. It is the developmental task of the psyche to bring order to this original chaos of unintegrated memory traces or early object relationships.

In this view the psychological defence of splitting is a return from an integrated or ambivalent condition to an earlier state of being. As in Klein's theory, the defence mechanism is used to keep 'good' away from (or protected from) 'bad'. However, the splitting is of complete object relationships rather than simple inner-objects. Thus the internal splits are the result of a secondary process, or, as Josephine Klein puts it, people who use the defence mechanism of splitting 'crack again along the original split' (personal communication).

Rolfe used splitting extensively. He (for a time) idealised new friends, placing on their relationship unrealistic expectations. At the same time he denigrated others, seeing no good in people who might have been willing and able to assist him. Splitting is not only a feature of infancy or pathology. Hanna Segal pointed out that:

> There are other aspects of splitting which remain and are important in mature life. For instance, the ability to pay attention, or to suspend one's emotion in order to form an intellectual judgment, would not be achieved without the capacity for temporary reversible splitting.
>
> (Segal 1964 and 1973: 35)

George and splitting

Let us consider how George used a process of splitting in the psychodrama.

He was a not very happy, rather neurotic individual who used the relatively mature defence mechanisms of repression, sublimation, and displacement. Normally he did not use, to any significant extent, the defence mechanism of splitting, although he tended at times to use projective identification.

The techniques of psychodrama allowed for the reduction of his lifelong use of repression. He became aware of his anger towards his much loved mother. He then, however, became very anxious and distressed. He could not continue the scene with his mother as he once more gained contact with the object relationship in which he hated this controlling parent. It was his need for her, and no doubt his love, that in childhood resulted in the repression of the object relationship containing the self-representation 'I hate my mother'.

The psychodrama had allowed unconscious material to surface. In the session the director wished George to remain in conscious contact with his anger and hate of his mother. He hoped that George could in time produce a more satisfactory use of defence mechanisms that did not result in total repression (indeed suppression) of important aspects of himself. The knowledge of his conflicts would also allow George to use his cognitive processes to gain some understanding and control over his inner world and its consequences in the external world.

However, at this point in the session, when George became very anxious, his spontaneity and creativity were reduced and he felt completely stuck.

So the director assisted George by suggesting that he consciously split the aspects of his mother in the externalisation on the psychodramatic stage. To do this he used two chairs, one for the 'loving good mother', the other for the 'hateful bad mother'. George could, of course, now relate to these two externalisations of his inner mother with the appropriate *I*-object roles formed when George was a child. He could shout at his 'bad' mother without the concern for his 'good' mother who sat in a separate chair.

In the psychodrama George is encouraged to use splitting as a defence against his ambivalence and guilt, with their associated feelings of anxiety. As this defence mechanism is a psychological process normally associated with early infancy and with Mrs Klein's paranoid-schizoid position, it might be said that he had regressed (in terms of the maturity of his defences) to assist the therapeutic process.

And of course people do regress in real life, under psychological or social stress. 'Others' become increasingly 'black' or 'white', 'good' or 'bad'. Ambivalence is lost as is concern for the damage that might be caused by our rage directed towards the 'bad' people around us. All becomes simple.

In extreme situations the integrated experience of the 'self' and 'others' fragments, the I identifying with any of these fragments. The individual loses contact with adult reality and psychosis develops.

George certainly isn't psychotic in the session. The dramatic use of 'splitting' in the session helped George to reduce his anxiety and to express long repressed feelings. Thus his spontaneity and creativity increased, and he was able to find new emotional and cognitive solutions to his dilemma.

This situation challenged reality. George did not have two mothers, one bad, one good. However, he maintained aspects of his adult 'observing ego' which watched him talking to the two, now split, aspects of his mother. If George had actually believed this situation, it would have been said that his 'reality testing was impaired'. He would have been deluded and psychotic.

A regression to this defence, while it may be of short-term use, in the long term significantly reduces the individual's ability to have an integrated, reality-orientated, and thus sane relationship with the world.

The use of splitting, involving the therapeutic illusions of psychodrama, allowed George to make progress. As the session progressed he was able to reach a conscious acceptance of his ambivalence towards his mother. In a child this developmental progress could take months or years to come about. And in a borderline individual, such as Fr. Rolfe, it may never fully occur.

Projection and projective identification

Splitting is normally associated with the defence mechanisms of 'projection' and 'projective identification'.

We need to be careful when talking about these processes. Psychoanalysts use the terms in rather different ways. For example, Melanie Klein used the term 'projection' for a psychic mechanism that was a fundamental feature of tiny infants (see Hinshelwood 1989 for a discussion), while Kernberg applies the word to a mechanism used by neurotic adults (Kernberg in Sandler 1988: 94). Likewise, for some, the use of projective identification by adults may be considered to be a sign of pathology (e.g. Segal 1964, or see Sandler 1988 for a review), while for others (e.g. Moses, also in Sandler 1988) projective identification is associated with the much more mature defence mechanisms of the neurotic individual.

I have always considered projection to be a very primitive mechanism used by the tiniest infant and by the deeply psychotic, deluded and hallucinating, adult (see Segal 1973) and I use this term in this way in this book.

Projection

The processes of projection are powerful when they occur in adults. The psychotic or schizophrenic throws out aspects of themselves in a random and unfocused manner. Anyone (or indeed anything) can become the repository of the projected aspects of the self. Indeed such people will often imagine that they hear these individuals or objects talking about them using their *own* words. They live in a threatening world where many people or objects feed their delusions of persecution.

The persecutory 'others' are entirely passive, and may be human or inanimate (for example, a television set). The psychotic *'knows'* that the other person is 'angry', for the responses of the other are immaterial, requiring no validation from another person. He hears voices from the refrigerator and thus does not require the fridge to talk. The delusions and hallucinations are independent of external reality.

Projection for Melanie Klein was an essential element of the infant's psyche. She believed that:

> The immature ego of the infant is exposed from birth to the anxiety stirred up by the inborn polarity of instincts – the immediate conflict between the life instinct and the death instinct. . . . When faced with the anxiety produced by the death instinct, the ego deflects it. This deflection . . . in Melanie Klein's view, consists partly of a projection, partly of a conversion of the death instinct into aggression. The ego splits itself and projects that part of itself that contains the death instinct outwards into the original external object – the breast. Thus, the breast . . . is felt to be bad and threatening to the ego, giving rise to a feeling of persecution.
>
> (Segal 1964 and 1973: 25)

In this process an individual projects part of himself (with associated affects) onto someone else, in infancy usually the mother. According to Klein, the projected parts of the self also include the good and loving aspects of the inner world. In this circumstance the other is felt to be the repository of 'good' while the self may be experienced as fragmented and lacking in positive qualities (see Segal 1964 and 1973; Sandler 1988).

The association of this process with the psychic mechanisms used by tiny infants is a fundamental aspect of Kleinian theory. However, research (and everyday experience) shows that even the newborn has an acute awareness of the reality of others (Stern 1985).

Projective identification

The process of projective identification is both more subtle and more selective than that which occurs in projection. It is a feature of the psychic functioning of infants, and many adults.

As in projection, objects from the individual's inner world are projected outwards, not towards *any* object but onto specific individuals. These projections, reflecting a more integrated inner world, contain not only the inner object, but also the associated affect and role.

In adults it allows, for example, an individual who cannot stand the self-image of the 'angry destructive man' to get rid of his anger by projecting it into (and thus experiencing it from) someone else. Projection of the role occurs towards a person who is likely to respond; the actual responses of the other person confirm the 'fact' of the successful projection. It is for this reason that projective identification works only with another person, a person who must be role responsive and identify with the projection. George could not have used projective identification to rid his inner world of the 'bad father' unless Fred was able to respond appropriately.

Sandler described how in psychotherapy the patient unconsciously acts to manipulate or provoke certain actions or responses from the analyst that are congruent with the object relationship involved in the transference. He wrote that: 'In the transference, in many subtle ways, the patient attempts to prod the analyst into behaving in a particular way' ('Countertransference and role-responsiveness', Sandler 1976: 44).

The therapist will become aware of these manipulations and the associated projections through his own feelings and thoughts (his countertransference). Sandler believes that the therapist, in addition to his free-floating conscious attention (which is linked to emotional responses and cognitive understanding), *also* has a free-floating potential for a behavioural response. He may thus, all too easily, fall into the psychic trap and respond actively as, say, 'the uncaring father' or the 'over-protective mother'.

In the former role, if a patient behaves like a rejected and abused child and treats his therapist like a bad father it will not be long before the therapist begins to feel like a rejecting father. He may be late for his patient's sessions or at worst miss one altogether.

In the latter role he will perhaps express excess anxiety about any new move or project in his patient's life. The therapist has identified with the parent role and has begun to *act* like a father/mother to the patient who feels and acts like a child/son.

Such behaviour is described as the therapist's 'acting out' and as such cannot meet with approval, even though it may increase the drama of the treatment. It can, however, be understood as a consequence of the projections of the patient's inner objects. Ideally the therapist will pause and think about what is going on, and use his ideas to form an interpretation.

Such objectivity is one crucial difference between psychotherapy and everyday life where projective identification may be a feature of many of our interactions.

Rolfe's letters demonstrate his deep sense of persecution resulting from his use of projective identification. (The initials refer to the names of his persecutors.)

And P-G and B. and T. have made up their minds to take the fullest advantage of that condition [Rolfe's poverty and physical illness]. It isn't necessary for them to commit murder. *All they have to do is just keep quite still while I die.* . . . Now mark me well. I won't die, till I've had a good kick out all round. So this is what I've done. . . . Also, I have denounced P-G, and B. and T. to the Publishers' Association as *thieves* of my work giving particulars of the works stolen so that no publisher will dare issue them without my consent.

(Rolfe 1974b: 66–7)

No doubt people did misuse Rolfe, but they were sorely provoked by this difficult man.

George too was, in some ways, a passive-aggressive individual who needed to feel calm and collected. He could only achieve this peace of mind, since he had much internal anger, through the projection of his own angry inner-objects onto individuals likely to respond. For example, the projection of a 'father' inner-object (together with its role attributes and affects) is more likely to be made towards an older male father figure than, say, towards a teenager or a woman.

These people then had to be psychically possessed and controlled, for they now contained parts of George's self. The situation has been likened to a boy with a balloon into which he has projected some of his inner-objects. He must hang on for dear life if he is not to lose bits of himself. And as his father figures responded George felt himself to be surrounded by angry men, as indeed he was at times.

George's projections in the office will have been confirmed by the angry dismissive responses of Fred whose feelings were stirred up by George. The roles and affects of anger had been projected, or transferred, by the subtle manipulations and prods of his passive-aggressive behaviour. George denied his own anger but experienced it in Fred. Thus George could say to himself: 'Look, I'm not angry at all. It is you who has the temper, not me.'

Projective identification does not involve a complete loss of contact with reality. However, reality testing is somewhat impaired. Fred was *not* George's absent father, nor was Paul his controlling mother, none the less George acted (at times) as though they were. But note that Fred was often absent and that Paul could be controlling, behaviours independent of George which, however, created a dynamic interplay with his inner world and past experiences.

Different internal aspects of the individual (say 'angry man' or 'needy child') will be projected onto different people. Projective identification requires two people. When George projected the needy hurt child aspects of himself onto his social work clients, he lost contact with these parts of his personality *in himself* and experienced them as existing in others.

Of course those who were responsive to the projected roles may well have been projecting back the reciprocal role from their own inner world. George's needy clients found a social worker who needed to be needed.

The passive-aggressive woman, who had an angry abusive father, finds an angry husband who needs to attack his wife. All the partners in these types of relationship have the greatest difficulty in letting go. And if they do so they will often rush into a further repetition with someone else.

Violent men are often themselves victims, having experienced violence themselves as children. They may identify with their own aggressive fathers, projecting their 'abused helpless little boy' self-representation onto those they attack as adults. As aggressive men they no longer have to face the anxieties and terrors of the abused child.

Kernberg provided a summary of projective identification. It is a mechanism consisting of:

(a) projecting of intolerable aspects of intrapsychic experience onto an object,
(b) maintaining empathy with what is projected,
(c) attempting to control the object as a continuing defensive effort against intolerable psychic experience,
(d) and unconsciously inducing in the object what is the actual interaction with the object.

(Kernberg in Sandler 1988: 94)

The defence mechanisms of splitting and projective identification are most powerfully observed in the more disturbed individuals, such as those with borderline personality structures. Some see projective identification, when used as a psychic defence by adults, as a sign of serious emotional problems. Others, however, including myself, believe that this psychological process is a common, and a feature of more integrated and mature people and thus an aspect, at times, of most people's psychic functioning. The American psychoanalyst, Rafael Moses wrote:

Only in the last two or three decades has it become more generally accepted that many of the mechanisms previously described for psychotic patients (perhaps all of them) are ubiquitous. They are to be found not only in all our patients, but ourselves. (And of course, they abound in our colleagues!)

(Moses in Sandler 1988: 143–4)

THE BORDERLINE OR UNINTEGRATED PERSONALITY

Let us consider Fr. Rolfe in the light of our discussion of primitive defence mechanisms. He was clearly a most difficult and peculiar man. I have indicated that he might be described as having a borderline personality. What is meant by this?

Put simply, such individuals have not yet reached a solid integration of their inner worlds. Both *I*-objects and other-objects remain separated and split by valency or emotional charge (Kernberg 1976). Thus they do not have a realistic (and so ambivalent) internal representational world, nor do they have a consistent and integrated sense of self. This inner turmoil is reflected in their behaviour and in the relationships that they make.

Gunderson and Singer (1975) reviewed the vast literature (which has of course greatly increased since then) on this topic and decided that they could describe a series of symptoms that seemed to be a consistent feature of borderline individuals. They listed the following (1975: 8):

1 The presence of intense affect, usually of a strongly hostile or depressed nature.

Such individuals have powerful affects (often negative) associated with their internal object relationships. This may be the result of excessive negative experiences in infancy leading to difficulties in psychic integration.

Rolfe fell for people, who often initially liked him. Rapidly, however, the angry aspects of his inner world were externalised and he lost friends and supporters.

2 A history of episodic or chronic impulsive behaviour which is often self-destructive (e.g. self-mutilation, drug taking, suicide attempts, or promiscuity).

Rolfe was highly self-destructive; indeed, because of his pride, he spent his final freezing winter in Venice camping outdoors on the canals. This destructive quality (of self or others) again reflects the high level of rage involved in the object relationships, and internal attacks on the internal 'good' self-images by the negative object relationships. He also wrote (in letters to friends in England) about his promiscuous and risky sexual encounters with young gondoliers (Rolfe 1974b).

3 Social adaptiveness in which the individual has an ability (through strong social awareness) to manifest a superficial adaptation to external social needs. However, this apparent strength may reflect a disturbed identity, masked by an ever changing mimicry of those around them.

Rolfe was accepted as a trainee for the Catholic priesthood and spent time at the Scott's College in Rome (he was eventually forcibly evicted, thrown into the street with his bags). He was also, at other times, both in England and in Venice, accepted into polite society. He was able to mimic or copy the social skills appropriate to his ambitions. However, in a more fundamental sense he never really felt that he fitted in. Deep down inside he was still an angry child, with no clear integrated adult view of himself.

4 Brief psychotic episodes, often of a paranoid quality and at times provoked by alcohol or drug misuse. (I would add that if hallucinations occur they are more often visual than auditory.)

Rolfe was often very paranoid, and spent much time, energy, and money (which he did not have) fighting those he *knew* had so misused him.

5 Such individuals produce bizarre, illogical and immature responses to unstructured psychological tests such as the Rorschach (ink blot) test. However, their performances on more structured intelligence tests (such as the WAIS) show the normal range.

Rolfe, as far as I know, saw no doctors or psychologists. However, his writings have a bizarre and dream-like quality. It seems that his primary processes were poorly repressed (if at all).

6 Interpersonal relationships vary between the transient and superficial and the highly dependent. Long-term relationships are often marred by devaluation, manipulation, and demandingness.

There can be no doubt about the transient nature of many of Rolfe's friendships. At first he tended to idealise people (and they at times him) but before long relationships changed to those of fury and denigration. However, with a few people (who perhaps saw him more as a difficult child in need) he was able to maintain relationships. These, however, still involved Rolfe's continuing demands for money and his bitter and hostile complaints when he was, yet again, let down.

Fr. Rolfe was clearly the victim of his inner world. He was often paranoid and deluded, and it is probable that at times he was more floridly psychotic. There can be no doubt that he used, predominantly, the psychic defences of projection, projective identification, and splitting.

Delusion, illusion, and sanity

Delusions and hallucinations (Slade 1976) are features of psychosis and madness while illusions are a feature of normality and of psychotherapy. The florid lunacy of psychotics may be a fairly permanent state or, as is the case of those with a borderline personality, intermittent.

The psychotic individual has the greatest difficulty distinguishing his inner world from the world of reality around him. The boundaries between self and other are blurred. He also has problems unravelling the different object relationships that form his inner world. Daily living becomes an almost impossible strain. For the psychotic in therapy the illusion (which maintains the sense of the 'as if' in the therapeutic relationship) may be lost to be replaced by a delusion. The psychotic may say of his doctor: 'This is my father in the chair opposite.'

Moreno worked with psychotic patients in his clinic at Beacon. He wrote:

the [psychotic] patients are aroused to reconsider their situation and to use auxiliary egos in their attempt at establishing a new and imaginary world for themselves which is more fitting for them than the world of reality. . . . The psychodramatic auxiliary ego plays a double role. In the therapeutic theatre he is an ideal extension of the patient's ego in his efforts to establish a sort of psychotic hierarchy, a self-sufficient world, and outside of the theatre he is an interpreter between the patient and the people of the real world.

'The psychodramatic treatment of psychosis'
(Moreno 1973 in Fox 1987: 77)

Moreno chose to work with psychotic patients. Any psychodramatist may find a psychotic individual in his group, although an appropriate process of assessment should reduce this risk. However, it is also possible for a group member with a borderline personality to slip from neurotic to psychotic defence mechanisms during a session. Such a (rare) event requires all a director's skill to maintain the protagonist's and the group's hold on the magical 'as if' quality of the process.

The stages of projective identification

Let us consider in more detail the mechanisms in the inner world which cause projective identification.

According to Sandler (1988), there are three different forms or stages in the psychological process. The first stage occurs entirely within an individual's psyche. In this circumstance aspects of the self-representation or *I*-object are, in phantasy, projected into an internal other-object or representation. This process involves projection in that characteristics are experienced in the other-object that have been split off from and expelled or projected from the *I*-object (Sandler 1987: 36). This stage one projective identification does not require the presence of another person. It occurs entirely in the inner world. (Note that Sandler uses the term self-representation rather than *I*-object.) Figure 8.1 illustrates the process.

The reverse of this process is introjective identification, when internalised representations of others (object representations) are introjected and incorporated into the *I*-object or representation (Sandler 1988: 16; Joseph 1988: 76). This mechanism is obviously crucial in childhood when the individual feels themselves to have characteristics originally experienced and remembered as existing in others. Children demonstrate this when they feel and act like their mothers when playing with dolls.

In second stage projective identification the analyst is able to identify with the unconscious phantasies in the patient using his countertransference. Thus the unconscious processes in the patient are conveyed to the mind of another. However, the analyst does not react in the active and concrete way that characterises the third stage of this process. Empathy, a process whereby we feel for or understand others, may represent an everyday example of the process of second stage projective identification.

Third stage projective identification is interactive and involves the externalisation of parts of the self or the internal other-object directly into the other person (Sandler 1987: 38) (see Figure 8.2). A young child may actually have the emotional experience and believe that such a concrete process has occurred. The process clearly remains in some ways a phantasy as nothing concrete is pushed into another person.

However, the mechanism does involve an active two-person relationship, and to that extent the process does not occur in phantasy. It can operate fully only if the other person is 'role responsive' (Sandler 1976). Thus the projections must be directed towards a specific person who is able (to a varying extent) to identify with and respond to the projected object or role. It

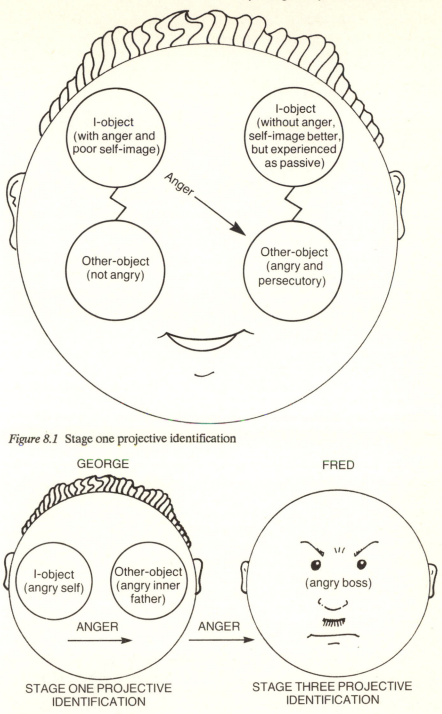

Figure 8.1 Stage one projective identification

Figure 8.2

is no good projecting the angry part of oneself onto an individual who continues to remain placid and charming. The projection must be confirmed by an angry response.

George and the stages of projective identification

George, as a child, internalised (as a representation of his father) an inner other-object 'father'. This resulted from his relationship with this unreliable and angry man. Through the further process of introjective identification aspects of this other-object became part of his self-representation; that is, George felt *himself* to be unreliable and potentially angry. This mechanism accounts for why we all often feel so alike to our parents.

Later George was, perhaps unconsciously, distressed by this self-image. If he was so angry, perhaps he too would be aggressive towards his mother just like his father had been. He thus defended himself against the psychic pain of this awareness by projecting the roles back into an other-object in his psyche (Sandler's stage one projective identification).

He was able to bring about a further, and more complete, disposal of these roles and the associated affects by the use of another person (Sandler's stage three).

Communication in projective identification

Projective identification is a process that aids interactions between individuals. It helps us to understand something more about another person's inner world. For infants (who do not yet have the use of language) such communication is essential. The mechanisms work through the use of various modalities including, in the infant, body posture, facial expressions, and its cries. Later, other techniques are added, such as language, tone of voice, and behavioural patterns that involve subtle (and unconscious) 'manipulations'.

All these mechanisms help the other person to accept and respond to the projected role, with its associated feelings. For example, if the patient behaves like a rejected and abused child and treats his therapist like a bad father it will not be long before the therapist begins to feel like a rejecting father. If he has professional insight he wonders why he's so nasty to this particular patient. It requires a degree of self-knowledge in the therapist to prevent these feelings becoming associated with actions with all the associated risks to the therapy.

Projective identification and psychodrama

In the previous chapter I described Racker's views of how, using the countertransference, a therapist may gain understanding of his patient. In a similar way an auxiliary ego gains understanding of the protagonist. This knowledge is acquired, in part, through the protagonist's use of projective identification.

Analytic psychotherapists are trained to have a 'predisposition to identify' with a patient and the ability to appreciate and analyse their own subsequent emotional responses. They thus reduce the risk of their 'acting out' as a result of their patients' projections. It is in part through the process of projective identification that they gain an understanding of their patients' inner worlds. The therapist must be available to respond to all the patient's inner roles, male and female, old and young. At any point in time he may not know who he 'is' in the terms of the transference and it takes time for him to make sense of exactly which roles are being projected and to understand their origins in terms of their patient's past.

Psychodrama is different, being, in some ways, a more conscious and indeed stage-managed process than psychoanalysis. When an auxiliary ego is chosen and agrees to play a role from a protagonist's inner world that person is usually given a name for this part ('my mother' or 'my brother') and a certain amount of factual information. This was certainly the case when Victor took on the role of George's father. If the protagonist begins to behave and talk like a child the auxiliary ego is strengthened in his identification with the role of 'father'.

Important unconscious additional communications also occur between protagonist and auxiliary ego through the mechanisms of projective identification. The protagonist also has less need to 'prod and manipulate' the other person, as the auxiliary ego has willingly taken on the task of becoming, for a time, this person who originates in the protagonist's inner world.

Thus, while Fred resented being unconsciously cast as George's father in their office, Victor had consciously accepted this role in the psychodrama. He was easily able to identify himself with George's projections of his father and was thus able to take on this role in the psychodrama. Victor had the role of 'father' as one of his inner 'other-objects'. It is a role in his 'role repertoire' although, having no children himself, it was not a role he used in everyday life, but he had access to it, and enjoyed playing a 'father'.

Through the process of psychodrama, including role-reversals, the 'performance' of the auxiliary ego is modelled and modified to increase the resemblance to the inner-object of the protagonist, a process that involves both conscious and unconscious communications.

It must be noted that the auxiliary ego is enacting a role from the protagonist's inner world, and *not* an objective dramatisation of the real historical person. In George's inner world his 'father' has been modified both by the perceptual abilities of George the child and by the internal mechanisms of the psyche.

The director and projective identification

We have considered how the protagonist's inner world is dramatically expressed using other members of the group as auxiliary egos to play his inner-objects or roles. The protagonist's relationship with the director is not the principal medium of the treatment process. In this respect it is unlike psychoanalysis. Indeed, the director must strive to maintain a relationship with the protagonists based in the here-and-now. This is facilitated by the method of psychodrama which encourages the protagonist to direct his projections (and the associated identifications) towards the auxiliary ego. The director will learn much about his protagonist from the way the auxiliary ego develops the role.

It is important that the contract (between director and protagonist) for the task in hand is supported by what psychoanalysts call the 'working or therapeutic alliance' (see Sandler *et al.* 1973). This contract for the session is made between two (in Moreno's terms) equal adults.

The complex feelings and thoughts that develop in the director, as the result of his relationship with the protagonist, are still crucial to the process of psychodrama. They can provide him with much subtle and useful information that can be used to facilitate the process of the session. The mechanism of the countertransference, involving as it does projections and identifications allows the therapist to understand and to assist the protagonist.

THE MECHANISMS OF DEFENCE OF THOSE WHO HAVE DEVELOPED CONCERN FOR OTHERS

In time the child begins to develop those defence mechanisms that it will use as an adult. Melanie Klein said of this period, which she called the depressive position, that:

> as the ego becomes better organised and projections are weakened, repression takes over from splitting. Psychotic mechanisms gradually give way to neurotic mechanisms, inhibitions, repression and displacement.
>
> (Segal 1964 and 1973: 75)

The British psychotherapist Harry Guntrip described these more mature defensive mechanisms. When conflicting emotions occur simultaneously in the same person, he said:

> such conflicts often result in the repression of some of the conflicting emotions, which never the less do not thereby cease to be felt, but continue to be experienced albeit unconsciously, with highly disturbing effects on conscious experience and behaviour. . . . Out of this inwardly suppressed mental turbulence, there arise the various symptoms of the psychoneurosis, both physical and mental.

He went on to say:

> Freud further discovered that one of the things that happens to repressed experiences in childhood is that later in life the emotions involved find outlet by transference onto some roughly analogous figure in the present

day. This phenomenon of 'transference' – so prolific a cause of disruption in friendships, marriages and adult partnerships of all kinds – inevitably erupts, unrecognised by the person in the treatment situation.

Psychoanalytic Theory, Therapy and the Self (Guntrip 1971: 8–9)

In a neurotic defence the inner-object relationships associated with conflict are repressed. This mechanism, however, has the associated consequence that there is a loss, from the individual's role repertoire, of certain roles that may be of use in their adult life.

For example, George was rather passive and found it very hard to be directly angry with his boss or his clients. He had, without doubt, reached the 'depressive position', or the phase of 'ruth or concern for others'. He was worried for his wife, his boss, and his clients. He felt confused and guilty about his relationships. This indeed was the reason he came into psychotherapy. None the less at times he used the defence mechanism of projective identification, considered by some psychoanalysts to be a sign of significant pathology.

It is at this stage of psychic development that the super-ego becomes a more significant aspect of the inner world. This psychic force can be considered to be an association of those object relationships derived from the child's experiences of external prohibitions and controls from parents and society. In as much as the super-ego is an association of roles and object relationships, it resembles the role clusters we have considered previously: the two simple clusters – 'good-positive' and 'bad-negative' – of the early paranoid-schizoid period and the more mature clusters associated with 'father and men' or 'mother and women' of a later stage of development (but see Laplanche and Pontalis 1967; Kernberg 1976, for more complex accounts of the super-ego).

The role cluster of the super-ego adds to the psychic stress of the child as it defends against (in a classical Freudian sense) the id instincts, or against the tendency towards expression of conflicting self-representations. Anna Freud wrote that:

The instinct is regarded as dangerous because the superego prohibits its gratification and, if it achieves its aim, it will certainly stir up trouble between the ego and the superego. Hence the ego of the adult neurotic fears the instinct because it fears the superego. Its defense is motivated by the superego anxiety.

The Ego and the Mechanisms of Defense (A. Freud 1936 and 1966: 55)

Anna Freud listed the methods of defence. I have already discussed the more primitive ones: regression, projection, introjection, and splitting (a later addition to her list). The more mature or neurotic defences are: repression, reaction-formation, isolation, undoing, turning against the self, reversal, and sublimation or displacement.

By these means, she believed, the ego is able to defend (or protect) itself from the dangers of the uncontrolled expression of the id impulses which, if expressed without control, would cause the individual anxiety.

She also described how the ego also defends itself against certain affects or feelings for:

> Whenever [the ego] seeks to defend itself against instinctual impulses ... it is obliged to ward off also the affects associated with the instinctual process. The nature of the affects in question is immaterial: they may be pleasurable, painful or dangerous to the ego. It makes no difference, for the ego is never allowed to experience them exactly as they are. If an affect is associated with a prohibited instinctual process, its fate is decided in advance. The fact it is so associated suffices to put the ego on guard against it.
>
> (A. Freud 1937 and 1961: 61)

Anna Freud followed, on the whole, the classical model of her father in her concern with the expression of the instincts. Object relations theory is more concerned with the internal and external tensions resulting from the conflicts between the incompatible aspects of the inner world. However, object relations are associated with memories of affectual states, which are, in Kernberg's words, drive derivatives.

However one views it, the defence mechanisms of the mind act to prevent aspects of the individual (which one might call the psyche, self, or ego depending on one's choice of term) being overwhelmed by distress caused by internal conflicts.

Kernberg and projection

Let us for a moment review, for the sake of clarity, Kernberg's use of the term projection. For him it describes:

> a more mature type of defense mechanisms. Projection consists of (a) repression of an unacceptable intrapsychic experiences, (b) projection of that experience onto an object, (c) lack of empathy with what is projected, and (d) distancing or estrangement from the object as an effective completion of the defensive effort. ... Projection is seen typically in the defensive repertoire of patients with neurotic personality organisation.
>
> (Kernberg in Sandler 1988: 94)

As an example of the use of this defensive mechanism, Kernberg described a patient who fears that someone (perhaps her analyst) 'has become sexually interested in her, without any awareness of her own sexual impulses or a parallel communication of such impulses by non-verbal means' (Kernberg in Sandler 1988: 94).

This situation would not be overtly erotic, due to the lack of a behavioural or manipulative component on the part of the patient, who will have completely repressed, then projected and disassociated herself from these aspects of herself. This is of course very different from a defence by projective identification in which the analyst (or other person) would be prodded and manipulated into appropriate role-responsive behaviour when the interaction might be overtly erotic if the analyst does not become aware of and control his countertransference reactions.

GEORGE

Some individuals, such as Fr. Rolfe, are never able to develop an adequate level of psychological integration and remain on the borders of psychosis, for ever seeing the world as all 'good' or all 'bad'. Others of us regress to this state under stress, or in the psychotherapeutic process.

It is possible to observe in George's behaviour the more mature defence mechanisms described by Anna Freud. He repressed his self-representation 'I hate my mother' as this was in conflict with the self-representation 'I love and need my mother'. As a child, he was very distressed at the thought of upsetting his mother, whom he both loved and needed, and very concerned about the potential damage he feared his rage could do to his mother, a terror greatly increased by the omnipotence of childhood. How could he be angry with this woman who had dedicated her life to her son, even if she had failed to provide him, her only darling son, with a father in the home?

In his family there was the myth that it was his father who was 'no good' and 'angry'. In accepting this belief he had to lose his awareness of the agony of his ambivalence. These emotional conflicts (which emerged again in the psychodrama) caused him pain and distress. The troublesome inner-object, 'the hurt angry child' with its associated role 'Georgie loves and needs his father', was pushed aside in his inner world. His conscious self was unable to gain access to or use this aspect of himself.

His level of emotional development and the intensity of the situation in the family did not allow him to create a spontaneous and more integrated solution. He need to protect himself against the intense anxiety of his ambivalence. This he did through the use of psychological defence mechanisms. He had to 'lose' one aspect of the conflict.

He sublimated his anger, guilt, and confusion through his devotion to his work, and he displaced his needy 'child' onto his clients. The intensity of his feelings was inhibited and his concerns for the 'mother' he had 'damaged' were also displaced onto his needy social work clients.

He had, on the whole, developed productive (and pretty normal) neurotic defences, most of which tended to make him a hard-working and respected social worker. Adult George did not *feel* himself to be a person who needed a father figure. But he became very angry when he felt let down or deserted by his bosses. This behaviour confused him. He really did not need Fred's supervision. He knew that he was a man capable of working independently. He felt himself to be caring and loving, if at times rather put upon; he was after all a good and hard-working social worker much appreciated by most of his clients.

But, just as Guntrip described, the inner self-object emerged from time to time to confront and distress him.

George in the psychodrama

In the psychodrama the initial focus of his difficulties related to the situation at work. These problems were after all why he had come into psychotherapy. However, as the session progressed from the present to scenes from his childhood, the possible origins of his difficulties became clearer. This psychodramatic exploration followed the form described by Goldman and Morrison (1984).

He began to get in touch with both his father's point of view and his own anger towards his mother. As 'father' George found himself saying things that he had not previously remembered. His father too had his side to the story. For years George had accepted his mother's account of family life. He suddenly became aware that he had loved and needed his father. Playing himself as a child, he recalled the terror and fury he experienced listening to his parents fight in the room below his bed.

In the session he had difficulties relating to his 'mother'. Ambivalence and anxiety began to overwhelm him as he got in touch with his anger (about his absent father) directed towards his mother. He became increasingly tense and the psychodrama slowed down as he lost some of his spontaneity.

As a child George must have experienced the same psychological conflicts and distress. He began to use his neurotic defences to cope with the almost intolerable. He repressed his conflicting 'object relationships' which included his angry self-image. Following the principle of the association of like inner-objects, other object relationships in which George was angry would be repressed as well. George thus lost access to an important inner role, the assertive angry boy/man. His role repertoire was diminished.

In the session these roles began to re-emerge. Only time would tell if he would be able to use his new-found assertive self in the real world outside the psychodrama theatre.

9 Conflicts and anxiety
Holding and containment

The group

While George was talking to the two aspects of his mother Paul had moved to the back of the room, allowing him to get a clear view of the session.

'I love you mum. You'll never leave me will you?'

'No, of course not Georgie. . . . I love you too.'

The protagonist was deeply involved in a cathartic confrontation with his mother which was now possible because the 'mother' he hated was now split off, on a separate chair, from the mother he loved. For the first time for many years, his ambivalence was avoided through the use of a technique of psychodrama. The group had been absorbed and involved as they watched the session. Paul felt pleased and began to think about what might happen next in the psychodrama.

He then noticed that the group had become rather restless. Peter was leaning towards Thelma and Paul realised that they were talking together. Maggie, it appeared, was asleep. George had stopped talking to his 'good mother' and was once more looking tense and anxious.

The session was now not going well. The group members had become rather distracted and anxious. George, too, was once more losing his spontaneity. Paul moved back into the stage area and spoke to George.

'What's happening? How should we finish this scene with your mother?'

George looked worried.

'I don't know what to do. I feel very stuck.'

Paul was aware that he felt uncertain about what to do next. The scene with George's mother had to be completed. And there was then the issue of George and his father. The psychodrama session had started with George and his problems with father figures/superiors at work. The group seemed ill at ease. Perhaps this related to the increasing anxiety and uncertainty in the protagonist. And to make matters worse, the director was also feeling a bit uncertain about what to do next. Paul turned to the group.

'Any suggestions about how to proceed?'

Debby spoke up from the back of the room:

'You know, if George could express his feelings of anger and frustration towards his boss like he has just done to his mother, life might be easier for him at work.'

Debby clearly had ideas about the directions in which the session might go. David added: 'I think George must finish the scene with his mother.'

The group knew, from previous sessions, that David also had a very powerful mother in his life.

'OK George, how should we finish the scene with your mother?'

Paul was now standing close to his protagonist, with a hand resting lightly on his shoulder. Paul was clear about how to proceed, but no progress was possible while George was so tense and anxious. Paul's proximity and the active involvement of the group appeared to give George courage. David indicated that he would like to double George, Paul agreed. David (standing close to George as his double) said: 'I think that I want to talk to both my parents together! They were always so separate when I was a child.'

'Yes, that's what I'd like to do.'

Paul was relieved and continued: 'Great. Where do you wish this meeting to occur? Remember that this is psychodrama and anything is possible.'

George looked thoughtful then delighted.

'I know, I'll talk to them in the staff room at work. Neither of them ever thought I should be a social worker, "not a man's job" said my father. My mother wanted me to be a doctor like her father. They would never come to see me at my office!'

'So, you mean we're going to return to the room we started in. Set it up again.'

The room was re-created. George clearly had ideas of how he wished the scene to progress, and was directing the auxiliary egos.

'I want mother and father to sit together on the tatty sofa. That's right, side by side. Good, I'll sit over here in Fred's chair. The one he uses when he does come in! Well, nice of you to come and see me mum and dad. . . .'

George was losing steam as he became anxious again. Paul moved closer to him.

'Go on. What do you want to say?'

'Well. . . .'

'Would it be easier if you were higher than them? Stand on this high stool. Take this.'

(He handed George a long stiff cushion.)

'Now tell them!'

David and Victor indicated that they would like to help George as doubles or supporters.

'Thank you. Come and stand by George so that he feels safer on his stool.'

George still looked very worried.

'Tell them three things that angered you. Just three things.'

'You should have stayed together. I needed two parents at home.'

'Yes, a second thing.'

'When I was a child you both blamed me for your problems. Yes I know you got married because you were pregnant. You didn't want to be a single parent. But I didn't asked to be conceived!'

'Three.'

Turning to his 'father', he added:

'Why did you never come to see me when you promised? I know I was close to mother and that she hated you, but I was still your son. I needed you. . . .'

George was now in full flight. David and Victor withdrew a few paces from the stool so that George was able to experience the full force of his own feelings and expressions. George, for once, felt powerful.

Continued on page 151.

GEORGE'S FEAR OF HIS RAGE

George had been able in the psychodrama to express his rage with his mother, a feeling previously repressed as he needed, as a child, to maintain a good relationship with her, especially after his father left home. He was also able to tell his 'mother' in the session how much he needed her. Through the use of the two auxiliary 'mothers' he was able to get in touch with his long-lost experience of ambivalence towards her. Thus he brought back into his active role repertoire the 'little boy who hates his mother'.

This role was associated with the role cluster 'George and women'. It is probable that in his marriage aspects of this angry object relationship were externalised and enacted, without conscious motivation, with his wife. Now the role was once more conscious it might be expected that George would be able to better understand and control his behaviour at home.

At this point in the session George became anxious again and felt stuck. He had lost his spontaneity and creativity. Through the techniques of psychodrama, and with the support of his director whose presence helped contain George's anxiety, George became aware of his need to confront *both* his parents with his confusion and fury about the conflicts that existed in his childhood family.

ANXIETY

Anxiety is a powerful and unpleasant sensation which has been experienced by each of us at some time or other. Emotions, be they pleasant or nasty, have a function. Freud pointed out, for example, that the universal feeling of anxiety acts as a signal to warn the individual of approaching danger, be this real and external (realistic anxiety) or internal and within the psyche, in which case the anxiety might be described as either psychotic or neurotic depending on the individual's degree of disturbance.

In addition to the feelings, both types of anxiety are associated with physiological changes. The pulse rate increases, the pupils of the eyes dilate, and the mouth becomes dry.

Realistic anxiety strikes us as something very rational and intelligible as it is the reaction to the perception of an external danger. It may be regarded as a manifestation of the self-preservation instinct (Freud 1916–17: 441).

Indeed the body is preparing for either 'flight or fight'. The physiological changes prepare the body for action, while the associated psychological changes are indicators to the individual that something is afoot and that a decision must be made. Freud wrote that there 'is a preparedness for the danger, which manifests itself in increased sensory attention and motor tension' (Freud 1916–17: 442).

However, the anxiety, which is initially both the signal to the self of forthcoming risk and the precursor of a communication to others, can become overwhelming. Then one neither fights the problem nor runs away, but stands frozen to the spot. Anxiety has become both self-destructive and counter-productive, unless, as a result of the, perhaps non-verbal, communication, someone comes to your rescue.

In psychotic or neurotic anxiety states the body and the mind respond as if there is an external threat, but the horizon is clear of risks, challenges, or desertions. There are dangers, but they are internal, existing within the psyche, resulting from tensions in the complex internal world of object relationships.

Psychotic anxiety

As the integration of the self-object or representation and the internal representations of others progresses, the rage incorporated in the object relationship associated with, for example, the 'mother who doesn't feed me' may be felt to be attacking the 'mother who cuddles me'. The intrapsychic assault on the good other-object results in guilt, and brings a risk to the positive or good self-image.

I have described how an early defence against this risk is to make separate once more the object relationships that are starting a tentative integration. A split occurs. The infant then has the possibility of two separate states of self-awareness: put simply, either that associated with positive affects and self-image or that associated with negative affects and self-image.

Associated with splitting, the infant defends its psychic calm by projecting outwards, into space or into (m)others, aspects of self which cannot be integrated. When an adult uses these mechanisms, which reduce the individual's contact with reality, the anxiety which is being defended against might be described as psychotic, and is associated with a fear of disintegration, loss of boundaries and indeed of the structural failure of the self.

The psychoanalyst W.R. Bion, describing the psychic mechanisms of adult psychotics (who in many ways may resemble infants), wrote:

> In the patient's phantasy the expelled particles of ego lead to an independent and uncontrolled existence outside the personality . . . either containing or contained by external objects.
>
> *Second Thoughts* (Bion 1967: 39)

In the psychotic's world these projected parts of the self exist (and indeed in Bion's view multiply) outside so that the individual feels surrounded, attacked, and persecuted by what become 'bizarre objects'. Such people are indeed mad and out of touch with reality. They find no receptive containers in space to hold and modify the terrors.

Most infants are, however, luckier. Their projections, forced outwards by anxiety, go towards those adults closest to them, usually their mother, who accepts, contains and holds these externalisations of their inner worlds. I will return to this point later.

Neurotic anxiety

In time the developmental forces for integration are such that the child begins to use the defence mechanisms associated with repression (a process that represses integrated object relationships). This is the start of Klein's 'depressive position'. Initially the tensions are still those created by a two-person or dyadic relationship; for example, mother and son. When anxiety is experienced by an adult using these mechanisms to control an inner psychic conflict it is described as neurotic.

George coped with his rage with his mother by the loss (through repression) of his 'I hate mother' self-image together with the associated other-image. How could he ever have hated or been angry with such a loving woman? How could he ever get angry with motherly women now in his adult life? Women needed him, as son, as social worker, as husband.

As his wife discovered, the repressed 'I hate women' object relationship was not destroyed, just buried. And at times this image crept to the surface with resulting neurotic anxiety, partly because of the threat within George's mind, but also because of his guilt when he was angry with his wife.

The object relationships of the little boy who really needed and loved his daddy, but also hated him for his desertion, were also repressed, only to emerge, like Banquo's ghost, in his relationships with boss–father figures. He lost his awareness of his need for his father, agreeing with his mother that this man was not worth caring about. The senior social worker, Fred, in his relationship with his demanding and difficult junior, had also experienced aspects of the externalisation of George's inner world.

However, in time George as a child began to develop concerns, tensions, and intense anxiety about his relationships with his parents as a *couple*. Psychoanalysts refer to such difficulties as being 'Oedipal' after Oedipus who killed his father and then married his mother. George's distress about triadic conflicts occurred both in childhood and again in the session.

As a child, some of George's anxiety related to an external threat: perhaps his parents would fight again and separate and he might lose, perhaps for ever, one or other of his primary love objects and caretakers. This sense of anxiety related to a real perception of danger.

Later in life, with his parents internalised as inner-objects, he experienced anxiety related to the conflicts between his internal parents, conflicts that also involved his own self-representation. The aspect of his parents that represented authority and external controls will have become, in his inner world, part of his super-ego. The cluster of object relationships involved in this intrapsychic structure would be in conflict with the aspects of George that wished to be naughty (to take a day off work) or angry (to shout at Fred): another internal conflict resulting in neurotic anxiety.

OF HOLDING, BEING HELD, AND THE NEED FOR COMMUNICATION

Perhaps one of the earliest experiences of a real threat (in the perceptions of the infant) is the mother's departure (if only to get a fresh bottle of milk). The resulting separation anxiety can leave the baby in a terrible emotional state which usually passes when the mother returns, to comfort and feed him.

John Bowlby, who wrote on these issues in his books *Attachment and Loss* Volumes 1–3 (Bowlby 1969, 1973, 1980), saw the infant as needing the attachment to others for both emotional and physical reasons: (m)others providing both support and protection. The feelings of anxiety roused by separation are important indicators to the child that its situation is not correct. For Bowlby, man's anxiety has its roots in his biological past.

> The heart of the theory ... which derives directly from ethology, is that each of the stimulus situations that man is genetically biased to respond to with fear has the same status as a red traffic light or an air-raid siren. Each is a signal of potential danger.
>
> (Bowlby 1973: 167–8)

The infant's responses to anxiety and perhaps the fear of total disintegration (after all it still has a limited and fragile sense of self) involve tears or screaming. This will have one highly desirable effect: mother comes rushing back. The baby has made a successful communication.

The mother may initially feel worried herself (taking in her infant's terrors). This process involves projective identification in which the infant places the distressed aspects of itself into another, its mother (Sandler 1987: 39). She may herself become distressed until she discovers that everything is all right. A 'good-enough' mother must have the ability to test reality and think rationally about the situation.

The infant is safe once more. Its anxiety is contained by the mother's psyche and its body is held by her arms. Its developing (but still vulnerable) sense of self is once more intact. The mother talks to her baby, calms it, and reassures it: 'There's nothing to fear now, I am back.' The infant's anxiety, projected into mother through the mechanisms of its screams is now, after being altered or metabolised in mother's psyche, fed (or projected) back to the child: that is, if the mother is not too disturbed herself, for if she has her own emotional problems she may not be able to contain her infant's distress. A good-enough mother knows that the infant is only scared and hungry, nothing serious is amiss, and she is open and available to her baby's projected needs (Grinberg *et al.* 1975 and 1985: 39).

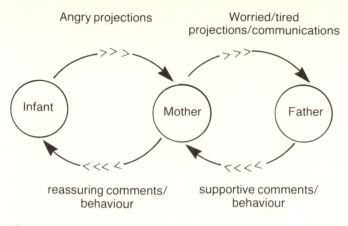

Angry projections   Worried/tired
                         projections/communications

Infant   Mother   Father

reassuring comments/   supportive comments/
behaviour   behaviour

Figure 9.1

This projective mechanism involves two real people, and thus does not occur in phantasy. It therefore corresponds to Sandler's stage three projective identification (Sandler 1988). The process is shown diagrammatically in Figure 9.1.

Following the work of W.R. Bion this process has been called 'containment', with its implication of the need for boundaries. The British psychotherapist Josephine Klein (1987) prefers the term 'emotional holding', as these words are more in tune with the language of mothers and infants. Perhaps 'containment' can sound too much like 'imprisonment'.

You will note that I've added the father to the scheme, because, in part, his role is to support and contain the mother's anxiety and needs, for she may become overwhelmed herself (by her infant's needs) or her *own* internal anxiety might be projected onto her child. In these circumstances she would be psychologically unavailable to calm her baby, and indeed may add to its distress.

Depressed mothers too are sometimes unable to hold or contain their infants psychologically as they cannot respond to their infant's needy projections.

Bion believed that this process of projection and containment (which is associated with both the infant's developing ability to tolerate frustration and the quality of the relationship with its mother) is a fundamental part of the growth of the infant's psyche (see Grinberg *et al.* 1975 and 1985 for a review of Bion's ideas). The infant learns from and starts to think about this interaction, a process which becomes a crucial step in the ordering and integration of the inner world.

The infant's inner world contains the memory traces of the relationship 'distressed baby–comforting mother'. In time the inner-object 'comforting mother' will be able to provide the child with comfort even when the real mother is absent. A child who lacks these positive internalisations will have to continue to seek comfort from the external world, perhaps as an adult in relationships or through the use of alcohol or drugs. Subsequently, through the process of introjective identification, the child will itself be able to provide comfort to its dolls, and eventually other people. The ability to be a 'comforter' will have become a role in the self-representation in the psyche and (unless repressed) in the role repertoire.

George, a well-liked social worker, clearly had internalised a good supportive and containing inner-object. This might be expected as his difficulties related to a later time in his childhood when his parents' rows and separation caused him much distress and anxiety. When he was an infant his mother was 'good enough' (Winnicott 1971 and 1974).

This process of containment or holding is not confined to infant and parents. Many adults continue to need help or holding when they become anxious. For example, a therapist or a social worker in a panic will go and talk to a supervisor or colleague. The behaviour or conversation may be (unconsciously) designed to spread or project the fears. 'My patient is threatening to commit suicide. I'm sure he'll do it.' Or 'I'm sure Mrs Smith will kill her baby.' A good supervisor will listen, may initially begin to share the panic but will then think, realise that not all is lost. He will then be able to feed back more positive thoughts and ideas. The professional's initial panic subsides, his anxiety has been contained and he feels held. Much of the process of individual psychotherapy also involves the emotional holding of patients by their therapists (see J. Klein 1987).

Anxiety and the group

The reappearance of an internal conflict, in the conscious part of George's mind, stirred up anxiety, and he felt distress in the psychodrama. The group became aware of this, the information being transferred and responded to, initially without thought. Communication involved the group's innate (and socially learnt) understanding of the emotional signals that George was emitting, for example, his tense face, his body language, and perhaps even the smell of his sweat.

Some individuals, including Paul, developed a conscious awareness. 'George is anxious. I wonder why?' Other members of the group responded by becoming uneasy or anxious themselves, perhaps without being aware that the changes in their emotions might be the result of George's state.

The mechanisms of the communication of emotions form part of the processes that have been called countertransference, tele, and empathy.

ANXIETY AND SPONTANEITY: FREUD AND MORENO

Anxiety, when it becomes a problem rather than an indicator of dangers that can be avoided, is not pleasant. It may act as part of the communication of an individual's need for others, but it also destroys creativity and spontaneity. We become stuck, frustrated, and dysfunctional. Defence mechanisms play an essential role in the control of the levels of anxiety in the psyche.

Freud saw the role of anxiety as central in the functioning of the psyche and it was one of his principal concerns in his theories. 'The topic of anxiety occurs in a very large number (perhaps in the majority) of Freud's writings' (editorial comment 1961: 89 to Freud 1926). The psychic processes concerned with anxiety were also an interest of Moreno's. However, he believed that it is a loss of spontaneity which results in an increase in anxiety. He wrote:

> Anxiety is a function of spontaneity. Spontaneity is ... the adequate response to a present situation. If the response to the present situation is adequate – 'fullness' of spontaneity – anxiety diminishes and disappears. With a decrease of spontaneity anxiety increases.
>
> (Moreno 1934 and 1953: 336)

He added, writing about an 'actor' (which could be taken to mean a protagonist or any individual in life):

> [Anxiety] may start with his striving to move out of an old situation without having the spontaneity available to do so; or, the anxiety may set in as soon as some 'external' force pushes him out of the situation and leaves him hanging in air. The terrifying thing for an actor is this wavering between a situation which he has just abandoned and to which he cannot return and a situation which he must attain in order to get back into balance and feel secure.
>
> (Moreno 1934 and 1953: 336)

There can be little doubt about the reciprocal relationship between anxiety and spontaneity. However, unlike Moreno, I see the presence of anxiety as being the cause of a loss of spontaneity. I would suggest that it is increasing anxiety, associated with the physiological changes needed for an adequate physical response to danger, which reduces spontaneity and the ability to find creative solutions.

Anxiety has its roots in man's biology. The state of anxiety is based on biochemical and physiological mechanisms which can be altered by medication (for example, anxiolytics such as diazepam or valium). I know of no pharmacological way in which spontaneity, or its associated force creativity, can be so affected. Although alcohol may initially apparently increase 'spontaneous' behaviour, this is probably due to the reduction of performance anxiety.

An individual may be able (to some extent) to hide his feelings of anxiety from the world. However, those around him might notice his sweaty palms and more fixed facial expression. They might also note a decrease in his spontaneity and creative powers. As the fears increase, the need to hold things in (for example, rage or anger) or to hold himself together (from fears of disintegration) may result in a more rigid and limited manner of relating to the world. The anxiety may also communicate the individual's needs to other people.

Spontaneity is the human facility to create new solutions to conflicts in which, if these are in the mind, different aspects may be integrated, thus reducing anxiety. When no creative resolution occurs the situation is resolved by ignoring or burying one part of the conflict (i.e. through repression) which then has the potential to reappear to haunt the individual.

George experienced anxiety in the session when a role, long suppressed, surfaced again. Initially he did not feel held or contained by Paul or by the group. He lost his spontaneity and creativity. He found it difficult to continue the session.

No doubt, when George was a small child, the same emotional conflicts (which emerged again in the psychodrama) caused him pain and distress. His level of emotional development and the intensity of the situation in the family did not allow him to create a spontaneous and more integrated solution.

His warring parents were unable to offer sufficient emotional safety for him to confront his fears and worries more openly. Since they could not help him, he needed to protect himself against the intense anxiety of his ambivalence. This he did through the use of psychological defence mechanisms. He had to 'lose' one aspect of the conflict. He was unable to find any other solution.

As the result of his use of defence mechanisms his conscious self was depleted and his freedom for actions reduced. The loss of roles through repression will have resulted in a reduction in George's spontaneity in life too; peace of mind may sometimes be found only at a cost. Too much spontaneity might have risked the repressed inner 'self-objects', with their associated roles, rising to the surface and causing anxiety. Without psychotherapy he would have to remain in the role of the 'good, caring' boy/man for ever.

BOUNDARIES OR CHAOS – CONTAINMENT OR HOLDING IN PSYCHOTHERAPY

In the session George was surrounded by people different from his parents. Perhaps they would be better able to help him with his increasing terror.

If anxiety is not to become overwhelming then the individual may need to be provided with 'holding' or 'containment' by those around him. This may be provided, as has been described above, by a mother, a father, a supervisor, or a psychotherapist, each providing the emotional holding through the two-person relationship.

Containment or holding can also be provided by physical spaces; we often feel less anxious in a room or house we know well. The rules of law of society or the family, external factors and constraints acting to contain the impulses and conflicts that relate to the feelings of anxiety, may also help.

Thus, to hold or contain someone's emotions, limits or boundaries are required. These can be created or provided in various ways both in life and in psychodrama. If a child is to grow emotionally and develop the capacity for thought it must be psychologically 'held' by an-other (often the mother).

If a protagonist is to explore his inner world, recover repressed object relationships, and attempt new solutions or integrations, he too must be 'held' in the session. It is one of the tasks of the techniques of psychodrama to hold or contain the mounting anxiety of the group, the protagonist, and at times the director.

George, in his session, is provided with such holding or containment by a variety of means. The one-to-one relationship with his director is important as are also the other members of the group, and the rules and techniques of psychodrama.

Boundaries, in psychodrama, as in life, may be conceptualised as existing in three categories:

1 Those that relate to the *emotional* aspects of interpersonal relationships (here I include 'containment' in Bion's sense and 'holding' as described by Josephine Klein).
2 Those related to *rules, permissions, policies*, and *techniques* of a specific therapeutic group, of the therapeutic method, or of society at large.
3 Finally there are boundaries that are dependent on the *physical* situation: the arms of a member of the group, the safety of the familiar walls of the psychodrama theatre, or the boundaries of the building or centre.

These categories are illustrated in Figure 9.2. Within each category a hierarchical arrangement of containers (with their boundaries) exists. These range from the most intimate situation closest to the protagonist to those more general and most distant (levels 1 to 5 in Table 9.1).

During the course of any psychodrama session different boundaries are containing protagonist's, director's, or group members' anxiety. The shifts in which boundary is the principal 'container' holding anxiety will depend on various factors; for example, the level of anxiety in the protagonist or the group or the level of skill and experience of the director. Indeed, some directors will opt to encourage the use of one 'container' (say the director's close one-to-one relationship with the protagonist) while others will depend more on the containing properties of the group or trust in the dramatic aspects of psychodrama. Directors, of course, cannot ever maintain control of all these factors or, indeed, always be aware of them during the running of a group.

BACK TO GEORGE AND THE PSYCHODRAMA

At this point in George's psychodrama he became more anxious as his internal psychic conflicts over his relationship with his mother (both internal and external) became more overt. The group too became anxious, demonstrating that George had communicated his feelings to them (perhaps through the mechanism of his projections). They lost concentration. Peter and Thelma engaged in a one-to-one conversation, perhaps unconsciously seeking to reduce each other's anxiety. Maggie was avoiding the tension by having a brief sleep.

Table 9.1 The hierarchy of boundaries or containment

| | | | Level of boundary | | |
| | *Intrapsychic*
1 | *2* | *to*
3 | *4* | *society*
5 |
		one-to-one	*one to group*	*group to group*	*person to society*
Emotional	Protagonist's own psychic defence mechanisms, e.g. splitting or repression.	Protagonist's therapeutic relationship with the director. The director's relationship with the co-therapist.	Protagonist's relationships with other members of the group. Co-therapist's relationship with supervisor.	Protagonist's involvement with his own family and friends. Membership of other groups. Own individual therapy.	Place in society. Respect at work. Involvement in the community.
Rules and permissions	Protagonist's 'super-ego 'processes	Rules' and techniques of psychodrama, e.g. the use of a double or role-reversal.	Rules, policies, and temporo-spatial arrangements specific to this group, e.g. coffee at start of group. Visit to pub after the group.	The position of the therapist and the group in the therapeutic community. General rules of therapeutic practice.	(Especially for adolescents) supervision and external controls. Family expectations.
Physical	Protagonist's defensive use of action, e.g. some tics or hair twisting.	Varying the physical distance between the director and the protagonist. Other members of the group moving closer to the protagonist.	Protagonist's use of the room. Use of a favourite chair. Trips to the lavatory.	Consistency of the group room. The use of its doors and windows as a boundary of the psychodramatic space.	The boundaries of the clinic or psychodrama centre. The front door, the garden gate.

Paul used various techniques to contain the rising anxiety. Initially he moved closer to George, providing him with an increased *emotional* and *physical* containment. He also supported the group in their desire to contain anxiety by allowing them to make helpful suggestions. In doing this they were able to feel less lost and helpless and were also able to demonstrate concretely to George their continuing support of him and his psychodrama.

Paul also increased 'containment' by trusting in the intrinsic quality of the method of psychodrama; he asked the group for help. The group's assistance and support acted to reduce Paul's anxiety and he was thus better able to help George. This process resembled the way in which a father might help an anxious mother with their infant. Paul was trusting in one of the *rules* or *permissions* of psychodrama; the director should never be afraid to ask the group for help.

Later he further helped George by the use of the two doubles. Men who were able to offer support, both *physically* while George stood on the stool, but (perhaps more importantly) *emotionally* through the symbolism of this action and their physical proximity.

When George's anxiety once more began to rise, Paul structured his statements to his 'parents' in the psychodrama. 'Say three things to them.' This instruction, stated firmly, acted to contain and limit the myriad of things George could have said. A richness of accusations and complaints that began to overwhelm the protagonist, resulting in an increase in anxiety. George could manage three clear statements. His anxiety level did not rise too high.

The same technique can be used when assisting a protagonist to describe someone important in his life needed in the psychodrama. 'Say three things about your mother to help Maggie play her.'

With a very anxious protagonist it is sometimes useful for the director to lay a hand on the protagonist's shoulder and to hold up three fingers, adding a *physical* and *visual* component to the containment. 'One.... Two.... Three.... good!'

These are other examples where the *rules* (or *techniques*) of psychodrama can be used to contain anxiety by the provision of structures.

Thus, in this short section of the session, anxiety (of the protagonist, the director, and the group) was reduced by techniques from each of the three categories: emotional, rules and permissions, and physical methods.

An analysis of containment or holding in the session

The holding or containment of anxiety in the group is important from the beginning to the end of a psychodrama. Should the level of anxiety rise too high the smooth process of the session may be interrupted. Of course, if the level of anxiety is too low, members of the group may not feel the motivation to undertake any therapeutic work.

It might be useful to consider briefly what I think was happening in the various phases of George's psychodrama. The reader may, of course, differ from my assessment of the nature of the containment or holding at different points in the session.

Group members often arrived at sessions tired, preoccupied with issues from work, and rather anxious about the evening ahead. Starting with coffee in the staff room provided a degree of the 'known' as did the informal discussions between group members (although interpersonal difficulties might also arise, as they did on the evening described in this book).

The emotional holding or containment was offered by 'rules and permissions': the ritual of coffee (*rules*, level 3); 'emotional' means: the talking (*emotional*, level 3); and 'physical': the security offered by the known space of the staff room with its walls and door (*physical*, level 4).

The group room (or 'theatre') with its large colourful cushions (comfortable to sit on or even hide under) provided a sense of the familiar. It was a space the group had grown to trust. Good (if at times painful) things could and did happen in it. Containment involved the contents of the room (*physical*, level 3).

Warm-ups are used for various reasons. These include: the learning of group members' names, the increasing of group cohesion, the raising of spontaneity and creativity, and a method to help people focus on issues on which they might like to work in the session. A good warm-up must contain and reduce anxiety, for no one is going to think about a problem, let alone risk being a protagonist, if anxiety rises too high. So the structures and routines of the warm-up must provide a sense of safety.

In the session described, Paul used a game about toys and a guided fantasy. Both these warm-ups involve the use of symbolism. Freud pointed out that part of what he called 'dream work' was the reduction of anxiety and psychic censorship by the psyche's use of symbols to tell the story (Rycroft 1968). In psychodrama the use of symbols has the same effect, allowing conflicts to emerge slowly from the depths of repression. In this session the element of playing a game, 'be a toy', assisted George who could begin to think about his father only through the *emotional* containment (intrapsychic therefore level 1) in the warm-up.

However, as in most warm-ups that utilise an element of fantasy, the process is containing through the group's relationship with the director, both individually (*emotional*, level 2) and as a group (*emotional*, level 3).

George found the warm-up difficult at first, he was anxious and tense, but the containment offered slowly allowed him to participate. Perhaps without much thought, he chose a toy soldier from his childhood. It was only later that he realised that this little figure was associated with much pain and frustration: conflicts that he'd been allowed to approach through the holding aspects of the warm-up game. However, his anxiety still remained too high. He was becoming aware of the significance of his toy but still could not allow himself to become the protagonist.

Paul, having no protagonist, decided to use a guided fantasy. His rising anxiety was contained by his experience and belief in the methods of psychodrama (*rules*, level 1) as this was initially an internal decision. When the whole group began to feel more secure following the suggestion of a guided fantasy, containment involved *rules*, level 3.

Everyone felt a degree of relief as the session continued. A guided fantasy offers an apparently rather rigid boundary (as with the description of early stages of the journey). Within these safe boundaries the individual is freed to be creative (for example, through the choice of objects). These choices have a similarity to the free association process of psychoanalysis. Containment is at both the private and personal level (*emotional*, level 1) and is also related to the group members' relationship with the director who leads the fantasy (*emotional*, level 2).

George now felt able to become the protagonist. He felt held by the group who supported his becoming the focus of the session (*emotional*, level 3).

Slowly his anxiety began to rise again. It was held by Paul's relationship with him (*emotional* and *physical*, level 2). An anxious protagonist can be held by the initial dialogue between him and his director. The closeness and intimacy can reassure. However, should this continue for too long and psychodramatic action be avoided, anxiety may rise again. A trust in the very methods of psychodrama can offer an individual and a group comfort. George's anxiety was reduced by Paul's insistence that they moved to *action* (*rules*, levels 2 and 3).

Throughout the session Paul used his relationship with George to hold and contain his rising panic as buried conflicts surfaced. At times he was close, both physically (sometimes touching George gently on the arm or back) and emotionally (again *emotional* and *physical*, level 2). At other times he moved away, allowing George to discover his own strengths and skills (*emotional*, level 1).

George was also held by the correct use of the techniques of psychodrama. When Paul needed to know more about George's boss, Peter, he used role-reversal to help George describe him without falling, once more, into his habitual role with this man.

Paul knew that the scene with George's father was going to be difficult. He used his relationship with George and the rules of psychodrama to be firm. 'Show us this coffee shop. Set it up for us.' And then, as anxiety rises, 'Stand in the doorway of this coffee shop. What is its name?' Clear, firm directions and questions (*rules*, level 2). George is able to continue the scene.

Later, when Paul begins to anger George, he again uses his relationship with his protagonist to lower anxiety and allow the psychodrama to continue. He also uses his professional rule: think about your own feelings, try to understand your countertransference (*rules*, level 1).

The psychodrama group was held, with the permission of his colleagues, in Paul's clinic. Although not directly involved in the group, the social worker Tom knew about it and approved. Paul's knowledge of this support provided both him and other group members with further boundaries and containment at level 4 (*emotional*, Tom's support; *rules*, Paul's colleagues' permission to use the room).

The psychodrama group was provided with further containment by the knowledge that group members' families and friends supported the therapeutic work of the sessions. Such containment occurs at level 5.

THE MAGIC OF PSYCHODRAMA

Anxiety in a psychodrama session can be the result of many influences and forces; for example, each individual's own internal conflicts, the possibility of conflicts arising (in the here-and-now) between members of the group, the group's awareness that the director has 'lost his way' or his control over his use of the techniques of psychodrama.

These factors, and of course many more, can produce unproductive anxiety with the associated loss of spontaneity in the protagonist, the director, and the group. It is the director's task to sense these changes and to be aware of at least some of the ways the situation can be held or contained.

Psychodrama, like other forms of psychotherapy, can provide the magic that allows for emotions to be held. A containment that many people (especially those who seek therapy) may not have experienced adequately in childhood.

It must not be forgotten that without the awareness of anxiety we might never know that the approaching lion was a threat. A protagonist without some anxiety may very well not challenge those issues that require psychodramatic work. A director without a degree of anxiety will become complacent, his psychodrama session boring and routine.

The skill in psychodrama, as in life, is to get the balance right. Never an easy trick.

10 Playing and reality

The group

George found much energy in his confrontation with his 'parents'.

'Would you like your parents to react differently?'

'Yes, they always criticise and blame me. They don't approve of my work and they have rarely supported me in my marriage.'

'Who could tell them about the good work you do?'

'Well, some of my clients. Not all of them of course. Some are never satisfied! They'd never say nice things about my work!'

'OK. But some would. Describe one or two clients who would be positive about you.'

'Well, there's Mrs A. with three small children under five. I helped her get nursery school places and she talks to me about her worries.'

Paul indicated with his hand that Maggie should play Mrs A.

'Then there's Joe. His wife left him with the kids. I see him every week for an hour in this office. He's got a job so money isn't his biggest problem, but he gets very tense and depressed at times. He finds it difficult to feel angry with his wife. She just went off with another man!'

Paul asked Peter to play Joe.

'So Mrs A., Joe, and some of your other clients think you're a good social worker. Here they come into this office to talk to your parents.'

'They would never do that!'

'This is psychodrama, George. Let it happen.'

George's 'clients' came into the room and began to tell his 'parents' about their really positive feelings for their social worker, how much he has helped them and how much they respect and like him. George's 'parents' listened, then began to ask a few questions. They expressed surprise and real pleasure in hearing so many good things about their son.

Paul indicated that more group members could, if they wished, come into the office as 'clients' and talk to George's 'parents'. Soon the stage was full, people clustered around George and said really positive things about him. Paul realised that some were in role as clients, others were being themselves, as group members; all were expressing positive things. George looked very pleased, his 'parents' were for the first time listening and responding in the way he wished them to. He felt good, more assured and confident.

'Let's finish this scene. You've got to talk to Fred now, and perhaps your wife!'

Paul was feeling that George must pull together some of the strands of his psychodrama. ·

'Who should we start with?'

'I'd like to start with Fred. Maria is much more important to me. I'd like to finish the session tonight with a scene with her.'

'So, the clients and your parents leave the room, and in comes Fred.'

Victor came back onto the stage area as 'Fred'. George started: 'Fred, I've really had enough of you. I know that you're a good social worker and try hard to keep this unit afloat, but you don't give me enough support.'

'Reverse!'

'But George, you're a very experienced social worker. I can't hold your hand all the time!'

'Reverse!'

'I don't want my hand holding! I just want some normal support and supervision, after all that's what you get from head office!'

'OK George, should we make a regular weekly slot again? Then you can tell me about your case load.'

'Thanks Fred, that would be great. And what about lunch in the pub one day?'

Fred agreed. It was clear that George's forceful but not hysterical demands had been heard. George had found, at least in the psychodrama, a way and a language to talk to his boss. The scene ended.

'You said you wished to talk to Maria? Where?'

'In the kitchen at home. I want to tell her about my new relationship with Fred.'

And, thought Paul, perhaps she will tell you a thing or two about your relationship with her.

'Who could be Maria?'

'Thelma.'

'OK Thelma?'

'Yes.'

'Set up your kitchen. . . . Start talking.'

Paul was aware that the evening was passing and that he must allow time for the group sharing, the crucial last phase of a psychodrama.

'Well, Maria, I don't feel that you always listen to me.'

(He's trying the same line that worked with Fred, thought Paul.)

'Reverse!'

'What a nerve George! I try very hard to listen to you, but you're in so late, and when you're really in a state about work you just retreat into yourself. Just like your father. Moody and absent!'

As 'Maria' George really knew his own faults, and in role-reversal was able to voice them loudly and clearly. He really could be, at times, very like his father.

'I don't know about you George, sometimes I feel I'm living with an over-grown toddler. One minute you're all charm and cuddles, the next moment you're having a tantrum, just as if you had broken a new toy. You really can be very childish.'

The group laughs, they like George's own account of himself from the role of

Maria. The scene continued; George played both himself, and sometimes, in role-reversal, his wife. Thelma (as 'Maria') was able to help George externalise and discover more about his marriage. George looked thoughtful but relaxed.

'Let's finish this scene. You can continue it at home!'

Continued on page 164.

THE PSYCHOLOGICAL TERRITORY OF PSYCHODRAMA

George looked really pleased when his 'clients' told his 'parents' in his 'office' what a good and well-respected social worker he was. For George the scene was *real*. His emotional response was powerful and positive. He felt as if he was at work, experiencing what he wished would happen but never had.

This is the magic of psychodrama. The drama has moved into the realm of surplus reality.

> It can well be said that the psychodrama provides the subject with a new and more extensive experience of reality, a 'surplus' reality, a gain which in part justifies the sacrifice he has made by working through a psycho-dramatic production.
>
> (Moreno 1946 in Fox 1987: 16)

The stage can become anywhere we choose, peopled with those important to us from our past, our present, and indeed our future. A bare room, a few cushions, and group members we may have known for months can be converted into other worlds and other people for the duration of the session.

This transformation is one that those who have only read about psychodrama sometimes find hard to accept. 'You mean someone my age might actually feel like my 70- year-old mother?' Yes indeed. And in another psychodrama the same young woman might be someone else's ageing father or young child. The auxiliary egos playing 'roles' in the drama *become*, for the protagonist (for the duration of the session), these other people.

How might we explain these strange and powerful experiences? Do protagonists become briefly psychotic, losing contact with the shared reality in the group room?

No, for their experiences are illusory. It is a form of 'therapeutic madness' (Klauber in Klauber *et al.* 1987). They remain aware of the 'as if' aspects of the session while at the same time entering (in an emotional sense) into the 'reality' of the drama.

PLAYING AND REALITY

I believe that the writings of the British paediatrician and psychoanalyst D.W. Winnicott offer much to help us in our attempts to understand this magical process. Indeed I've taken the heading for this chapter and this section from the title of his small but powerful book. My copy is worn and tattered, rather like a favourite teddy bear. His writings have powerfully influenced my theoretical understandings of human psychology and interactions and added much to my awareness of the processes of psychotherapy. In this chapter, however, I can touch upon only those aspects of Winnicott's theories that seem to me to be most pertinent to my themes in this book.

So far we've talked about two closely linked worlds: that of personal psychic reality, the 'inner world' of object relationships, and the corresponding 'outside world' shared by others in which real relationships exist. Winnicott proposed that there is a third psychological world. He wrote:

> Of every individual who has reached the stage of being a unit with a limiting membrane and an *outside* and an *inside*, it can be said that there is an inner reality to that individual, an inner world that can be rich or poor and can be at peace or in a state of war. This helps, but is it enough?
>
>   My claim is that if there is a need for this double statement, there is also need for a triple one: the third part of the life of a human being, a part that we cannot ignore, is an *intermediate* area of experiencing, to which inner reality and external life both contribute. It is an area that is not challenged, because no claim is made on its behalf except that it shall exist as a resting-place for the individual engaged in the perpetual human task of keeping inner and outer reality separate yet interrelated.
>
>   *Playing and Reality* (Winnicott 1971 and 1974: 3; my italics)

In Winnicott's view, this third area (which he called a 'potential or transitional space') is the realm of play and, in my opinion, it is also the realm of illusions. In his paper on 'Transitional objects and transitional pheno-mena', his primary concern is an infant's early relationships with the world, which, as I hope this book has demonstrated, continue to influence the adult's life.

> I am here staking a claim for an intermediate state between a baby's inability and his growing ability to recognize and accept reality. I am therefore studying the substance of illusion, that which is allowed to the infant, and which in adult life is inherent in art and religion,

– and I would add 'and in the processes of psychodrama' –

> and yet becomes the hallmark of madness when an adult puts too powerful claim on the credulity of others, forcing them to acknowledge a sharing of illusion that is not their own.
>
>   (Winnicott 1971 and 1974: 3)

The psychoanalyst Joyce McDougall, also talking about psychosis, wrote:

> Fortunately, in coming to grips with life's Impossibles, most of us have at our disposal other theaters than that of delusion. There is another stage, on which many impossible and forbidden wishes may find substitute expressions. This stage, lying between the limitless inner universe and the restricting world of reality, coincides with what Winnicott ... called

'transitional space'. This potential 'space', according to Winnicott, is the intermediate area of experiencing that lies between fantasy and reality. It includes, among many other phenomena, the place of cultural experience and the area of creativity.

Theatres of the Mind (McDougall 1986: 10)

I believe that it is in this third area, this potential space of transitional phenomena: of play, creativity, phantasy, imagination, and illusions, that the magic of certain aspects of psychodrama is enacted. But not all, for it must be emphasised that members of a psychodrama group also have very real here-and-now interactions.

McDougall described how some adults in everyday life, unconsciously, enrol people into external enactments of their internal dramas.

[T]he wish behind such complicated dramas . . . is to try to make sense of what the small child of the past, who is still writing the scripts, found too confusing to understand. Constructions that use others to play important parts of oneself of one's inner world are neither psychotic nor neurotic creations, but they borrow techniques and ways of thought that belong to both. The social stage on which such psychic productions are presented and the nature of the tie to the characters who are maneuvered into playing roles in them characterize what I call the Transitional Theater.

(McDougall 1986: 65)

George's 'parents' and 'clients' are in his 'potential space'. To him they seem very real. Although they are not hallucinations, they are his creations. He retains his sanity and his awareness that it is only 'as if' his parents were on the psychodrama stage with him, a stage which is a special part of the transitional theatre of life.

We have thus seen George act out his drama with his father on three different stages in the three different theatres.

The theatre of the original drama

The café 'Tea for Two'. It must of course be stressed that this meeting with his father, re-enacted in the psychodrama session, was but one of many frustrating and traumatic interactions with his father (see 'The concept of cumulative trauma', Khan 1963).

The transitional theatre

The social work office. Here George unconsciously enrolled Fred to assist him with his re-enactment of his childhood drama with his father. And, as Fred was role responsive, the drama continued.

The psychodrama theatre

The stage. In the session George's tendency to re-enact his childhood dramas with father figures is therapeutically clarified with Victor as the auxiliary ego.

The psychodrama stage, like the transitional theatre of everyday life described by McDougall, involves a bending of reality or an illusion. As she suggested, these dramas occur in a space that is neither psychotic nor fully real. The technique allows the protagonist, who might normally keep much of his psychic conflict secret, to externalise his internal world in a clear and dramatic manner. It is a theatre in which projective identification is used, as in infancy, as a means of positive and therapeutic communication.

Transitional objects

We must now consider what Winnicott thought might occur in this 'potential space': processes that might involve the infant on its own or the relationship between an infant and its mother. We must discover what he meant when he referred to the 'transitional objects' of a child, for perhaps these relate (in some way) with the auxiliary egos of psychodrama.

For Winnicott, a 'transitional object' is the first 'not-quite-me' possession an infant chooses for itself from the array of colourful toys and objects that fill its small world. These very important objects are recognised, well-known, and respected by 'good-enough' parents who know with what intense significance their babies endow their special blanket or teddy bear.

When I was a small child, my mother tells me, I clung to a wooden spoon (which cannot have been a very comfortable object, but perhaps explains my tendency to stir in adult life). The small child Linus, in the Peanuts cartoon strip, has a more usual object. He becomes distraught when he loses his blanket, as do other infants when their favourite sheet or soft toy disappears.

The infant's relationship with this object lies between that which it has with its thumb (which is clearly part of its own body) and those true external object relationships which it develops with the world around it. The transitional object exists in the realm of illusion, and becomes its substitute for its mother when she is absent.

However, this object is not, for the infant, a symbol. It is endowed with all the attributes of the breast. It is experienced as real, existing in the outside world. Winnicott said:

> The infant assumes rights over the object. . . . [it is] affectionately cuddled as well as excitedly loved and mutilated.
>
> It must never change, unless changed by the infant. It must survive instinctual loving, and also hating. . . .
>
> Yet it must seem to the infant to give warmth, or to move, or to have texture, or to do something that seems to show it has vitality or reality of its own.
>
> It comes from without from our point of view, but not so from the point

of view of the baby. Neither does it come from within; it is not a hallucination.

(Winnicott 1971 and 1974: 6)

It is the baby's comforter, its friend in times of need, its mother's breast in times of unmet hunger, its first playmate, being both its own creation *and* a separate object, for:

> It is true that the piece of blanket (or whatever it is) is symbolical of some part-object, such as the breast. Nevertheless, the point of it is not its symbolic value so much as its *actuality.* . . .
>
> When symbolism is employed the infant is already clearly distinguishing between fantasy and fact, between inner objects and external objects, between primary creativity and perception.

(Winnicott 1971 and 1974: 7; my italics)

The transitional object exists at a point in time on 'the infant's journey from the purely subjective to objectivity', for it is not an internal psychic object, it is, after all, a concrete external possession. However, nor is it (for the infant) an external object either. It exists in the magical world of the transitional space.

In Winnicott's view, it is an externalisation of an 'alive and real and good-enough' internal object. The transitional object may represent the real external object (say mother and her breast) but only indirectly, through standing for the 'internal' breast. That is, the transitional object derives its psychic significance because it is endowed with the characteristics of an internal good (and comforting) object from which the child needs to obtain support in the absence of the real external object (mother).

Parents acknowledge the crucial importance of these transitional objects to their children. It is their child's first possession, their first creation. Should the object get lost, the infant's omnipotence is challenged, resulting in great distress. The child alone can release the transitional object from its dramatic role. The mother adapts to her infant's needs, thus allowing the infant the illusion that what it has created really exists, for:

> Of the transitional object it can be said that it is a matter of agreement between us and the baby that we will never ask the question: 'Did you conceive of this or was it presented to you from without?' The important point is that no decision on this point is expected. The question is not to be formulated.

(Winnicott 1971 and 1974: 14)

Back to adults and to George

Winnicott suggested that transitional objects are, originally, created by the infant for comfort and support in the absence of the mother. In adult life we may still, at times, use the same psychic processes, creating objects that are endowed with great psychological significance by the individual. At times my garden in London seems to have replaced the wooden spoon of my childhood, at other times it is just a place to sit in, on a sunny afternoon.

McDougall (1986) said that adults use the 'transitional theatre' in attempts to reduce psychic distress when they 'adopt' real external people and treat them (or use them) as if they were their own psychic creations. George 'used' Fred in his attempts to disown his unreliable and angry self. This process involves projective identification and the others in the drama must, unlike a teddy bear, be role responsive in an active way.

For George, in his psychodrama session, his 'parents' and his 'clients' feel rather like his creations. Through the method of role-reversal he has brought them alive on the stage, and the auxiliary egos, through their subtle under-standing (involving tele and countertransference), complement George's creation. Like a mother they allow George the illusion that they are *his* creations, his parents and clients, indeed his externalised inner-objects.

Let me adapt Winnicott's description of transitional objects to psychodrama.

The auxiliary ego in a session is 'used' and 'played with' in a way that is similar to that with which a child uses his teddy bear or blanket.

The protagonist assumes [some] rights over the auxiliary egos, who must allow themselves to be cuddled, loved and at times attacked or symbolically mutilated [how many auxiliary egos have been passionately hugged or 'attacked' with cushions in sessions?] but must survive both the loving and the attacking. They must maintain contact with the protagonist's view of their roles, and must shift their 'performance' to meet the protagonist's perceptions of the role. If they don't do this the 'magic' of the session may vanish and here-and-now reality intrude.

(adapted from Winnicott 1971 and 1974: 5–6)

From the group's view point the auxiliary egos' roles come from 'without', but for the protagonist they come from 'within' himself. They are his creations.

The child at play

Winnicott had more to say about transitional objects and phenomena in childhood, but we must move on to consider his applications of these theories to play. He wrote that he made his idea of play concrete:

by claiming that *playing has a place* and a time. It is not *inside*. . . . Nor is it *outside*, that is to say, it is not part of the repudiated world, the not-me, that which the individual has decided to recognize (with whatever difficulty and even pain) as truly external, which is outside magical control. To control what is outside one has to *do* things, not simply to think or to wish, and *doing things takes time*. Playing is doing.

(Winnicott 1971 and 1974: 47)

Many analytic psychotherapists (including Winnicott and myself) believe that play occurs in the relatively actionless verbal relationship between therapist and patient. In psychodrama a central element is the playfulness (with the associated humour and fun) which can be seen both in the warm-up and in the central action.

For Winnicott, play in childhood takes place in the potential space that exists between mother and child or between two children in a sand-pit both agreeing to believe in the reality of their 'children's tea party' or of the 'battle of the giants'. Winnicott believed that play was a universal phenomenon which facilitates growth and health. It leads to the development of interpersonal relationships and 'can be a form of communication in psychotherapy' (Winnicott 1974: 48).

He saw that the origins of play had a place in the developmental sequence that exists between the world of the tiny infant and that of the adult. At first the baby has only a subjective view of an object with which it is merged and the 'mother is orientated towards the making actual of what the baby is ready to find'. She cannot force her games on her infant, she may only (with her maternal preoccupation) respond to the ever changing needs of her child. Slowly the infant discovers that its objects are indeed external and thus separate from itself. It begins to gain pleasure from the 'marriage' of the omnipotence of its inner psychic world with its growing control of objects in the real world.

The mother is crucial for this process because she must participate in it, being at times experienced as merged with her child and at others as separate from it. Winnicott saw these changes occurring in the 'playground' between the two individuals. At times the baby experiences the apparent 'magic' of its omnipotent control over its mother and its toys. At other times (and increasingly with age) it enjoys the reality of the separation between them.

Psychodrama allows the protagonist to re-enter this magical world of childhood development and once more 'play' with his psychic inner world, a process that encourages change and growth. An infant initially needs another person to join them in play in their potential space (the same is true of psychodrama), however, in time the child moves onto:

> the next stage [which] is being alone in the presence of someone. The child is now playing on the basis of the assumption that the person who loves and who is therefore reliable is available and continues to be available when remembered after being forgotten. This person is felt to reflect back what happens in the playing.
>
> (Winnicott 1971 and 1974: 55–6)

Thus, for the capacity to play to develop, the infant must learn the skill in the context of a relationship with someone who is (initially) experienced, at times, as the omnipotently controlled. As is the associated transitional object that in the infant's mind stands for this external person.

Eventually the child is able to allow for its playground to overlap with that of another. No longer must the mother carefully adapt her play to fit with her baby's activities. The child in time will also begin to play with other children, each allowing the other into their own 'potential space' or psychic (and concrete) playground.

But woe betide the other child or adult who too firmly imposes or intrudes their own wishes or ideas into this space which is inhabited by the child with such concentration and tenacity. Tears, tantrums, and a withdrawal will follow.

PSYCHODRAMA AND PLAY

In *Playing and Reality* Winnicott summarised his views on children's play (1974: 60–1). Let us consider the process of psychodrama in these terms.

Psychodrama, like play, occurs outside the individual. It does not occur only in the mind, in the reality of the inner world, but nor is it fully in the reality of the external world.

In psychodrama the protagonist draws into his 'drama' or 'play' objects, phenomena, or people from external reality through the use of auxiliary egos and certain props. These are all used in the service of something derived from inner or personal reality. As in play this process does not involve hallucinations.

In psychodrama, as in a child's play, the protagonist manipulates external phenomena in the service of his inner world. To this extent the process of psychodrama resembles the externalisation of a dream with chosen objects or auxiliary egos, being invested with a dream meaning and feeling.

Winnicott wrote that 'There is a direct development from transitional phenomena to playing, and from playing to shared playing, and from this to cultural experiences' (1974: 61).

The protagonist must trust the director and the group, for, like a child, he becomes dependent, and cannot play unless a safe transitional space exists between himself and others in the session.

Psychodrama, again like play, involves more than the mind, for the body is essential. Interactions involve the manipulation of objects (toys or props) and the movement of people.

Winnicott added that: 'Playing is essentially satisfying. This is true even when it leads to a high level of anxiety. There is a degree of anxiety that is unbearable and this destroys playing' (1974: 61). He adds that playing is essentially exciting and precarious. This too is characteristic of psychodrama. The apparent danger derives from the precariousness that belongs to the interplay in the protagonist's mind of that which is subjective (near-hallucination) and that which is objectively perceived and part of the actual or shared reality with others in the group.

George and the group had enjoyed the vitality and laughter he brought into his scene with his wife, especially when he was role-reversed as Maria. Moreno said that he wished to be remembered as the psychiatrist who brought laughter to psychotherapy.

For psychodrama is after all an active and playful form of psychotherapy. The creation of this atmosphere of fun is a task of the psychodrama director who, like a parent with her child, must foster the growth of the group and of the protagonist.

And yet there is a potential paradox in psychodrama, for the content of our playfulness in the therapeutic theatre may often involve not only pain and torment but death itself. But we must not be surprised for we go to the theatre to see the bloody dramas of Coriolanus or Macbeth. The play of children is often suffused with aggression and terror. These seem to be innate features of the human condition (Lorenz 1963).

The 'good-enough' psychodramatist

Marcia Karp describes the essential characteristics of the director if they are to be 'good enough' at their job. They must:

have an optimistic and affirmative view of the group potential;
create moments when all is possible: the director is able to create an atmosphere of potential magic;
have a true sense of play, fun, freshness and embody the humour of life as well as the pathos;
have the ability to take risks, to encourage, to stimulate and be able to transfer these into actions;
be able to engender in others the free-flowing of the creative and spontaneous spirit that promotes change.

(adapted from Karp in *Psychodrama: Inspiration and Technique*, Holmes and Karp 1991: 3)

And how important all these qualities are in good parents. I believe that the very special relationship that develops between a psychodrama director and the protagonist has indeed many of those same special qualities of a mother playing with her child. The director must facilitate the 'play' (in a therapeutic and theatrical sense), must provide containment and holding of anxieties, and must (as must a good mother) allow for or create changes and developments in the play. However, these must not be too intrusive or forced upon the protagonist, they must grow out of their joint work/play together.

It is not uncommon for a protagonist to say, after a powerful and successful session: 'I really didn't know that the director was there at all. I was just aware of my mother and my brothers and sister!'

Like a 'good-enough mother', the 'good-enough' psychodrama director provides a playground (assisted by the group) in which the protagonist plays, sometimes allowing others (the director and auxiliaries) to play too.

As psychodramatists none of this will surprise us, as Moreno himself saw the roots of psychodrama as being in the Augarten, the park in Vienna, where in 1911 he played with the children and encouraged their imagination and creativity (*Preludes to my Autobiography*, Moreno 1955: 10).

George entered his psychodrama through his memories of playing with his toy soldier with his smart red tunic.

The process of change

In childhood, reality slowly begins to assert itself and the child learns that its transitional object really is external and not an extension of its psyche. Such a step is painful but crucial if the child is to continue to grow and face the real world. This process, which takes time, is initiated and indeed controlled by the growing and developing child. For there are innate drives that force the psyche to become more ordered and allow thinking to develop, processes that require the child to come to terms with external reality. At times of crisis the child will regress and once more endow the blanket or teddy bear with magical, supportive properties.

In a single psychodrama session, however, something occurs that may only rarely, or never, happen in a baby's life. The director or indeed the creative auxiliary ego may decide to change or mutate the original 'transitional object/ auxiliary ego' (re)created in the session. Thus the protagonist's perceptions and experiences of his inner world are challenged. External reality is stressed, highlighting the difference between internal and external reality. This is a step in the therapeutic process. This sort of confrontation with reality occurs for an infant when its essential teddy bear gets lost.

Alternatively, the protagonist may choose to change his auxiliary ego's behaviour himself and thus make alterations in the externalisations of his inner world. It was George who said he wished his parents to behave differently. *He* decided they should visit his social work office together. *He* decided to risk the experience of meeting parents *different* from his childhood perceptions.

George was rather like a child who decides to change his teddy bear's mood and personality. Through the externalisation of his inner-object relationships into the potential or transitional space of the psychodrama stage, he began to take control of his inner world, with all its conflicts. He could thus 'play' with and explore issues and relationships without the terror they caused him when he was a child.

Zerka Moreno says, 'psychodrama allows one to take risks in life without the fear of punishment' (personal communication). George was able to create on the psychodrama stage situations he had been avoiding since childhood and he could take the risk to find new solutions. This is an aspect of the therapeutic process of psychodrama.

The protagonist can not only gain knowledge of those object relationships previously repressed, but they can bring about shifts and alterations in the inner world. As the session develops the inner world is,

Projected, Externalised, and Enacted,

and as the psychodrama continues the external drama on the stage is (as in childhood),

Sensed, Perceived, Remembered, and Re-internalised,

becoming a new, or at least altered, part of the protagonist's inner world. This seems to me to be an essential aspect of the therapeutic process. The protagonist in a role-reversal is playing that part of himself that may be, at other times, projected onto others. This process allows the protagonist's self once more to regain contact with those lost parts of himself. This promotes psychic growth in the protagonist.

George, as the session progressed, had learnt about forgotten aspects of his childhood. He could, as a result, think about his problems and their possible solutions. He had also had an emotional or cathartic experience (Scheff 1979), which also assisted him in his emotional growth.

11 The dynamics of the group

The group

George hugged 'Maria'. He knew that his psychodrama was over. Thelma held onto him. Somehow the physical contact seemed necessary. George had had a long evening and Thelma (partly still in the role of his wife) wanted to help him end on a positive note, to help him so that he could return home to his real wife and begin the slow process of allowing shifts and changes in their relationship and marriage.

'Let's share.'

The group all moved onto the stage area and formed a circle. This phase of the psychodrama allowed those in roles to shed them and become fully, once more, themselves. And it allowed those whose feelings or memories had been stirred up to share with the protagonist.

Joyce continued to sit next to George. Paul looked around the group. There was a long mellow silence. Suddenly Joan was seen to be in tears. Thelma reached out and put her arm around her.

'Joan?'

'George is so like my son, Gerald, so distant. I can see the pain in Gerald, but cannot reach him. His father left when he was a baby. He's only seen him twice since then! I know he misses having a dad. I know he blames me. I blame myself at times, but his dad was a mess. Our marriage wouldn't have lasted. And I've been happy, on the whole, as a single woman. But I feel for Gerald!'

George then crossed the room and put his arm around Joan, a gesture which she accepted. A real son with a real mother. George's action seemed to offer Joan some hope with her own teenage son back home.

'I really liked being your dad, especially in the last scene.'

The group knew that Victor was gay, but would have liked children.

'It's great being your dad. I don't think that your parents knew what they were missing.'

George looked pleased, he liked Victor, who was a fair bit older than he was, but he had not always found him easy to relate to in the group. Victor added: 'But there are times when I also feel I'm like Fred, I can see why you asked me to play him tonight!'

Maggie looked up.

'I always tend to avoid difficult or painful situations. I don't like being like that! As you know, I've had great difficulties with Jack, my boss.'

Maggie had been the protagonist three weeks ago. Like George she seemed to confuse her boss with her father, although in her case her father had sexually abused her. Now she feared that all men wanted the same thing. A fear that made her life troublesome at times.

Debby had two children, both about to leave home. She shared with George that although 'to the outside world we're a happy family' she and her husband have had their problems.

'I worry about how these might have affected our sons, especially John, the younger. However, they seem happy enough, but who can really tell?'

Paul shared that he too had had difficulties, in different ways, with both his parents. But now he felt he was getting on much better with them. One by one everyone in the group said something.

Joan was still tearful.

'Are you all right?'

Paul as director felt a concern for her. He wasn't really sure why she was so upset.

'I'm feeling a bit better. While the others have been sharing I've realized that the problem is not only with my son, but also with my father. He's still alive and we see each other quite often so I'm not really sure why I'm so upset. It feels as if something wasn't quite right when I was a girl.'

Maggie said: 'I had the same sort of feeling too, then I discovered that my father had abused me. I'd forgotten all the events, I just remembered the pain and the loneliness.'

Joan went over and put her arms around Maggie, who was now looking distressed.

'I don't think that my father abused me, but I do know that he was a rather distant dad.' said Joan. Paul added: 'It seems that we are finding material for another psychodrama, but not tonight. Do you feel that you can cope until next week?'

'Of course!' replied Joan. She was known in the group for being 'strong'. Joyce said: 'You've got my phone number, do ring me during the week if you want to.'

'Anyone for a drink?'

'I've got to meet a friend,' said David. 'I'll come next week.'

So the group and Paul left the 'theatre' and went downstairs to pick up coats and umbrellas from the staff room. As they left the building George said:

'It's still raining out here! I'd really forgotten this awful weather during my session! Perhaps because it was always sunny when I was a child!'

He laughed and Debby put an arm over his shoulders. The group hurried down the street, avoiding the puddles. They soon entered the Duke of Cambridge and settled with their drinks around a table. A lively conversation about politics and the local council developed. The psychodrama group was over for the week.

GROUP PSYCHOTHERAPY

In 1932 J.L. Moreno coined the phrase 'group psychotherapy' initially to describe his own psychodramatic and sociodramatic methods. However, subsequently the term has been used to describe many different styles of group psychotherapy with their associated theories of group dynamics. These include those developed by psychoanalysts (analytic group psychotherapy) and gestalt and client-centred therapists (see Perls *et al.* 1951; Rogers 1970; Yalom 1985).

This chapter will explore some of the ideas that psychoanalysis has brought to the understanding of group dynamics. It will focus in particular on the contributions of the British schools of S.H. Foulkes and W.R. Bion (see Pines 1983, 1985).

GEORGE AND THE GROUP

This book describes in detail one session of protagonist-centred psychodrama (Holmes 1991). The session concentrated on George and the ways in which his *inner world* was explored *outside* on the psychodramatic stage. His relationships both in childhood and in the present were examined, linked as they were by his inner-object world.

The matrix of internal identity

George's inner world could be thought of as a 'matrix of internal identity', each object relationship being embedded in the psyche, indeed each being part of the surrounding matrix of all the other internal relationships, the whole representing his own unique identity or self. George's psychodrama was 'classical', the focus being on the protagonist and his matrix of internal identity as presented to the group.

The matrix of external identity

We have heard something about his relationships at work and at home and looked at George's relationships with his director, Paul, and with other members of the group. These might all be said to form part of his 'matrix of external identity' as who we are is defined by our external realities (job, family, friends, and our position in society) as well as our internal realities.

The matrix of the group

The group analyst S.H.Foulkes used the term 'matrix' to describe the rich and diverse relationships which exist between individuals in a group. Within this matrix are embedded all the members with their individual and shared dynamics (Foulkes 1964, 1975; Foulkes and Anthony 1957; Pines 1983).

It might be useful to state once more (what must seem very obvious): every member of this group, including the group leader and director Paul, has his or her own complex and rich inner world which to varying degrees becomes actively involved in the session. There is a constant interaction of the matrices of internal reality of all the members of the group.

During the evening various aspects of group members' interpersonal relationships became apparent. For example, before the group began, while coffee was being drunk, Joyce became angry and verbally attacked George. Maggie came to his rescue. Later in the session George became, for a moment, very angry with Paul. Their positive contract and therapeutic alliance seemed threatened. At the end of the evening Debby put her arm around George.

How can we understand what was happening between Joyce and George at the start of the group? Did it have any links with George's anger with Paul? And why did Debby become so close to George? What was the significance of these interactions?

Should the group leader ignore them? The contract was for protagonist-centred psychodramas, but this was after all a 'psychotherapy group'; perhaps these interactions were important. Should Paul have given some time and space to consider the group dynamics? Would the problems continue and perhaps adversely affect the session?

The theories of group analysis answer some of these questions.

S.H. FOULKES AND ANALYTIC GROUP PSYCHOTHERAPY

Foulkes developed group-analytic psychotherapy in the 1940s when, with others, he was involved in attempts to treat the large number of soldiers who had experienced emotional difficulties during the second World War. He wrote that:

> Just as the individual's mind is a complex of interacting processes (personal matrix), mental processes interact in the concert of the group (group matrix). These processes relate to each other in manifold ways and on a variety of different levels.
>
> *Group-Analytic Psychotherapy: Methods and Principles*
> (Foulkes 1975: 130)

Previously, psychoanalysts had been more interested in the psychology and treatment of individuals. Foulkes began a detailed psychoanalytic study of the processes that occur within groups of people.

Before we consider the complexities of a whole group let us review the relationship between two individuals (and their respective realities and inner worlds). This situation is shown diagrammatically in Figure 11.1.

Figure 11.2 extends this diagram to three people. Each person in this triad can relate to the other two in ways governed by reality (and modulated by tele). Their relationship may, however, be dominated by their own, individual

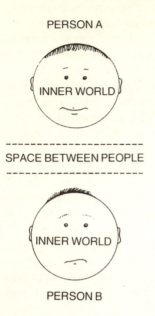

PERSON A

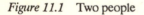

SPACE BETWEEN PEOPLE

PERSON B

Communication across the space between people involves aspects of transference, tele, and empathy

Figure 11.1   Two people

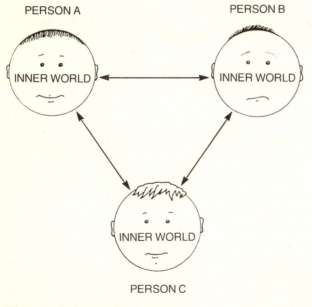

Figure 11.2 A group of three people

inner worlds; that is, by the unconscious processes that create the transference in therapy and the kinds of confusion George experienced at work.

Normally in a group, if all the members know something about each other's here-and-now realities, sanity and reality will be the order of the day. The group will be able to focus on the agreed task: for example, in an office the provision of services to clients, in a psychodrama group the exploration of the strengths and problems of one individual, the protagonist.

However, if one or more of this group of people have difficulties in reality testing *or* the group members lack much (or any) real information about each other, then the mechanisms and contents of their inner worlds will begin to dominate. Transferences will develop between group members.

For example, if the trio consisted of George, Joyce, and Victor, George might relate (yet again) to Victor as a father figure and to Joyce as a mother. Joyce herself might see in George her spoilt younger brother who 'got away with everything', while she had to support and care for their ageing father. She might see in Victor the possibility of yet another doomed relationship with an unavailable man, yet another repetition of her life with her father.

Victor had been attracted to Roy, and perhaps wondered if he had frightened him away from the group, a fear that stirred up his guilt about aspects of his childhood: and so on. Each person in the group had a complex mixture of reality-based and unconscious aspects in their relationships and feelings about each other. This network is part of the matrix of the group, which can be extended, according to Foulkes, to the whole group, as illustrated in Figure 11.3. In this figure each connecting line represents the full richness of the relationship between those two individuals.

In *Who Shall Survive* Moreno included a complex sociogram of the 435 inhabitants of the Hudson School for Girls, a reformatory for delinquents in New York (Figure 11.4 taken from Moreno 1953). This is a highly complex diagram of relationships (as seen by the girls) within the institution. Large circles represent residential houses, the small circles the individual girls. (For more about sociograms see Hale 1981.)

I include this figure here because of its marked similarity to diagrams of the group matrix produced by group analysts (e.g. James 1980). If one moves up a level and takes the large circle to represent individuals then the smaller circles (and the lines connecting them) represent each individual's inner world. Thus the inner worlds and their outer relationships are included. It must be stressed that Moreno, in his sociometric explorations at Hudson, was more concerned with the real external relationships between the girls than with the unconscious aspects of their likes and dislikes for each other.

Group-analytic psychotherapy focuses on the reality-based relationships in the group *and* on the transferences that develop both between members and with the therapist. This emphasis is not surprising in a therapy based on the theories and techniques of classical psychoanalysis.

Transference phenomena . . . can be clearly observed in this 'group-analytic

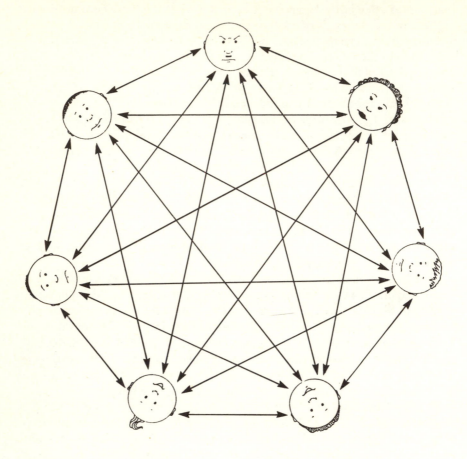

Figure 11.3 A whole group

situation'. They are naturally distributed among a number of persons and
not concentrated exclusively on the therapist.

>   Foulkes, in *Group Psychotherapy* (Foulkes and Anthony 1957: 28)

Foulkes believed that here-and-now reality was also important in analytic
groups and he pointed out that the transferences that develop differ from
those seen in classical individual psychoanalysis. As a consequence:

> the group situation discourages the development of a regressive
> transference neurosis, that is one which repeats early infantile
> attachments, on the part of the individual, by contrast to the psychoanalytic
> situation.

>   (Foulkes and Anthony 1957: 28)

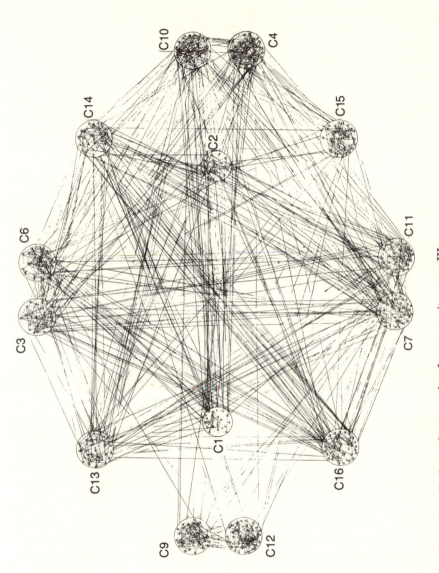

Figure 11.4 Sociometric geography of a community – map III

The process of treatment in group analysis uses the interpretation of the relationships and interactions of group members with each other and with the therapist, for:

> treatment groups ... are 'transference groups' (T-Groups), where every member is a potential auxiliary ego and a focus of projections, and where every relationship can be a model by proxy of relationships in society outside. Transference and projection operate of course in every type of group, but in these treatment groups they are thrown into relief.
>
> (Foulkes and Anthony 1957: 252)

So, in group psychoanalysis, it is the relationships within the group, between group members including the therapist, that form the matrix, that are analysed. They provide the basic material for the therapeutic process (just as the patient's relationship with the therapist does in psychoanalysis).

For any individual in such a group the transferences are 'shared around'. The leader (if male) may receive the paternal transference, while a motherly woman might receive maternal transferences from many (if not all) group members. In such a rich matrix many other transferences are possible (brothers, sisters, etc.), and of course not all group members will direct their projections and transferences in the same direction.

The rules that govern the running of such groups are obviously consequent on these theoretical and practical considerations. For after all it is a therapeutic process developed from psychoanalysis.

Certain 'rules' are shared with psychodrama groups: for example, the expectation of regular and punctual attendance and the maintenance of confidentiality. However, other rules are radically different; for example, contact between members of an analytic group, after or outside sessions, is strongly discouraged. (In psychodrama the social aspect, often in my experience focused around food and drink, is very important and I believe therapeutic.) 'The specific condition for treatment ... is that the patients are strange to each other and have no relationship in life' (Foulkes 1975: 93).

For most of us, reality challenges the transference. If we know too much about our analyst, or other members of the group, they become too real and can no longer so easily become the focus of projections and transferences. Additionally:

> Whilst in treatment it is essential to avoid taking any decisions in life which have serious consequences in reality, quite particularly such as are irreversible, as for instance a change of profession, marriage or divorce. This is a precaution which one cannot overrate ... for motivations and reactions of an infantile, immature character are mobilised during an intensive form of psychotherapy. To act on them ... is disastrous for the patient's life and future.
>
> (Foulkes 1975: 94)

Furthermore, abstinence is required:

> from tension-relieving devices as smoking, eating or drinking in the session
> ... and from any physical contact, tender or hostile, towards other patients.
> This has to do with the suspended action which is so characteristic for an
> analytic approach.
>
> (Foulkes 1975: 94)

A comment on 'T' groups

It appears that confusion exists over the term 'T Group'. Foulkes is clear that
for him such a group involves T-ransference and T-reatment. However, other
styles of 'T group' also exist which are used for sensitivity or T-raining
purposes. De Board wrote:

> One of the features of the workshop [at the National Training Laboratories
> in the USA] was a small, ongoing group called the Basic Skills Training
> Group, where behavioural data collected from observation was made
> available for discussion and analysis by their group. This method of
> education and training is now universally known as 'T-group' training.
>
> (de Board 1978: 63–4)

Although the underlying philosophy of these groups may be psychoanalytic, based in part on the theories of Bion, it is clear that they are not
intended for treatment. In the light of this confusion it is probably better not
to use the term 'T group'.

Psychodrama and analytic groups

It must be clear by now how different in terms of the process group
psychoanalysis (as described by Foulkes) is from psychodrama. This
difference must remain, I believe, for the clarity or therapeutic potency of
analytic group therapy. In such a group treatment occurs through the analysis
and interpretation of the transference relationships in the group matrix.

Conversely, one of the strengths of psychodrama is the encounters and
sharing that occur between equals, both in and between sessions. This
freedom is possible because the therapeutic process occurs in the drama
between the protagonist and the auxiliary egos who, after the psychodrama,
shed their roles in the sharing and become, once more, themselves. There are,
however, psychotherapists in Britain who are actively working on an
integration of group analysis and psychodrama.

On a personal note

I have learnt much, both personally and professionally, from my six years as a
patient in group analysis. I also gained from my experience of running such a

group, for two years under supervision, while I was working at the Maudsley Hospital in London.

The therapeutic model of group analysis is well established and much respected. I am aware that I cannot possibly, in this very short account, do justice to the richness of its theoretical and treatment formulations.

However, I have some reservations about the therapeutic processes of group analysis which reflect the theoretical and philosophical differences between Freud and Moreno. It seems to me that this technique contains at least one potential paradox.

The group brings together people who may all have interpersonal difficulties. Some will lack friends, others will have only over-intense or otherwise disturbed relationships. Yet the rules of the group (for understandable theoretical reasons) forbid the development of any friendships in everyday life from within the group. Effective changes may only occur when the therapeutic process generalises to others outside the group.

In this respect the logic follows that of psychoanalysis. Freud was cautious both about action in therapy and about over-familiarity between doctor and patient. You will remember the trouble that Dr Breuer got into when the boundaries of early psychoanalysis and friendship became blurred.

In my experience of both styles of group, I have greatly valued the positive power of the real friendships and support that can be offered by members of a psychodrama group. I hope that this book has demonstrated that the methods and techniques of psychodrama allow for an exploration and change in the uncon-scious, in which respect such groups resemble those of the group psychoanalysts.

Moreno and Foulkes

Before moving on to discuss more fully how I've found the theories of group analysis useful, I'd like to quote Foulkes's acknowledgement to Moreno. In *Group Psychotherapy* he described how he liked the processes of the theatre: 'because it [the theatre] demonstrated so many of the mechanisms we see at work in the therapeutic group'. As a footnote he added:

> In this context we would like to acknowledge the particular debt which we owe to J.L. Moreno. In his system the insight into the dramatic situation is basic, and he uses dramatic techniques as the main vehicle of psycho-therapy. Moreno's so-called psycho-dramatic and socio-dramatic techniques and his theoretical concepts have also become significant in the field of group psychotherapy, and are in accord with many viewpoints expressed in this book.
> (Foulkes in Foulkes and Anthony 1957: 223)

Moreno too was positive about Foulkes:

> There are developing a number of combinations between psychodrama and psychoanalysis in recent years. . . . Last not least is the work of courageous

English group psychotherapists and psychodramatists, Dr Maxwell Jones at Sutton General Hospital, Dr SH Foulkes at the Maudsley Hospital and Dr Joshua Bierer at the Institute of Social Psychiatry.

(Moreno 1953: cvii)

The outcome of this 'encounter' of group psychotherapists, was, I fear, less positive. Foulkes wrote in 1975 about the use of psychodramatic processes of role playing and acting:

> Some otherwise analytically orientated colleagues find psychodrama useful and practise it. I do not doubt that acting or role playing are valuable means of communication; this, however, is very different from an analytic approach. . . . The question is whether it is really necessary. . . . Personally, I find that in the analytic group there is sufficient dramatic action going on between people on deep emotional grounds, and have found 'action' unnecessary. During the last war, I experimented with psychodramatic methods and used the material produced for further analysis and consideration.

(Foulkes 1975: 93)

Indeed, when I trained in the psychotherapy unit at the Maudsley Hospital in the late 1970s (where Foulkes had worked), there were few or no signs of the influence of psychodrama. Psychoanalytic individual and group therapy was the order of the day. It is interesting to note that Marcia Karp had started to re-introduce psychodrama to the hospital in the early 1970s. I learnt about this only after leaving the Maudsley's august portals to work elsewhere. Perhaps the influence of the more orthodox psychoanalysts in the psychotherapy unit was too powerful.

It is only fair to add that in my training as a psychodramatist in the early 1980s I heard nothing about the theories of group analysis.

Classical psychodrama

This book describes the process of protagonist-centred psychodrama. In any session other members of the group play crucial roles as auxiliary egos, doubles, audience, and (as I've explained) holders or containers of anxiety. However, their individual 'inner worlds' are *not* the focus of attention and nor are the complexities of their personal inter-relationships. The time and the stage are given over to that session's protagonist.

I would most certainly not deny that important things *do* happen to all group members in a session. The taking of certain auxiliary roles can be a powerful (and at times therapeutic) experience, as can the actual process of watching someone else's psychodrama.

In New York Moreno established the use of psychodrama as a very theatrical medium. People paid to come and watch sessions (with the possibility that they might become more involved). Marcia Karp (who directed such sessions in the early 1970s) described how one woman attended these weekly sessions for several months, always sitting in the back row, never saying a word. She eventually came up to Marcia and thanked her, saying that her problems were now solved through watching the psychodramas of others (personal communication). Indeed perhaps the more orthodox theatre has the same power to help and change us all (Scheff 1979).

So, in classical psychodrama the space is given to the protagonist, other group members are there to assist the session through the taking of auxiliary roles, doubling, and so on.

Indeed the auxiliary egos need not be in the group for their own therapeutic benefit. Moreno, in the 1930s at his hospital in Beacon, used paid theatre students to be the auxiliary egos in the psychodramatic treatment of a psychotic young man. He also used paid and trained therapeutic staff, for example, nurses, in his psychodrama sessions.

Psychodrama and group dynamics: an analytic understanding

But we are all human. The powerful tendency for us all to interact with others and to confuse these interactions with aspects of our inner worlds (through the transference) cannot be denied. Joyce's irritation with George before the session started was almost certainly influenced by a mixture of here-and-now reality: 'Why should *he* be late when I've made such an effort to get here on time?' and aspects of her inner world (the transference): 'Why is that my spoilt younger brother always gets away with everything? What about me?'

Indeed, it was this same 'spoilt' younger brother who suggested that she join a psychodrama group. In psychoanalytic terms her anger with George may be the repetition of her fury and envy with 'little boys who get away with things'. In an analytic group such possible links could be voiced and interpreted and her relationship with George in the group would provide the material for the analysis.

This feature of Joyce's inner world, which continued to cause her pain in her adult life, would be explored very differently in protagonist-centred psychodrama. Joyce's difficulties with her envy and her brother would not, usually, be focused on in George's psychodrama. Her problems could be raised in the sharing at the end of the group, although a fuller exploration would have to wait for her next session, when perhaps George would be the auxiliary ego playing her brother.

But in the psychodrama session described in this book something rather unexpected happened as she was asked by George to play his mother, a request that clearly challenged this difficult relationship.

Could Joyce forget her irritation and move away from her unconscious transference reaction to play his mother? This was a potentially difficult role for Joyce, relating as it did to her own problems with mothers. She could certainly play the 'depriving' mother (this was after all part of one of her own inner-object relationships, 'deprived little girl–unavailable mother'). Could she, however, provide George with a different type of mothering if the session called for this?

George clearly felt (through his tele) that she could. And she did so with great success. Joyce had, in reality, confronted him that evening. Perhaps George felt that she was tough enough to play his 'bad' mother. Perhaps he also sensed something else, perhaps her ability and wish to be a 'good' mother.

Later in the sharing Joyce was able to talk about her worries that she may never be a mother (after all she had reached an age when motherhood is far from certain) and her fears that if she ever did have a baby she would be an inadequate parent. Again, issues of her own inner world emerged. Her relationship with her mother (explored in a previous session) was very poor. Inside Joyce there is an 'uncared for baby–young depressed mother' object relationship. Her mother had resented her (as a child) just as perhaps George's had him (for 'causing' an unwished-for marriage). At the start of the session perhaps she was identified with her inner 'resentful mother', a role she then acted out on the young boyish man who arrived almost late for the group. 'Men are always like that!'

The reality of the session was that Joyce was able to take on the role of George's mother and develop it to provide George with a different and perhaps new experience of good mothering. In the sharing she was able to get in touch with her wish to be a mother. She was able to give George some real comfort and support from which both gained benefit.

Perhaps Paul was lucky. The potentially difficult dynamic between George and Joyce seemed to be resolved *without* the need to focus on their relationship (in either reality or the two-way transferences).

This is not always the case. At times I have had to give some time in a session to an issue between group members. This I do by focusing on the here-and-now problems, for the interpretation of the transferential aspects of a relationship (in groups as well as in individual psychotherapy) can initially strengthen the unreality of the relationship and of the transference. Some knowledge of the theory behind the process of interpretation is, however, relevant. Malan (1979) described how a full interpretation in psychoanalytic therapy links three areas:

1   The patient's transference towards the therapist.
2   Their relationships in the real world of the present.
3   And the inner world with its roots in childhood relationships.

Such interpretations, which would emphasise the unconscious aspects of the group's interactions, make these relationships more exciting, dramatic, and important. To make such an interpretation in a psychodrama group would risk a change of emphasis away from 'protagonist-centred psychodrama' and towards another sort of psychotherapy group.

Paul used his understanding of the transference when he asked George who else had kept him away from his father. It was this question that shifted George from his frustrated anger with his director to an awareness that it was his mother who had kept his father from him.

At times it is essential to be aware of how inner worlds and inner pains affect group dynamics. This may be of particular importance with certain types of patient. For example, the young man who *always* fights with father figures in the group or the older woman who is terrified that *all* men will be abusive can have powerful consequences on the development of trust in a group. In these circumstances I will use my understanding of these individuals' dynamics carefully.

The fact that I think *I know* what is going on may be enough to contain my, and the group's, anxiety and distress. After all parents do not have to tell their children everything, nor do therapists have to explain all the dynamics to the group, to be 'good enough'.

Sometimes understanding is not enough and a gentle interpretation is helpful, perhaps following a piece of 'acting out' in the transference, as happened between Joyce and George in a previous session:

> 'You know, Joyce, you do seem to find younger "brothers", or younger men in the group, a real pain. They always seem to upset you. Perhaps they remind you of your childhood when your brother seemed to get everything from your mother.'

I would, however, use such interpretations sparingly in a protagonist-centred group, preferring to keep the focus on a protagonist and the techniques rooted in classical psychodrama.

W.R. BION'S CONTRIBUTION TO AN UNDERSTANDING OF GROUP DYNAMICS

Bion, like Foulkes, developed his interest in group dynamics in the 1940s while attempting to treat neurotic soldiers (Bion 1961: 11–12; Pines 1985).

We have seen that Foulkes considered the group as a collection of individuals linked by reality and transferences. He was also aware of the collective aspects of the group's behaviour, for in some ways a group functions as a single unity.

Bion's views on group dynamics placed the emphasis firmly on the group as an organic whole, rather than as a collection of individuals. He believed that people could form two types of group: 'work groups' and what he described as 'basic assumption groups'.

In the former there is an agreement to focus on a task through mutual co-operation. In such groups people relate to each other and the external world with a degree of reality testing and maturity. The reasons for the group coming together and meeting are remembered and the agreed task is pursued. The work of such groups obviously varies: it might be the provision of a clinical service to disturbed children, it might be the planning of a political campaign, it might be the manufacture and sale of butter, or it might be the exploration of a protagonist's inner world through psychodrama.

Bion believed that such a group 'depends on some degree of sophisticated skills in the individual' (Bion 1961: 143). Without such skills, and the associated structures, a group's functioning can easily slide into chaos.

When this happens a basic assumption group results. Contact with reality is lost and the group can be considered to be (in psychoanalytic terms) functioning using psychotic mechanisms. Bion observed that in groups without clear tasks, or in a group under stress, there was a tendency for them to lose contact with external reality. Then the members began to function *as if* they were but a part of a single organism, 'the group', a psychotic regression occurring both in individuals and in the group as a whole.

> The belief that a group exists, as distinct from an aggregate of individuals, is an essential part of this regression, as are also the characteristics with which the supposed group is endowed by the individual. Substance is given to the phantasy that the group exists by the fact that the regression involves the individual in a loss of his 'individual distinctiveness'.
>
> (Bion 1961: 142)

Perhaps this description of a group sounds rather far fetched. However, I am always surprised how many apparently 'sane' groups of people behave in ways typical of a basic assumption group. Certainly clinical teams or committees I have worked in have at times regressed to basic assumption functioning. It is also true of political parties (especially when they are under stress from the opposition). Even whole countries can slide into a basic assumption mode of operation (say at a time of war).

Although the individuals in such a group have unconscious psychotic phantasies about the group (including that as a part of a group they have no personal autonomy), it must be stressed that they are not themselves, in a clinical sense, psychotic or mad. On leaving the group their rational objectivity will return.

Bion described how a group in such a state uses primitive defence mechanisms to defend itself (the group) from increasing anxiety. He was a Kleinian and followed the theoretical formulations of that school. Individuals within the group become like inner-objects within a single psyche in which splitting and projective identification are the main defence mechanisms.

Thus, just as aspects of the self-representation can be projected onto the other-objects or representations in the psyche (Sandler's stage one projective identification, 1987, 1988), so can people within the group project onto each other. This is used within the group to defend against the *group's* anxiety rather than the anxiety of *individual* members. In these circumstances people lose their individuality and ability of independent action. They become but inner-objects within the group psyche.

It is easy to think about the strange contortions that overcome any group that becomes anxious. The stress may be due to the threat of a loss of funding (note that this was a feature in George's social work office). It might be because the group's task was in itself anxiety provoking. Nursing very sick and dying patients is very stressful. Isabel Menzies (1970) described how a hospital nursing system uses very primitive (psychotic) defence mechanisms to cope with the emotional strain. Or the fear might originate from the increasing success of the opposition political party with the associated fear of losing the next general election.

Bion (1961: 146) described how such groups adopt (as part of their unconscious defence mechanisms) one of three basic assumptions: dependency, pairing, or fight/flight. His descriptions of these styles of group are complex; some would say obscure or even poetic. However, as I have indicated, I believe these assumptions can be observed to be held by many types of group.

A well-run protagonist-centred psychodrama group *should* remember and stick to its task. If it does, it will avoid a regression into basic assumption functioning. Because of this fact I will present only a brief outline of Bion's views (see Bion 1961; de Board 1978; Grinberg *et al.* 1975).

In a *dependency* group an individual is in (or is pushed into) the role of 'leader'. This person is unrealistically idealised for a time, and may as a result become omnipotent or megalomanic. But the group expects too much from this person. He or she cannot fulfil the group's grandiose expectations of them, and is then toppled, as the attitude shifts to one of denigration. Another leader must be found from within the group, who, too, will be idealised. . . .

It must be noted that these leaders are role responsive to the group's need to project power and responsibility onto one person. As Bion says, such a leader is the 'creature of the group' and thus cannot act in a genuinely independent manner. How many political leaders can be considered in this way?

In a *pairing* group two (or perhaps more) individuals will get together to create a new solution to the group's problems and thus reduce the group's stress and anxiety. Bion described this process in the sexual terms of a couple getting together to produce a new baby or 'Messiah'.

Perhaps groups do have this unconscious sexual phantasy. However, the concept can also be understood in terms of two people getting together to produce a new idea or plan 'that will solve all our problems'. Again such expectations are often unrealistic and magical. Any new baby (or idea) cannot but fail to live up to these grandiose expectations. The baby or idea, once born, must fail.

Again, how many groups under threat or stress have created a 'sub-committee', or written a strategic planning document, to look at the problems and find a solution? Anxiety is always reduced until the idea is born and then fails.

A *fight/flight* group deals with all its anxiety and difficulties by projecting them outwards onto another group which is then seen as being the cause of *all* the group's problems. The group can forget its own internal problems and tasks, placing all its energy into the attack on the other group which is seen as threatening. Such a group is paranoid and unrealistic about its relationships with the external world.

How many City taker-overs result from an avoidance of stress within the predatory company? How many countries have been invaded and wars fought in order that the state may not think about its own internal stresses and turmoil?

All three basic assumptions allow the group psyche to operate in primitive and magical ways as a defence against internal anxiety. Contact with reality is lost. The group task is forgotten.

BASIC ASSUMPTION GROUPS AND PSYCHODRAMA

As I have stated above, I believe that a psychodrama group *must* maintain its hold on the realities of what Bion defined as a 'work group'. The task is to confront the needs of the protagonist. However, I am sure that from time to time a psychodrama group may shift from a 'work' group to a 'basic assumption group'. I am fairly sure I've been in more than one psychodrama group that has followed this path to chaos.

When this shift occurs the director *must* (by definition) be taken along by the process. He too will lose contact with the original task. The only solution is that one or more members will be resistant to the threat of the loss of their individuality and will maintain some hold on external reality. They will remember the task and *why* the group is meeting. Such individuals may be able to assist the group's return to 'work group' functioning, allowing it to continue the task and its development.

If this recovery does not occur, the group is doomed and will eventually disintegrate, much as a borderline personality may become floridly psychotic under stress.

It is important to note that some psychodramatists place a much greater emphasis on the interpersonal dynamics of the group than I do in my account of a session in this book. This is certainly true of those schools of psychodrama which already integrate Moreno's techniques with the theories of psychoanalysis.

Moreno too acknowledged unconscious, shared processes that occur in groups, which he called the co-unconscious (Moreno in Fox 1987: 63; Monica Zuretti, personal communication), even when psychodrama sessions are apparently protagonist centred.

In my experience, when a psychodramatist focuses on the group dynamics (rather than on a protagonist-centred task), there is the possibility that the members may behave, when in the group, in a manner quite different from that which they adopt as individuals outside the session. Such a shift may make classical psychodrama difficult.

THE HEALTHY PSYCHODRAMA GROUP

> A meeting of two: eye to eye, face to face.
>
> (Moreno quoted in Blatner and Blatner 1988)

Moreno talked about psychodrama as an encounter between equals, although I sometimes wonder how equal *he* felt with others. Meeting one's equals and sharing emotions, pain, history, fun, and laughter can be a most healing experience. The nature of protagonist-centred psychodrama allows for this to happen. The powerful inner-object relationships are not ignored, nor are their influences on everyday life dismissed. However, the exploration and therapeutic work are undertaken on the psychodrama stage, using the magic of the process to convert friends, associates, and other group members into those important 'others' from the world outside the group, from history, and from each individual's inner world.

Sharing

The final stage of a psychodrama session is the sharing when we all return to be ourselves: 'father' became once more Victor; Joyce lost the magic psychodramatic mantle of 'mother'; Thelma became herself again. Group members talk about their feelings and thoughts during the session both when in role (as an auxiliary ego) and as themselves.

This process facilitates 'de-rolling' in which members return to themselves, shedding the burdens (or pleasures) of the auxiliary roles they have occupied during the session. Some group leaders prefer a more ritualised process: 'I'm not George's father. I'm Victor, and I feel good to be in this group.'

I find that sharing, if sufficient time is allowed, will provided for a fuller and more meaningful de-rolling, allowing auxiliaries first to share from role and then to share with the group as themselves. Group members may gain as much therapeutically through playing auxiliary roles, or even just watching a psychodrama, as through being the protagonist in a session.

THE *OUTER WORLD* ON THE PSYCHODRAMATIC STAGE GOES BACK *INSIDE*, AND THE GROUP GOES OFF TO THE PUB

After this session only George remained as he was in the drama, himself. However, now his inner world had been explored, put forward onto the psychodrama stage outside his private psychic world. As the session ended these experiences were taken into himself once more, as memories and understanding of his difficulties, and perhaps as significant changes in his inner-object relationships.

Hopefully, in time, this session will help him alter his relationship with the world around him: with Fred and with his wife. But at the end of the session he was, in Moreno's words, 'like a patient in the recovery room after major surgery' (Zerka Moreno, personal communication). Fragile, tired but relieved that the 'operation' had gone well.

Both Paul and George knew that this evening's session, with its cathartic expression of anger, was not an end in itself. George would still have to undertake the hard work, within himself and at home and in the office, of developing the more mature aspects of his role repertoire.

However, at that moment he was pleased to receive support from the group as they made their way down the wet and windy London street to a much needed pint of beer in the local pub, the Duke of Cambridge.

Coda
How does psychodrama change people?

The group

Three sessions later George came into the theatre and told the group that two days ago he had had a row with Fred at work. To his great surprise not only had this made him feel better, but his relationship with his boss seemed to have improved.

'That's great!' said Thelma. 'But how's your relationship with your wife?'

'Oh, much as always. But I don't suppose that I can expect everything to change at once.'

WHAT HELPS IN PSYCHODRAMA?

Paul and the other group members had committed a number of hours every week to this group for several months. Time taken away from other pressing or enjoyable activities. What did they hope to gain?

Some of their reasons were given in Chapter 1. Joyce hoped the group would help with her depression and with her problems with men. David had also joined the group to work on interpersonal difficulties. Debby joined to learn more about psychodrama.

Only George's problems have been described in detail in this book together with an account of his treatment in one psychodrama session, but several members of this group reported changes in their lives during the next few months. They felt better, and some of their difficulties were reduced. Many of these improvements were attributed to the psychodrama sessions. George certainly felt that his session had helped him with his problems at work.

However, just because group members reported improvements in their lives, this does not mean that the psychodrama group actually *caused* these changes. It is well known that people's lives alter and shift, for better and for worse, without any help from psychotherapy.

It is also true that people who seek therapeutic help have already made the first step to change by acknowledging that something in their lives is not going very well. Just the process of accepting that they may need professional help may lead to significant alterations in someone's life.

It is of course important to listen carefully to an individual's interpretation of what has brought about change. They may even be correct when they attribute these alterations to certain events or activities!

Attacks on psychotherapy continue in the medical and scientific literature (see, for example, Shepherd 1985; Sutherland 1991). This situation will continue unless psychotherapists stop to consider very carefully both the processes and the consequences of their treatment methods. Research into the techniques and outcome of psychotherapy is essential, especially in these times of financial control and stress in the Health Service. Now, more than ever, any particular therapeutic school will have to argue its effectiveness against the other types of available treatment (Garfield and Bergin 1986).

Good empirical research is, however, still limited in dynamic psychotherapy (see, for an example, Firth *et al.* 1986), and psychodrama is no exception. For psychodramatists to be able best to help people they must have some clear ideas about what it is in the process that is actually therapeutic. Only then will they be able to enhance and improve their clinical practice. This situation does not, however, mean that research is unnecessary, and I would encourage any interested and concerned psychodramatist to consider undertaking properly organised investigation.

I have discussed possible therapeutic factors at various points in this book. However, I know that personally I make the assumption that psychodrama is helpful, not as the result of formal research results, but because of my positive experiences both as a patient and as a therapist.

Both Freud and Moreno developed their therapeutic techniques through observations of their own clinical practice and personal experiences. This is a position the psychologist Stuart Sutherland finds untenable. He would perhaps attribute my enthusiasm to the fact that 'I have made sacrifices to enter a profession and if I am now making a decent living out of it, I am likely to think that I am doing some good even if I am not' (Sutherland 1991: 120; quote transposed to first person).

WHAT MIGHT HAVE HELPED GEORGE?

In the absence of much formal research into psychodrama let us consider a general account of the therapeutic factors in group psychotherapy. Irvin Yalom in his large and well-known textbook *The Theory and Practice of Group Psychotherapy* (3rd edition 1985) reviews the therapeutic factors in group psychotherapy.

I will use his structure to consider the therapeutic factors in psychodrama. The interested therapist, however, should look at Yalom's book where he has space to consider this important topic at much greater length.

Yalom believes, from his extensive clinical experience, research, and reviews of the literature, that the therapeutic factors in group psychotherapy can be described under eleven headings:

1 Instillation of hope.
2 Universality.
3 Imparting of information.
4 Altruism.
5 The corrective recapitulation of the primary family group.
6 Development of socializing techniques.
7 Imitative behaviour.
8 Interpersonal learning.
9 Group cohesiveness.
10 Catharsis.
11 Existential factors.

(Yalom 1985: 3)

It is worth observing that these are factors that might be found in a variety of different types of therapeutic group. None of them can be considered specific to psychodrama. Indeed it has been shown that therapeutic effectiveness appears to have more to do with the personal characteristics and professional experience of the therapist than with the formal style or techniques of the treatment provided.

Let us explore in a little more depth what occurs in a psychodrama group in terms of Yalom's factors.

1 Instillation of hope

Psychotherapy is a time-consuming and often costly process which people undertake only when they are really distressed by aspects of their lives. Often many other attempts at change have been tried: will-power, new friends, a new wardrobe, a new job. George had moved jobs, perhaps in unsuccessful attempts to resolve his interpersonal conflicts.

By the time patients are driven to start in therapy they are often despondent if not despairing about the possibility of a better future. Treatment in groups allows them to regain hope through the experience of seeing others change and grow. They also soon discover that they are not alone or unique in their predicament, fears, wishes, or experience.

2 Universality

The process of psychodrama, perhaps especially in the crucial third stage, *sharing*, encourages both hope and the discovery of universality between group members, factors attributed by patients as being associated with their recovery.

They are also relieved and encouraged when they discover, in their therapist, an individual who not only has certain skills but also (one hopes) an optimistic belief that their therapeutic technique works. I doubt George would have been helped in this session if he suspected his director Paul did not have faith in psychodrama.

3 The imparting of information

Yalom sees this process as involving two rather different activities: didactic instruction and direct advice.

The former involves educating both individuals and the group about various issues relevant to their difficulties and to the therapeutic process. As Yalom pointed out, we all use our knowledge of the world to cope with anxiety of daily living. It is possible that Roy, who left the group after three sessions saying 'Psychodrama is not for me; it scares me', might have been able to survive in the group had Paul prepared him more fully about what to expect in sessions. This knowledge would have given him a cognitive structure which might have helped him cope better in the, for him, unusual and stressful situation of the group.

Individuals also learn about the basic nature of human functioning and difficulties through the experience of psychodrama, knowledge that will help them in a more personal way make sense of their lives. Again a cognitive understanding reduces the terror of the unknown.

In my groups I often talk (as does Marcia Karp) in a didactic way about the history and process of psychodrama. This information is given for two reasons: some group members already work with clients, and may be considering using certain techniques in their clinical work; others may be considering training more fully in psychodrama. Perhaps more importantly, the sharing of knowledge emphasises my fundamental equality in the *encounter of equals* in the group and gives each individual an idea of the structure and process of a session: information that helps contain or reduce their anxiety.

Yalom sees the giving of direct advice in psychotherapy groups as a frequent phenomenon, but:

> Despite the fact that advice giving is common in early interactional group therapy, I can recall few instances when a specific suggestion concerning some problem was any direct benefit to any patient.

(Yalom 1985: 12)

In my experience this is true in psychodrama. It is one of the tasks of the director, especially in the sharing, to stop people giving advice or unsolicited 'interpretations' to the protagonist. However, as noted above, the true sharing of personal feelings or experiences is of benefit, increasing as it does the protagonist's sense of hope and universality.

4 Altruism

Yalom pointed out that altruism is seen as positive and healing in many situations other than therapy.

Psychodrama emphasises the ability of group members to help each other for altruistic purposes, assistance given by playing a nasty auxiliary ego or through physically holding someone in distress. The very nature of psychodrama encourages such giving.

Paul, who had started the session feeling rather angry and ill at ease, felt better having given George and the group a positive experience.

5 The corrective recapitulation of the primary family group

A weekly psychodrama group is an intensive and powerful experience which in some ways comes to resemble a family. There are parents, siblings, and children. The theories of group analysis explain these phenomena in terms of the transference (Foulkes and Anthony 1957; Foulkes 1975). However, even without formal interpretation of these dynamics a group can offer the individual the chance to change through new experiences in a 'family' setting.

Joyce benefited from a warmer and less tense relationship with a brother figure, while George was able to find a less controlling mother in Joyce, and more reliable father figures in Paul and Victor. These experiences occurred not only in the more formal part of the session but also in the important social life of the group before and after the psychodrama.

6 Development of socialising techniques

Without social skills we are all lost. Even the apparently well adjusted individuals in this group benefited from modifying their techniques of social interaction.

The concept of role rehearsal (Goldman and Morrison 1984) in psychodrama offers an addition to a simple social skills training group. Through a regressive psychodramatic exploration George was able to discover something about the personal history of his difficulties with father figures. This information (both emotional and cognitive) was then used to assist him in a final scene with Fred in which he rehearsed how he would confront him in the office.

When this confrontation did occur in reality George's manner was more adult, and as a consequence his boss took him more seriously.

7 Imitative behaviour

Yalom pointed out that we all have a tendency to imitate or copy people we like or respect. Such behaviour does not, easily, become a fundamental aspect of the inner world, but it may allow for the acquisition of useful social skills. Perhaps if Roy had stayed longer in the group he might have 'imitated' some of the older men who were well established in work and thus gained more confidence as a young adult.

8   Interpersonal learning

Under this heading Yalom considered several crucial factors in the therapeutic process, all of which involve interpersonal relationships. These include the role of corrective emotional experiences, the transference, and the importance of relationships. He quotes William James:

> We are not only gregarious animals liking to be in sight of our fellows, but we have an innate propensity to get ourselves noticed, and noticed favorably, by our kind. No more fiendish punishment could be devised, were such a thing physically possible, than one should be turned loose on society and remain absolutely unnoticed by all members thereof.
>
> (James 1890: 293 quoted in Yalom 1985: 20)

Clarkson (1990) helpfully divided the types of therapeutic relationship that may occur in psychotherapy into five different kinds:

the working alliance,
the transferential/countertransferential relationships,
the reparative/developmentally needed relationships,
the I–You encounters
and what she calls transpersonal or spiritual relationships.

Aspects of all these styles occur in psychodrama. This is part of its therapeutic power. As I have stated, J.L. Moreno placed more emphasis on the I–You relationships, while Zerka Moreno sees the use of auxiliary egos and role-reversals, which (as I hope this book has demonstrated) parallel the transferential interactions of analytic psychotherapy.

Group members can also experience new relationships which may, in part, act to heal the wounds or gaps caused by what was missing in childhood. The use of surplus reality by a director may well allow the protagonist to experience for the first time a mother who *really loves her son* or a father who is *reliable* as well as loving.

Relationships such as these fall under the heading of the 'corrective emotional experience' (Yalom 1985: 25) or the 'reparative/ developmentally needed' interactions described by Clarkson (1990: 152).

Through all these varieties of experience with other people the individual learns about himself and the world. Psychic and social growth is possible.

9   Group cohesiveness

Yalom stresses the importance of this factor which is seen as a significant factor in successful outcome of group psychotherapy (1985: 69). Members of cohesive groups attend better, and fewer people leave. The atmosphere favours self-disclosure, risk taking, and the constructive expression of conflict in the group – phenomena that facilitate successful group therapy (Yalom 1985: 69).

The increasing self-esteem, which seems to relate to the resolution of personal problems, is also a more prominent feature of a cohesive group.

In my experience psychodrama groups are often very cohesive. The possibility of mixing deep therapeutic work with more relaxed social interactions, such as eating together or visiting a public house, allows for the development of very real and often deep friendships between group members. The importance given to hospitality and good food is a notable feature of the Holwell Centre. I have always enjoyed the atmosphere and found it very soothing and healing at times of personal distress.

My experience there was a marked contrast to my former psychoanalytic group. Each week the therapists needed to interpret the fact that the group members met after every session for a drink in the local pub. These comments failed to stop the meetings, and only seemed to serve to increase our guilt and hostility towards the therapists.

10 Catharsis

Catharsis is often seen as an important aspect of the therapeutic process of psychodrama, and indeed many other therapies. However, as Yalom points out, research studies have shown that incidents of catharsis were as likely to be selected (as the most significant personal experience in an encounter group) by members with poor outcomes as by those with good outcomes. Catharsis was not unrelated to outcome; it was necessary but, in itself, not sufficient (Yalom 1985: 84).

I have had personal experiences, as a group member, of both bio-energetic and encounter groups in which there was a high level of freely expressed emotions (catharsis). These groups did not seem to me to help me or the friends I went with. Indeed, I found the lack of a cognitive element very frightening.

In one such group, following an exercise involving childhood relationships, I found I had very violent feelings towards a male friend in the session, feelings that the group encouraged me to express (or act out). My friendship with this man was deeply stressed for some weeks. Only with time, in another therapy, did I make the link between this event and my childhood rage with my younger brother.

I am a psychodramatist because I enjoy and respect the method's ability to integrate the cathartic, the cognitive, and the unconscious inner world in a creative and enjoyable atmosphere.

11 Existential factors

Yalom sees such factors as important to any therapeutic process. In this he reaches back to the same philosophical roots as Moreno. He lists them:

1 Recognizing that life is at times unfair and unjust.

2 Recognizing that ultimately there is no escape from some of life's pain and from death.

3 Recognizing that no matter how close I get to people, I must still face life alone.

4 Facing the basic issues of my life and death, and thus living my life more honestly and being less caught up with trivialities.

5 Learning that I must take responsibility for the way I live my life no matter how much guidance and support I get from others.

(Yalom 1985: 92)

A PRACTICAL PHILOSOPHY FOR PSYCHODRAMA

Psychodrama, with its roots in Martin Buber's and Moreno's existential philosophy (Cooper 1990), encourages many of these attitudes.

I have been asked, often by therapists with a psychoanalytic background, how it is that I can run a 'one-off' psychodrama workshop and then not return to the group. They feel that I should continue to care for the protagonist.

I respond by saying that such behaviour would encourage the group member's dependency on me. Eventually each of us must take (as far as is possible) responsibility for our own actions and future. This is as true for a protagonist as it is for a man in the street. This is not to say that I don't care and worry about my group members. I certainly do: indeed, I may even be active in my offers of support or further help. But in the end real emotional growth comes only from an acceptance of our adult independence from others.

It must be said, however, that the emotional difficulties of certain individuals can be helped only through their developing a deep and dependent relationship with their therapist. I doubt that Fr. Rolfe would have made much progress in a short series of psychodrama sessions.

This is not to say that we don't all need help and support at times. However, in psychodrama this is available from other group members, and family and friends outside the group. The ethos encourages an increasing self-reliance and a widening and deepening of the support network.

This is an aspect of the existential philosophy of psychodrama, a philosophy which for me is in no way at odds with a psychoanalytic understanding of the human personality.

Bibliography

American Psychiatric Association (1980) *Diagnostic and Statistical Manual of Mental Disorders (DSM III)*, Washington, DC: AMA.

Ancelin Schuzenberger, A. (1985) *Vouloir Guerir*, Toulouse: Eres; Paris: La Meridienne.

Ashbach, C. and Schermer, V.L. (1987) *Object Relations, the Self, and the Group: A Conceptual Paradigm*, London: Routledge & Kegan Paul.

Aveline, M. and Dryden, W. (1988) *Group Therapy in Britain*, Milton Keynes: Open University Press.

Balint, M. (1968) *The Basic Fault*, London, Tavistock.

Benkovitz, M.J. (1977) *Fredrick Rolfe: Baron Corvo: A Biography*, New York: Putnam.

Bertalanffy, L. von (1967) *Robots, Men, and Minds: Psychology in the Modern World*, New York: George Brazillier.

Bertalanffy, L. von (1968) *General Systems Theory*, New York: George Brazillier.

Bion, W.R. (1961) *Experiences in Groups*, London: Tavistock.

Bion, W.R. (1967) *Second Thoughts*, London: Heinemann.

Bion, W.R. (1970) *Attention and Interpretation*, London: Tavistock.

Blatner, H.A. (1970) 'Psychodrama, role-playing, and action methods: theory and practice', Thetford, Norfolk: private publication.

Blatner, H.A. (1988) *Acting-In: Practical Applications of Psychodramatic Methods*, New York: Springer.

Blatner, A. with Blatner, A. (1988) *Foundations of Psychodrama: History, Theory, Practice*, New York: Springer.

Bowlby, J. (1969) *Attachment and Loss, Vol. 1, Attachment*, London: Hogarth Press; Penguin, 1971.

Bowlby, J. (1973) *Attachment and Loss, Vol. 2, Separation: Anxiety and Anger*, London: Hogarth; Penguin, 1975.

Bowlby, J. (1979) *The Making and Breaking of Affectional Bonds*, London: Tavistock/Routledge.

Bowlby, J. (1980) *Attachment and Loss, Vol. 3, Loss: Sadness and Depression*, London: Hogarth; Penguin, 1981.

Brown, G.W. and Harris, T. (1978) *Social Origins of Depression*, London: Tavistock.

Buck, R. (1988) *Human Motivation and Emotion*, 3rd edition, New York: Wiley.

Bustos, D. (1980) *El Test Sociometrico: Fundamentos, Tecnicas y Aplicaciones*, Buenos Aires: Editorial Vancu.

Casement, P. (1988) 'The experience of trauma in the transference', in J. Sandler (ed.) *Projection, Identification, and Projective Identification*, London: Karnac.

Changeux, J-P. (1985) *Neuronal Man: The Biology of Mind*, Oxford: Oxford University Press.

Clarkson, P. (1990) 'A multiplicity of psychotherapeutic relationships', *British Journal of Psychotherapy* 7 (2): 148–63.

Concise Oxford Dictionary (1990) Oxford: Oxford University Press.

Cooper, D.E. (1990) *Existentialism*, Oxford: Basil Blackwell.

De Board, R. (1978) *The Psychoanalysis of Organizations*, London: Tavistock.

Dockar-Drysdale, B. (1973) *Consultations in Child Care*, London: Longman.

Fairbairn, W.R. (1952) *Psychoanalytic Studies of the Personality*, London: Routledge & Kegan Paul.

Fairbairn, W.R. (1963) 'Synopsis of an object-relations theory of personality', *International Journal of Psycho-Analysis* 44: 224–5.

Firth, J., Shapiro, D.A., and Parry, G. (1986) 'The impact of research on the practice of psychotherapy', *British Journal of Psychotherapy* 2 (3): 169–79.

Forrest, A.D., Affleck, A.W., and Zealley, A.K. (1978) *Companion to Psychiatric Studies*, Edinburgh, London & New York: Churchill Livingstone.

Foulkes, S.H. (1964) *Therapeutic Group Analysis*, London: Maresfield Reprints.

Foulkes, S.H. (1975) *Group-Analytic Psychotherapy: Methods and Principles*, London: Gordon & Breach.

Foulkes, S.H. and Anthony, E.J. (1957) *Group Psychotherapy: The Psychoanalytic Approach*, Harmondsworth: Penguin.

Fox, J. (ed.) (1987) *The Essential Moreno: Writings on Psychodrama, Group Method and Spontaneity by J.L. Moreno MD*, New York: Springer.

Freud, A. (1936 and 1966) *The Ego and the Mechanisms of Defense*, New York: International Universities Press.

Freud, S. (1887 and 1954) 'A project for a scientific psychology', *The Standard Edition of the Complete Psychological Works of Sigmund Freud*, Vol. 1, London: Hogarth Press.

Freud, S. (1901) *The Psychopathology of Everyday Life*, Harmondsworth: Pelican Books, Pelican Freud Library (P.F.L.) 5.

Freud, S. (1905a) *Fragment of an Analysis of a Case of Hysteria ('Dora')*, P.F.L. 8.

Freud, S. (1905b) *Three Essays on the Theory of Sexuality*, P.F.L. 7.

Freud, S. (1910) 'The future prospects of psycho-analytic psychotherapy', *S.E.* 11.

Freud, S. (1912) 'Recommendations to physicians practising psychoanalysis', *S.E.* 12.

Freud, S. (1914) 'On narcissism: an introduction', P.F.L. 11.

Freud, S. (1915) 'Instincts and their vicissitudes', P.F.L. 1.

Freud, S. (1916–17) *Introductory Lectures on Psycho-Analysis*, P.F.L. 1.

Freud, S. (1921) *Group Psychology and the Analysis of the Ego*, P.F.L. 12.

Freud, S. (1923) *The Ego and the Id*, P.F.L. 11.

Freud, S. (1926) *Inhibitions, Symptoms and Anxiety*, London: Hogarth Press also P.F.L 10.

Freud, S. (1933) *New Introductory Lectures on Psycho-Analysis*, P.F.L. 2.

Freud, S. (1940) *An Outline of Psycho-Analysis*, P.F.L. 15.

Freud, S. and Breuer, J. (1895) *Studies on Hysteria*, P.F.L. 3.

Garfield, S.L. and Bergin, A.E. (1986) *Handbook of Psychotherapy and Behaviour Change*, 3rd edn, New York: John Wiley and Sons.

Goldman, E.E. and Morrison, D.S. (1984) *Psychodrama: Experience and Process*, Dubuque, IA: Kendall Hunt.

Goldstein, E.B. (1989) *Sensation and Perception*, 3rd edition, Belmont, CA: Wadsworth.

Gorell Barnes, G. (1984)'Systems theory and family theory', in M. Rutter and L. Hersov (eds) *Child and Adolescent Psychiatry: Modern Approaches*, Oxford & London: Blackwell Scientific Publications.

Greenson, R.R. (1967) *The Technique and Practice of Psychoanalysis*, London: Hogarth Press.

Gregory, R. (1966) *Eye and Brain*, 1st edition, London: Weidenfeld & Nicolson.

Grinberg, L., Sor, D. and Tabak de Bianchedi, E. (1975 and 1985) *Introduction to the Work of W.R. Bion*, London: Maresfield Library.

Gunderson, J.G. and Singer, M.T. (1975) 'Defining borderline patients: an overview', *The American Journal of Psychiatry* 132 (1): 1–9.

Guntrip, H. (1961) *Personality Structure and Human Interaction*, London: Hogarth Press.

Guntrip, H. (1968) *Schizoid Phenomena, Object Relations and the Self*, London: Hogarth Press.

Guntrip, H. (1971) *Psychoanalytic Theory, Therapy and the Self*, London: Hogarth Press.

Hale, A. (1981) *Conducting Clinical Sociometric Explorations: A Manual for Psychodramatists and Sociometrists*, Roanoake, VA: Royal.

Harris, T., Brown, G.W., and Bifulco, A. (1990) 'Loss of parent in childhood and adult psychiatric disorder: a tentative overall model', *Development and Psychopathology* 2: 311–28.

Heimann, P. (1950) 'On counter-transference', *International Journal of Psycho-Analysis* 31: 81–4.

Hinshelwood, R.D. (1987) *What Happens in Groups: Psychoanalysis, the Individual and the Community*, London: Free Association Books.

Hinshelwood, R.D. (1989) *A Dictionary of Kleinian Thought*, London: Free Association Books.

Hippias, H., Klerman, G.L., and Matussek, N. (1986) *New Results in Depression Research*, Berlin: Springer-Verlag.

Hodes, M. (1990) 'Overdosing as communication: a cultural perspective', *British Journal of Medical Psychology* 63 (4).

Holmes, P. (1983) 'Dropping out from an adolescent therapeutic group: a study of factors in the patients and their parents which may influence this process', *Journal of Adolescence* 6: 333–46.

Holmes, P. (1984) 'Boundaries and chaos: an outpatient psychodrama group for adolescents', *Journal of Adolescence* 7: 387–400.

Holmes, P. (1987) 'Boundaries and chaos' (revised version), in J. Coleman (ed.) *Working with Troubled Adolescents*, London: Academic Press.

Holmes, P. (1989a) 'The uses of sociodramatic techniques in providing consultation to institutions working with young people', *Journal of the British Psychodrama Association*, 4 (2): 29–49; reprinted (1991) in *Journal of the British Psychodrama Association*, 6 (1).

Holmes, P. (1989b) 'Wheels within wheels: systems within systems: the assessment process', *Children and Society*, 3 (3), 237–54.

Holmes, P. (1992) 'The roots of enactment in psychoanalysis, family therapy, and psychodrama', in press.

Holmes. P. and Karp, M. (1991) *Psychodrama: Inspiration and Technique*, London: Tavistock/Routledge.

Isaacs, S. (1948) 'The nature and function of phantasy', *International Journal of Psycho-Analysis*, 29 (2): 73–97.

James, C. (1980) 'Transitional phenomena and the matrix in group psychotherapy', paper presented at the VIIth International Congress on Group Psychotherapy, Copenhagen, 1980.

Joseph, B. (1988) 'Projective identification: clinical aspects', in J. Sandler (ed.) *Projection, Identification, and Projective Identification*, London: Karnac.

Karp, M. (1991a) 'Preface', in P. Holmes and M. Karp (eds) *Psychodrama: Inspiration and Technique*, London: Tavistock/Routledge.

Karp, M. (1991b) 'Depression: it only hurts when you can't laugh', *Bulletin of the British Psychodrama Association*, July 1991: 3–10.

Katz, B. (1966) *Nerve, Muscle, and Synapse*, New York: McGraw-Hill.

Kernberg, O. (1975) *Borderline Conditions and Pathological Narcissism*, New York: Jason Aronson.

Kernberg, O. (1976) *Object-Relations Theory and Clinical Psychoanalysis*, New York: Jason Aronson.

Kernberg, O. (1980) *Internal World and External Reality*, New York: Jason Aronson.

Kernberg, O. (1984) *Severe Personality Disorders: Psychotherapeutic Strategies*, New Haven & London: Yale University Press.
Khan, M. (1963) 'The concept of cumulative trauma', *The Psychoanalytic Study of the Child* 18: 286–306.
Kipper, D.A. (1986) *Psychotherapy Through Clinical Roleplaying*, New York: Brunner/Mazel.
Klauber, J. *et al.* (1987) *Illusion and Spontaneity in Psychoanalysis*, London: Free Association Books.
Klein, J. (1987) *Our Need for Others and its Roots in Infancy*, London: Tavistock.
Klein, M. (1946 and 1975) 'Notes on some schizoid mechanisms', in *Collected Works*, Vol. III, *Envy and Gratitude*, London: Hogarth Press.
Klein, M. (1957 and 1975) *Envy and Gratitude*, in *Collected Works*, Vol. III, *Envy and Gratitude*, London: Hogarth Press.
Klein, M. (1975) *Collected Works*, Vol. I, *Love, Guilt and Reparation*, London: Hogarth Press.
Kohut, H. (1977) *The Restoration of the Self*, New York: International Universities Press.
Laplanche, J. and Pontalis, J.B. (1967 and 1973) *The Language of Psychoanalysis*, London: Hogarth Press.
Leveton, E. (1977) *Psychodrama for the Timid Clinician*, New York: Springer.
Lorenz, K. Z. (1952) *King Solomon's Ring: New Light on Animal Ways*, London: Methuen.
Lorenz, K. (1963 and 1966) *On Aggression*, London: Methuen.
McDougall, J. (1986) *Theatres of the Mind: Illusion and Truth on the Psychoanalytic Stage*, London: Free Association Books.
MacFarlane, J. (1975) 'Olfaction in the development of social preferences in the human neonate', in M. Hofer (ed.) *Parent–Infant Interaction*, Amsterdam: Elsevier.
Malan, D.H. (1979) *Individual Psychotherapy and the Science of Psychodynamics*, London: Butterworths.
Marineau, R. (1989) *Jacob Levy Moreno 1889–1974*, London: Tavistock/Routledge.
Menzies, I. (1970) *A Case Study in the Functioning of a Social System as a Defence Against Anxiety*, London: Tavistock Institute of Human Relations.
Minuchin, S. and Fishman, H.C. (1981) *Family Therapy Techniques*, Cambridge, MA: Harvard University Press.
Moreno, J.L. (1934, 1953 and 1978) *Who Shall Survive*, 3rd edition, Beacon, NY: Beacon House.
Moreno, J.L. (1946 and 1977) *Psychodrama*, Vol. 1, Beacon, NY: Beacon House.
Moreno, J.L. (1947) *The Theatre of Spontaneity*, Ambler, PA: Beacon House.
Moreno, J.L. (1951) *Sociometry, Experimental Method and the Science of Society*, Ambler, PA: Beacon House, The Horsham Foundation.
Moreno, J.L. (1955) *Preludes to My Autobiography*, Beacon, NY: Beacon House.
Moreno, J.L. with Moreno, Z. (1959 and 1975) *Psychodrama*, Vol. 2, Beacon, NY: Beacon House.
Moreno, J.L. (1967) *The Psychodrama of Sigmund Freud*, Beacon, NY: Beacon House.
Moreno, J.L. with Moreno, Z. (1969) *Psychodrama*, Vol. 3, Beacon, NY: Beacon House.
Moreno, J.L. (1989) 'Autobiography', *Journal of Group Psychotherapy, Psychodrama and Sociometry*, 42 (1 & 2): 1–125.
Moreno, Z. (1991) 'Time, space, reality and the family: psychodrama with a blended (reconstituted) family', in P. Holmes and M. Karp (eds) *Psychodrama: Inspiration and Technique*, London: Tavistock/Routledge.
Moses, R. (1988) 'Projection, identification and projective identification: their relationship to political process', in J. Sandler (ed.) *Projection, Identification and Projective Identification*, London: Karnac.
Perls, S.F, Hefferline, R.F. and Goodmab, P. (1951) *Gestalt Therapy*, Harmondsworth: Penguin.

Pines, M. (1983) *The Evolution of Group Analysis*, London: Routledge & Kegan Paul.

Pines, M. (1985) *Bion and Group Psychotherapy*, London: Routledge & Kegan Paul.

Pines, M. (1987) 'Psychoanalysis, psychodrama and group psychotherapy: step-children of Vienna', *Journal of the British Psychodrama Association*, 2 (2): 15–23.

Pocket Oxford Dictionary (1924) Oxford: Oxford University Press.

Pope, H.G., Jonas, J.M., Hudson, J.I., Cohen, B.M., and Gunderson, J.G. (1983) 'The validity of DSM III borderline personality disorder: a phenomenologic, family history, treatment response and long term follow up study', *Archives of General Psychiatry* 40: 23–30.

Post, F. (1962) *The Significance of Affective Symptoms in Old Age*, Maudsley Monograph, London: Oxford University Press.

Racker, H. (1968) *Transference and Countertransference*, London: Maresfield Reprint.

Reich, A. (1951) 'On countertransference', *International Journal of Psycho-Analysis* 43: 25–31.

Rogers, C.R. (1970) *Encounter Groups*, Harmondsworth: Pelican.

Rolfe, Fr. (Baron Corvo F.) (1904) *Hadrian the Seventh*, London: Chatto & Windus.

Rolfe, F. (Baron Corvo) (1934 and 1986) *The Desire and Pursuit of the Whole: A Romance of Modern Venice*, Oxford & New York: Oxford University Press.

Rolfe, F. (Baron Corvo) (1974a) *The Armed Hands: and Other Stories and Pieces*, London: Cecil & Amelia Woolf.

Rolfe, F. (Baron Corvo) (1974b) *The Venice Letters*, London: Cecil & Amelia Woolf.

Rutter, M., Maughan, B., Mortimore, P., Ouston, J. and Smith, A. (1979) *Fifteen Thousand Hours: Secondary Schools and their Effects on Children*, London: Open Books; Cambridge, MA: Harvard University Press.

Rycroft, C. (1968) *A Critical Dictionary of Psychoanalysis*, Harmondsworth: Penguin.

Sandler, J. (1976) 'Countertransference and role-responsiveness', *International Review of Psycho-Analysis*, 3: 43–7.

Sandler, J. (1987) 'The concept of projective identification,' *Bulletin of the Anna Freud Centre*, 10: 33–49.

Sandler, J. (ed.) (1988) *Projection, Identification, and Projective Identification*, London: Karnac.

Sandler, J., Dare, C. and Holder, A. (1973) *The Patient and the Analyst: The Basis of the Psychoanalytic Process*, London: Maresfield Reprints.

Sandler, J. and Rosenblatt, B. (1962) 'The concept of the representational world', *Psychoanalytic Studies of the Child* 17: 128–62.

Sandler, J. and Sandler, A-M. (1978) 'On the development of object relationships and affects', *International Journal of Psycho-Analysis* 59: 285–96.

Scheff, T.J. (1979) *Catharsis in Healing, Ritual and Drama*, Berkeley & Los Angeles: University of California Press.

Segal, H. (1964) *Introduction to the Work of Melanie Klein*, London: Hogarth Press.

Segal, H. (1979) *Klein*, London: Fontana/Collins.

Shepherd, M. (1985) *Sherlock Holmes and the Case of Dr Freud*, London: Tavistock.

Skynner, A.R.C. (1976) *One Flesh Separate Persons: Principles of Family and Marital Psychotherapy*, London: Constable.

Slade, P. (1976) 'Hallucinations', *Psychological Medicine*, 6: 7–13.

Stafford-Clark, D. (1965) *What Freud Really Said*, London: Penguin.

Starr, A. (1977) *Psychodrama: Rehearsal for Living*, Chicago: Nelson Hall.

Stern, D. (1985) *The Interpersonal World of the Infant: A View from Psychoanalysis and Developmental Psychology*, New York: Basic Books.

Stern, D. (1991) *Diary of a Baby: What your Child Sees, Feels, and Experiences*, London: Fontana.

Stoddart, M. (1990) *The Scented Ape: The Biology and Culture of Human Odour*, Cambridge: Cambridge University Press.

Strachey, J. (1933 and 1959) 'The nature of the therapeutic action of psychoanalysis', *International Journal of Psycho-Analysis*, 50: 257–92.

Sutherland, S. (1991) 'Growing pains. A review of *Human Change Processes: The Scientific Foundations of Psychotherapy* by Michael J. Mahoney', *Nature* 350, 14 March.

Symons, A.J.A. (1934) *The Quest for Corvo: An Experiment in Biography*, Harmondsworth: Penguin.

Watzlawick, P. (1974) *Change: Principles of Problem Formation and Problem Resolution*, London and New York: Norton.

Webster, Dr N. (1864) *Complete Dictionary of the English Language*, revised by C.A. Goodrich and N. Porter, London: Bell & Daldy.

Williams, A. (1989) *The Passionate Technique: Strategic Psychodrama with Individuals, Families, and Groups*, London: Tavistock/Routledge.

Williams, A. (1991) *Forbidden Agendas: Strategic Action in Groups*, London: Tavistock/Routledge.

Winnicott, D.W. (1958) *Through paediatrics to psycho-analysis*, London: Hogarth Press.

Winnicott, D.W. (1965) *The Maturational Processes and the Facilitating Environment*, London: Hogarth Press.

Winnicott, D.W. (1971 and 1974) *Playing and Reality*, London: Tavistock; Harmondsworth: Pelican.

Wollheim, R. (1973) *Freud*, London: Fontana.

Wood, J. (1990) 'The good Freud guide', in *Weekend Guardian* 25–6 August 1990.

Woolf, C. (1974) Introduction to *The Venice Letters of Fr. Rolfe, Baron Corvo*, London: Cecil & Amelia Woolf.

Yablonsky, L. (1976) *Psychodrama: Resolving Problems Through Role-Playing*, New York: Gardener Press.

Yalom, I.D. (1985) *The Theory and Practice of Group Psychotherapy*, 3rd edition, New York: Basic Books.

Psychodrama bibliography

Blatner, H. A. (1988) *Acting-In: Practical Applications of Psychodramatic Methods*, New York: Springer.

Blatner, A. with Blatner, A. (1988) *Foundations of Psychodrama: History, Theory, Practice*, New York: Springer.

Fox, J. (ed.) (1987) *The Essential Moreno: Writings on Psychodrama, Group Method and Spontaneity by J.L. Moreno MD*, New York: Springer.

Goldman, E.E. and Morrison, D.S. (1984) *Psychodrama: Experience and Process*, Dubuque, IA: Kendall Hunt.

Holmes. P. and Karp, M. (1990) *Psychodrama: Inspiration and Technique*, London: Tavistock/Routledge.

Leveton, E. (1977) *Psychodrama for the Timid Clinician*, New York: Springer.

Marineau, R. (1989) *Jacob Levy Moreno 1889–1974*, London: Tavistock/Routledge.

Moreno, J.L. (1989) 'Autobiography', *Journal of Group Psychotherapy, Psychodrama and Sociometry*, 42 (1 & 2): 1–125.

Starr, A. (1977) *Psychodrama: Rehearsal for Living*, Chicago: Nelson Hall.

Williams, A. (1989) *The Passionate Technique: Strategic Psychodrama with Individuals, Families, and Groups*, London: Tavistock/Routledge.

Williams, A. (1991) *Forbidden Agendas: Strategic Action in Groups*, London: Tavistock/Routledge.

Yablonsky, L. (1976) *Psychodrama: Resolving Problems Through Role-Playing*, New York: Gardener Press.

Name index

Subject index

aggressive drive: children's play and 161; Kernberg 59; Winnicott 74

analytic group psychotherapy 167–78

anxiety 55, 137–40; defence against (Klein) 72; and the group 142; neurotic 139–40; psychotic 138–9; repression and 76–7; separation 140; splitting and 117; and spontaneity 142–4

auxiliary egos 49, 85–6, 93, 158, 175–6; countertransference in 102, 110, 128; projective identification and 129; tele and choice of 94

basic assumptions groups 179–81 *passim*

borderline personality 73, 123–6 *passim*; *see also* psychosis

boundaries in therapy 144–50; categories of 145, 146; *see also* containment

brain (the) 23; the infant's 56; and psyche 57

catharsis 189

containment 140–2, 144–50; *see also* boundaries in therapy

countertransference 45, 46, 97–111; in auxiliary egos 102, 110; defined 100–1; neurotic 102–4 *passim*; in psychodrama 102–4, 131; therapist identifications 108–9; use of in a session 109–10

death instinct 53; Klein on the 72, 117; projection and 120; splitting and 117

defence mechanisms 112–34; in groups (Bion) 179–81; *see also* introjection, introjective identification, projection, projective identification, regression, repression, splitting

depressive position (Klein) 73, 79, 130, 139

determinism 10–11, 95

dreams 78, 79, 83–4

drive theory: Freud's 37, 53–4; Kernberg's 59, 63–4; sexual 55

early life experience 54–7 *passim*; object relations theory of 58–81 *passim*; unintegrated 73–5

ego: defence mechanisms of the 131–2; early life of 116–23 *passim*; *see also* auxiliary egos, ego identity

ego identity (Kernberg) 73–5

emotions, early infant 55

empathy, as projective identification 126

enactment 90–3

existential factors 189–90

family dynamics 23; therapeutic enactment and 90–1

foetal experience 54

good-enough mothering 140, 142

group dynamics: basic assumption functioning 179–81 *passim*; Bion on 178–81; psychodrama and 176–8; *see also* group psychotherapy

group psychotherapy (analytic) 166–78; group matrix 166–7; Moreno and Foulkes 174–5; 'T' groups 173; therapeutic factors in 184–90; transference in 169–72 *passim*

hierarchical communications 25–6

holding (emotional) *see* containment

I–Thou relationship (Buber) 59

id 23, 53, 131, 132